SOCIAL
GARBAGE

Social Garbarge
edited by Henry Sturgis

© 2017 by Every Farthing Publications. All rights reserved.

Every Farthing Publications
P.O. Box 575, Lincoln Maine 04457 U.S.A.

Library of Congress Control Number: 2017936820
ISBN: 978-0-692-86047-2

*This work has been published with the support of the
William A. Percy Foundation.*

When an individual is protesting society's refusal to acknowledge his dignity as a human being, his very act of protest confers dignity on him.

— BAYARD RUSTIN

Social Garbage

Men in prison
for sex offenses
talk about their lives

**edited by
Henry Sturgis**

Every Farthing Publications

What if you wrote about
Just as it is
The waterfront
Just as it is
The boy on the bridge
Just as he is
The harbormaster
Just as he is
What if you wrote about
Just as it is

— *Wm. Ireland*

Table of Contents

t

Introduction

by Prof. Thomas K. Hubbard

The William A. Percy Foundation for Social and Historical Studies is pleased to support this collection of anecdotes, reflections, and case histories written by incarcerated men of the lowest reputation even within their own prisons. In the eyes of most normal citizens these particular criminals are "social garbage" so offensive to common decency that they must be isolated from the public for decades or life, and if allowed back into human society must be required to live only on specific blocks within their town, to notify authorities of any travel, to inform any potential landlord or employer of their status, and to submit new photographs of themselves each year to be posted online so that they may be recognized by their neighbors as pariahs to be avoided at all costs. I am speaking of sex offenders, who receive longer sentences on average than bank robbers and most other classes of violent criminals, and who are subjected to an unparalleled level of supervision and public disclosure even after release, even though their rate of recidivism for the same offense is lower than for those convicted of other categories of crime.

But most of these writers are among the lowest of the low, not merely criminal "sex perverts," but homosexual child molesters ("chomos" in prison slang). As the writers and numerous other correspondents of the Percy Foundation reveal, sex offenders generally rank very low in the prison hierarchy, with only the "snitches" being lower. But there also exists a triple hierarchy among sex offenders, with forcible rapists of adult females at the top (as the most "manly"), statutory rapists of underage females lower, and "chomos" lowest,

the bottom 1-to-2% among accused sex offenders.[1] It was not the intention of this collection to focus on gay offenders; at least two (B.C. and T.J.) admit to bi-sexual tastes in children, and others (K.J., O.D., E.J., S.R.) were married. However, it does seem to have been overwhelmingly the "chomos" who chose to write about their experiences openly. They are the ones with the most time on their hands.

The Percy Foundation has posted preliminary results from a detailed questionnaire filled out by 317 male sex offenders in both state and federal detention (William A. Percy Foundation 2016). The study reveals that contact offenses involving an underage male receive much longer prison sentences than exclusively heterosexual offenses (a median minimum sentence of 44 years vs. 20 years); the discrepancy is particularly pronounced for contact with minors in the 14-to-17 age bracket, which would not even be illegal in Germany, Italy, or until recently Canada (43.5 years median sentence for male-male, 12.5 for male-female). The sex of the juvenile victim correlates more strongly with the length of the sentence than any other factor, including age of victims, number of victims, and prior convictions; only whether a plea bargain was accepted had more impact in predicting sentence length.

Another study (Chaffin, Chenoweth, & Letourneau 2016), based on the National Incident-Based Reporting System, shows that authorities are far more likely to arrest and prosecute in statutory rape complaints that have to do with same-sex relations than complaints in heterosexual cases, even though the same-sex complaints are only about 1% of the total.[2] This bias toward more intense prosecutorial activity and harsher punishment for homosexual offenses most likely stems from dated misconceptions about pre-adult same-sex experimentation "turning" young people gay and thus forming a program of "gay recruitment," which in the eyes of most parents, police, prosecutors, judges, and juries, is a bad thing. As some of the contributions to this collection reveal, a large number of the boys with whom these

---

[1] Accurate figures concerning the percentage of incarcerated child sex offenders who committed same-sex offenses are not available, but this estimate extrapolates from the finding of Chaffin, Chenoweth, & Letourneau 2016, who report that same-sex offenses were only 1% of the complaints of statutory rape (see below).

[2] The low percentage of cases reported is probably not a reflection of fewer same-sex relations, but less detection due to the tendency of gay teens to keep their romantic lives secret from both peers and parents. It may also be related to higher levels of satisfaction with what happened, such that the minors never made a complaint.

men had contact grow up to be heterosexual; the issue needs to be studied further with both quantitative and qualitative methods.

The more severe punishment of gay MAPs (minor-attracted persons) cannot be explained by same-sex contacts between an adult and minor male causing greater psychological trauma or life-adjustment problems. The meta-analysis of Rind, Tromovitch, and Bauserman (1998) long ago established that male college students who were later questioned about childhood "abuse" more often rated the abuse a "positive experience" than a negative one, regardless of the gender of their abuser, whereas females reacted far more negatively. Indeed, a later study (Rind 2001) that examined only gay and bi-sexual college males revealed that 77% of them rated their sexual interactions as minors with adult men as a "positive experience" (vs. 15% negative). There are many reasons why this might be so: gay or gay-curious teens often feel more comfortable searching for partners outside their immediate peer group due to fear of exposure and ridicule, gay dating websites and apps require users to pretend to be at least 18, and uncertain male teens may want guidance from a man with more knowledge and experience of the gay lifestyle (parents seldom being a good resource in this area). Despite occasional persecution, pederasty has been a historical feature of Western civilization at least since the ancient Greeks (and of many non-Western cultures too). It has been argued that it may even have evolutionary roots in our primate history (see Rind 2013).

The purpose of collecting this material is not to defend what these men did as right or harmless, even if it might have been treated more leniently in other times and places. Some are unapologetic, while others express sincere remorse and say they deserved to be locked up. F.C.'s contribution contains excerpts from a longer work he is writing with the express goal of warning parents how pedophiles operate and admonishing other persons with his orientation to avoid acting on their impulses. Our goal is threefold: (1) to give a human face to men who have struggled with an illicit attraction that they found so compelling that even the severity of American law and social stigma did not deter them, (2) to help friends and family members of minor-attracted persons understand why their loved ones have suffered from this issue, and (3) to provide criminologists, legal scholars, psychologists, and other social scientists with qualitative case studies of how these men think and thought. Wherever one may stand in the

debate over the harmfulness of adult sexual contact with minors, it is useful to have more information about why these men did what they did, how they did it, how their own childhood experiences may have contributed to their orientation, and whether American penological and therapeutic approaches will deter them in the future. It is our hope that this evidence can contribute to future discussions of appropriate legal reform with regard to age of consent and guidelines that distinguish the most harmful (usually coercive or manipulative) incidents from those that were benign or had little negative effect on the minor.

The editor has changed names and sometimes places to preserve the anonymity of these writers, some of whom admit to crimes in addition to the one(s) for which they were actually prosecuted. He has not edited their manuscripts except to correct spelling or basic grammar in a few places, or to shorten a contribution that was too long to print in its entirety. It is best to let each of them speak in his own voice. Needless to say, the opinions they express are their own and are not necessarily endorsed by either the Percy Foundation or Every Farthing Press. We have not independently studied media accounts or court records in their cases. But by offering a sympathetic ear, we hope that we have from them words that are sincere and carefully considered after years of time to reflect on what they did and how it has affected others.

Chapter 1 – **Early Starters**

by B.C.

B.C. was targeted for incarceration because of his activism. He was carefully entrapped by a woman FBI agent. In this selection he describes the identity crisis that was precipitated by his arrest, and outlines some of the challenges that face a sex offender when he gets released from prison.

ભ

Prior to my arrest, I moderated a series of Yahoo groups for adults' personal intergenerational experiences. I use the term "early starters" as a way of self identifying for those who, like myself, enjoyed sexual activity as a child or youth. In the process of gathering the stories of members and prospective members certain key ideas emerged as common themes. In a nutshell, these involve the presence, or absence, of negative emotions such as guilt, shame, and fear, and conversely the cultivation of affirmative values like joy, empowerment, and love. These findings form the basis for much of what I put forward in these groups, both in my frequent postings and in the text files I uploaded for members' use.

Since the matter of how to relate these concepts to young people in the members' lives arose naturally in many discussions, I wrote on this subject as well. In my on-line persona, I became an outspoken advocate for an intergenerational-sex positive approach; connecting with others who share this view became the central focus of the group.

The principles themselves, in addition to the core premise of avoiding the use of guilt – shame – peer based approaches and fostering joy – love – empowerment, include concepts like "sex is good,"

"mutually volitional pleasure," "the ignorance of innocence," and "sharing values." I wrote extensively on these and related topics and this advocacy brought me to the attention of the authorities.

My entrapment was a year-and-a-half long campaign on the part of a female FBI agent who posed as a young mother in my group. Because I was married at the time, I initially took little interest in "Abigail," but over time I became interested and ultimately fell for this low-key (she never participated in the group) but seemingly very supportive (constant encouragement when we chatted, no requests or demands of any kind) member. So when my marriage ended, it made sense to meet this gal. I jumped on a plane on May 25, 2005 for a flight from my home in Wisconsin, and was arrested when it landed. Welcome to the federal justice system!

Although there was never any discussion of the purported minor, the body of work I described gave the feds more than enough to convince any jury that my travel was for illicit purposes. Further, the shock of my arrest and detention (bail was denied; I was a "flight risk") brought about an immediate repudiation of everything I believed and stood for before; for the next 3 ½ years, I lived in complete denial of my previous self. I considered myself "born again" from the ashes of a life that lay in ruins. The conversion launched me on a spiraling journey which has been the outstanding feature of my nearly ten years of incarceration. You ask about the impact this imprisonment has had on my life, and the surprising answer is that it has been tremendously beneficial, a truly transformational experience. Of course there has been a huge downside as well – the alienation from friends and loved ones, and the enforced separation from those who did not abandon me, being foremost. Nevertheless, on the whole my sojourn in the BOP has occasioned the most profound personal growth and authentic illumination of self which I can only call revelatory.

As this self-realization unfolded, I became increasingly aware of the contradiction between my re-born character and the aspects of my nature I had repressed in the wake of my fall. My watershed moment came on December 24, 2008, when for the first time since May 2005, I allowed myself the pleasure of self-gratification. Like the flood that follows the levee break, my prior passions and convictions came rushing back into consciousness, and over the course of a few weeks I was restored to my true identity, yet with the heightened perspective gained through 3 ½ years of relentless soul-searching. This

set the stage for what turned out to be the complete revising of my pre-arrest persona.

Basically I wrote several essays on the principles of sex-positive "intergen," a lengthy how-to piece, and numerous short fictional accounts of how such interactions might be conducted. The wisdom of doing this while in prison can certainly be questioned, but I felt impelled by my inner "demon" – the urgent impulse for creative self-expression, my soul-urge to resurrect and improve on the work of my earlier phase. When this material fell, as it was bound to, into the hands of the authorities, I had a new set of problems. However, these, like everything else that has befallen me along this strange road, ultimately led to my advantage.

My punishment, on the trumped up shots of violating the security of the institution by planning to mail this manuscript to a (nonexistent) confederate on the outside for on-line promulgation, was six and one half months in the SHU (Secure Housing Unit) and a transfer to the SOMP (Sex Offender Management Program) yard at Petersburg, Virginia. There I made the acquaintance of many unrepentant MAPs (I like that term! Minor-Attracted Persons) and was able to engage in frequent conversations around these sex-positive concepts and lifestyle preferences that brought us all to such a place. While for obvious reasons I eschewed any further writing on the subject, I actually expanded my advocacy beyond the very small circle I had drawn around me in Lompoc, where I spent nearly five years in all.

Furthermore, my three years at Petersburg saw a vast expansion of the self-realization and insights – gained through rigorous spiritual practice – that mark my prison years. I turned my writing efforts in this direction, and produced a couple hundred pages of publication-ready manuscript, which I plan to deploy upon my release in July. Because, despite the fact I was brought here to the federal correctional center last May for civil-commitment, I am indeed going home on schedule when my sentence (135 months less a year-plus of good time) is up. My release date is May 24, 2015.

The reasons behind my non-certification – "certification" being the term for the feds' panel of "experts" decision to hold an inmate for a hearing before a judge, who ultimately decides on commitment – boils down to the absence of a hands-on component in my offense, my status as a first-time offender, and the lack of any history of psy-

chological issues. I simply didn't meet the criteria, although the fact of those writings could have proven highly problematical had any of the other conditions applied. I knew from the outset that I wasn't certifiable, but the extremely controversial character of my text left open the possibility that I could be singled out for political reasons.

All the foregoing is a matter of record – the staff psychologist who wrote the report on my examination for possible civil commitment even cited my position that mine was a free-speech case when she briefed me about the interview process, indicating that my mail has been read and/or my phone calls monitored. Now that I'm off the radar, so to speak, I doubt that this letter will be scrutinized, but even if it is, I'm like, so what? I've made no effort to conceal my beliefs, and I've been fully prepared if necessary to enter the public arena and defend my right to express them ever since those documents were confiscated in June 2010. However it's not my preference to fight it out with these people on the very uneven ground of the civil-commitment process, so I am truly glad to be bypassing this battle.

With my release so close, the practical matters of residence and employment are at the front of my daily thoughts, along with my anticipation of reunion with my elderly parents – they're 85 and 82; (I'm 58 by the way) – and my son. For reasons only marginally related to my candidacy for commitment, I experienced a long delay in getting my release location changed from Georgia, where my case was initiated, to Wisconsin, where my entire family lives. As a result, my halfway-house application is still in limbo, 2½ months from my release date. That decision could literally come any day, and I could well be on a bus for Wisconsin as you read this. So my mind isn't really on the broader aspects of what I want to do when I get out. I'm focused on the basics.

These include, unfortunately, federal probation (I have 20 years of supervised release, if you can believe that. The judge took exception to some of the things I said in my on-line postings), sex-offending registration, and "treatment." This last item is particularly thorny, because completing the program is a condition of my probation, meaning failure to comply can result in a return to prison for as long as some judge sees fit. The difficulty this poses is that completion could entail a detailed disclosure of past and present thoughts as well as actions, and anything revealed becomes part of the record to be used in future commitment proceedings. Although I have no

actual skeletons in my closet, the prospect of discussing past conduct and current beliefs (using underlying detection technology), with the knowledge that doing so could jeopardize my vital liberty interest in the event of re-incarceration, is daunting. Since even a technical violation (missing a urinalysis test, for example, or failing to report an incidental contact with a minor) can trigger re-incarceration, and any return to prison means I will be again be subject to this ordeal; "treatment" poses a very real threat to my well-being.

Thus one of the first points on my reentry agenda is finding a friendly attorney to help me through the challenges of completing treatment without damaging myself. (I'll be looking for a sympathetic psychologist as well). I hope that this can be accomplished without undue conflict, but if push comes to shove, my contention will be that my Fifth Amendment right to refuse to incriminate myself stands with respect to court mandated sex-offender treatment.

Beyond this is the whole issue of civil commitment, which is patently unconstitutional, the Supreme Court rulings notwithstanding. The circumstances place this question before me again. I intend to take it on with all due diligence, and for this, too, I would hope to have a motivated counsel – that is, a right-thinking lawyer who understands what is involved and what's at stake.

Registration holds a whole other batch of potential annoyances, but I don't intend to let these bother me. This aspect of the SO debate doesn't really appeal to me. I respect RSOL and what they do, but lobbying for legislative change just doesn't interest me, as much as I agree these laws need changing. And in truth I'd rather avoid all these complications as adamantly opposed to civil commitment as I am. Resistance and opposition are not my preferred mode of expression. What I most want to do is write, publish, research, and teach, and if I can do so in peaceful coexistence with the powers that be, great.

If this seems a bit cowardly, oh well... After ten years dealing with this system, I've learned the enormous difficulty and overreaching futility of bucking. From the time the words "The United States of America vs. Joseph Conners" appeared in print, I faced the weight of the government's will, and it's something I'd rather not confront anymore. For this reason, I'm ready to abandon the idea of visible opposition. As passionate as I am about sexual freedom, I can't expect to write and speak my mind openly without repercussions, and consequently am willing to keep quiet on these matters publicly as

long as I'm allowed to go about my legitimate business essentially unmolested.

On a personal level, though, this means I must be allowed the space to be who I am, within the constraints my circumstances impose. What I intend to insist on is my right to express a healthy adult sexuality as part of my reentry into society. Having served the sentence for my "crime," having registered as required, and being in compliance with all the rules and regulations, the only equitable restrictions on my behavior are those imposed by the law and the terms of my supervised release. What this means is finding ways to get together with like-minded men and women for mutually rewarding exchanges of mind, body, and spirit energies.

You asked how I dealt with my feelings growing up, whether I shared them with others, and how it affected my self image and social relations. As you probably know from personal experience, such things leave indelible impressions on our psyche, and the exploration of the subjects remains a highly charged pursuit, as it was when I was running my Yahoo group. Definitely something I want to do more of once I'm free of BOP micromanagement of my daily life.

Discretion precludes my going into details here, but I'll answer broadly by telling you that my sexual experiences began with a younger family member and continued for three years. We did not share our intimacy, or even the fact of it, with anyone else until we were discovered together about 2 ½ years later. Enjoyable as it was, this relationship did not relieve the typical adolescent insecurity most kids go through; my feeling now is that adult guidance would have been invaluable in helping both of us to integrate what we were learning together into a more comprehensive, mature framework. While my experience was clearly positive for both, it was hindered by an ignorance that was only very partially mitigated by access to adult materials. Better would have been to receive loving and supportive hands-on instruction.

The simple heresy – the idea that adults and young people can share sensual and erotic pleasure as a part of a nurturing, empowering relationship – has become a life-in-the-balance position in these otherwise permissive times, a third rail of postmodern culture as taboo as the notion of trucking with the devil was 400 years ago. In this latter day witch-hunt, society has substituted long years in prison for burning at the stake, but the practical effect is the same. Fami-

lies are shattered, productive citizens condemned, stigmatized, and shunned, and child "victims" traumatized – not by playful and gratifying discovery of their inborn sexual nature but by the Inquisition of moralistic invaders who descend unbidden at the slip of the lip, or a busybody's tip, to upset their world forever. The demonizing you mentioned doesn't merely destroy the MAP – it devastates the lives of everyone around the alleged "perpetrator." This collateral damage has so far been an untold story in the deluge of "sex offender as monster" media reports.

This isn't to say that there is no such thing as harmful intergenerational sexual contact; just as with corporal punishment, there is a line between that which would generally be considered acceptable (although I personally reject *any* use of physical discipline directed by adults against children), and what constitutes obvious abuse. Any two people might disagree on where that line is, but when we call it all "abuse," the term loses any real meaning. One of my essays was titled "Sex-Positive and Sex-Negative" and treated this topic thoroughly. My point was that by refusing to acknowledge this essential distinction, the dominant paradigm actually enables the worst behavior by fostering expectations rooted in fear and violence. If our approach to children's sexuality were rational the determination that "this is okay but that isn't" would ensure that more of the former and less – much less, most likely – of the latter takes place.

In the current atmosphere of hysteria and panic it is not realistic to think that the kind of nuanced approach I am outlining can actually be implemented on a societal basis. However, small-scale and localized groupings dedicated to subverting the dominant paradigm are possible, and of course the Internet is a wonderful tool for promoting and supporting an enlightened perspective. While this isn't work that I can participate in, my future computer use being subject to close scrutiny (I could even be denied use of technology, although such across-the-board bans are being revised in court after court as unreasonably broad), it is certainly something I support.

I have a vision for how a sex-positive research institute might make a contribution, but this is not among my short-term projects. Where I do see possibilities for service is in providing support to the prison population in question. I hope to organize a prison literature project when I get out. One aspect of this is the distribution of my own spiritually-oriented writings, which I feel can be of real value to

those who are locked up but want to be free in mind. This is mostly a matter of finding suitable ways to communicate my fundamental message which can be summarized as "wake up and think for yourself!"

I've been thinking about a combination memoir-polemic on the whole SO question. The problem is that my own experiences really aren't that interesting, and researching other cases would be problematic even after I'm out, given the restrictions on the Internet usage I'm likely to face.

The polemical part, though – the argument against the witch-hunt and in favor of the sex-positive outlook – is something I've thought about extensively and could write on at length. I'm really not all that excited at the thought of being some kind of spokesperson for sexual freedom, even though that's an integral part of my identity. I prefer the approach of supporting the cause from the relative anonymity of private life, or under the cover of whatever success I might obtain through my other writing endeavors.

And this is the other side of my dilemma. In addition to the book I've nearly completed (a commentary on the ancient classic of Chinese wisdom, the *Tao Te Ching*), I have several other titles on self-realization in the conceptual pipeline. *Writing Chomo* (my title for the hypothetical SO book) would take time and focus away from this more conventional, and more acceptable, pursuit.

Another reason not to go public with my sex-positive views is that the increased scrutiny would surely constrict my freedom of expression and bring undue attention to those with whom I associate. What I've been holding in my mind, though, is that an opportunity might present itself to collaborate with someone similarly inclined that could serve to get the ideas I'm passionate about out there without the need to assume a visible role.

At a previous prison I was able to have some deep conversations, but here it doesn't really happen. The atmosphere is chilled by fear (of those being subjected to the commitment process) and intimidation (from those who are here for other reasons).

One of the biggest obstacles to the kind of solidarity we need in our campaign to change public perception around this issue is the artificial and unnecessary division into, for lack of a better term, "orientation camps." I've encountered a lot of this form of exclusivity, mostly from the straight side of the fence but also among those with

same-sex attractions. For my part, I identify as omni-sexual. I am a partisan of pleasure who adores Priapus as well as Venus, a partisan who rejects all arbitrary barriers to communion. As such I relate to LGBTQ-oriented MAPs as well as to those of a more traditional persuasion, shall we say. One of the most disappointing things I've observed is the "I'm okay but that guy's sick" reaction to someone whose preferences are merely different from their own.

When I was a student radical in San Francisco back in the mid-70s I saw how factionalism in the gay rights movement hindered progress: the outstanding gains of the past few years can be credited in large part to the unity forged in the decades since, as can the increasing acceptance by average Americans who came to see homosexuality as a legitimate part of social life. This is the kind of transformation we want to see our work produce. For that to happen, we've got to de-marginalize the ideas of sexual freedom and intergenerational love, and to do that we've got to come together. (Pun intended).

So this is a challenge for all of us – witch-hunts operate by isolating and marginalizing their targets, which is the function of demonization I'd like to serve as a bridge-builder if I can.

(As a note of clarification I'd like to add that I have remained celibate for the entire duration of my prison term. Thus what I'm expressing on this page represents a philosophical, and not a sexual, orientation. I was "bi" before I got locked up, but I didn't understand this part of the problem at all. Ironically, abstaining from sex with others entirely has brought me into a much deeper rapport, or vibrational alignment, to use a phrase that I use in my spiritual work, with those occupying a range of positions along the gender-identity / sexual-preference spectrum.)

In my view, the axis of this whole endeavor must be the sex-positive / sex-negative duality. As long as there is the misapprehension that all intergenerational contact is harmful to minors, the victimization of MAPs will continue. We have to be crystal clear on what we are for and what we're against, and why. Guilt, shame, fear, coercion, and violence – not sensual and erotic exploration – are harmful. Joy, love, empowerment, pleasure, even ecstasy… these are the birthright of every human being, and helping our children and youth to unfold these dimensions of self is not a crime, except in the repressed and moralistic mind of the hyper-alienated dominant paradigm.

Chapter 2 – The Death of Peter Pan

by P.R.

These are excerpts from a much longer work. In time I hope to make a slightly edited version of the whole manuscript available on uryourstory.org. Here I include his description of his growing up and then skip to some of his experiences in prison after he was apprehended for possession of child pornography.

ೞ

How it started

It all started innocently enough. My sixth-grade health class was studying the stages of sexual development. There were black-and-white photographs of boys and girls lined up according to age and size in order to show the gradual changes that take place from year to year. On one page, a boy and girl about three or four years old, posed together, with their genitals exposed, to show the difference between boys and girls. While my classmates giggled and joked, I experienced a much different reaction: I became sexually aroused – especially while looking at the pictures of the younger boys.

I went home and jacked off looking at those pictures. Nothing ever felt so good or right.

Jacking off had become my favorite hobby since I discovered it earlier that year. I'd done it looking at the women in lingerie and swimsuit ads as well as the porn that my friends lent me. But none of it got me as worked up as the other guys. I just couldn't understand

what the big deal was.

At first, I thought I was gay. But when I tried jacking off looking at pictures of men or thinking about boys from school, I still couldn't get off. Jacking off to those pictures of naked boys in the text-book, it became clear: I liked little boys the same way my friends liked girls.

Now that I knew what I liked, I sought out more pictures of naked or scantily clad little boys. I'd snatch up the Sears and JC Penney catalogs as soon as they came in because they always had pictures of boys in their underwear. *National Geographic* became my *Playboy* because it frequently contained pictures of naked boys. The naked baby on the cover of Nirvana's "Nevermind" album became my favorite visual aid.

Was I some kind of sick perverted freak? I wondered. I certainly felt like one at times. I didn't know anyone who shared my same interests. The closest I ever came was a homeless guy named Dirty Dan who hung around the neighborhood parks and play grounds, offering to buy me and my friends beer if we showed him our dicks. He'd gotten beat up a lot for being so creepy. If this was the fate that awaited me, I didn't want any part of it. So I kept my mouth shut and pretended to like girls like a "normal" teenage boy – all the while wishing that I could meet someone I could talk to about my lustful desires for young boys, preferably an older man who could also be the father figure I always wanted but never had.

Growing up as a misfit

Growing up, I was a misfit, and as a misfit, I was forced to hang out with other outcasts: fat kids, poor kids, nerds and all the other rejects who didn't fit in with the popular kids, who we called "preppies" because they wore the latest fashions and listened to pop music. They hated us and we hated them.

Like generations of outcasts and misfits before us, a trip to South Street was our rite of passage. Located just off the waterfront, with its eclectic mix of head shops, used book and music stores, sex shops and alternative clothing boutiques, South Street is the Shangri-La of Philadelphia's counterculture.

I was 13 when I made my first trip.

After I begged my mom for months, she finally agreed to let me go.

My best friend Wally spent the night at my house the night before. We were wearing our best punk attire. We were heavily into

punk rock, so we listened to the Dead Milkmen's "Punk Rock Girl," a song about a similar journey to South Street, on repeat, while spiking our mohawks as tall as they would stand.

My mom snapped a photo to preserve the moment while Wally and I raised our middle fingers in joyful defiance. When I looked at that picture years later, I winced at how awkward we were. But back then we thought we were the coolest guys in Philly as we stepped out the door and headed to catch the El.

We met up with our friend Hayden at the Fifth Street Station. Wally and I idolized Hayden because he was 18 and was a celebrity from the local punk rock scene. As the veteran South Street traveler, he would serve as our tour guide.

As we walked past the Liberty Bell and Independence Hall, I couldn't help but think about how appropriate they were as symbols of the freedom Wally and I were about to gain. Before stepping onto that mythical street, I had to catch my breath as I took in the warmth of the early afternoon sun beaming off signs and illuminating the whole street in a magical glow.

I was greeted by the most wonderful sights and sounds I'd ever seen or heard:

Punk rockers with even taller Mohawks, strutting proudly, free of harassment ...

Drag queens and gay men holding hands and kissing right out in the open ...

Bikers and tattooed babes ...

Homeless people and street performers panhandling on every corner ...

The freaks, outcasts and rejects of society.

I felt right at home and took it all in in wide-eyed wonder.

Following the route laid out in "Punk Rock Girl": we went straight to Zipperhead, an alternative clothing boutique. "Do you have a beau?" we asked the heavily tattooed girl with fiery red hair behind the counter, just like in the song, which was by then at least fifteen years old. She glared at us the same way she'd probably done the countless other punk teen boys who'd thought they were being cute by asking her that same question.

We then went to the Philadelphia Pizza Company, another landmark mentioned in the song, for lunch. Following the lyrics, we ordered hot tea, then jumped up on the table and shouted, "Anarchy!"

We were told they only served it iced. After getting kicked out, we headed to the record store across the street and asked for Mojo Nixon. The joke was on us when the clerk showed us some Mojo Nixon CDs.

We abandoned the idea of trying to relive the song and went to Tower Books instead. Tower Books was a popular hangout for teen boys because it stocked a wide variety of pornographic books and magazines, which were kept behind a tall pane of black glass, smeared with sticky fingerprints, on the top shelf of the magazine rack at the rear of the store.

A sign said you had to be at least eighteen to look at these magazines, but the place was always so crowded, the clerks rarely checked ID.

"Look at the gash on that bitch," Wally and Hayden shouted, elbowing one another as they gawked at the centerfold in the bleach-smelling isle. I faked an interest for a few minutes before moving on to find something more interesting. *Nude & Natural* jumped out at me. Skimming the pages I saw pictures of naked old people with flabby tits and sagging skin playing volleyball. Grossed out, I was about to put the magazine back when I spotted a photograph that instantly aroused me: a blond boy wearing nothing but a smile stood with his arms akimbo, thrusting his hips toward the camera. In my mind's eye, the look on his face was erotic and welcoming. A surge of excitement pulsed through my body. I shifted to hide my visible hard-on from Wally and Hayden but they were so distracted by gaping pussy, they didn't notice me.

After working ourselves into a sexual frenzy, we went back outside to calm down. By now, the sun was setting and a cool breeze was blowing. It was a perfect ending for such a memorable day.

"It's been real. We should do this again soon," I told Wally and Hayden before parting ways.

They agreed. And we did. Trips to South Street quickly became part of our weekend routine. Each time we'd follow the same route with Tower Books being our final destination. It never got boring – especially after I discovered the photography section at the back of the store.

I began noticing a cast of shady characters lurking in the back: guys with thick glasses, guys with bad comb-overs and ratty facial hair, guys wearing trench coats in the middle of the summer, the kind

of men parents warn their kids about.

One day, while Hayden and Wally drooled over a centerfold of a slut impaling herself with a huge black dildo, I was lusting over the latest issue of *Nude & Natural* magazine. I watched out of the corner of my eye as one of the regulars skulked past the children's section and stopped in front of a shelf labeled "Photography." Darting his eyes back and forth, he removed a book from the shelf. As he thumbed through it, he occasionally looked up to see if anyone was watching him. When he thought the coast was clear he placed the book back on the shelf and walked off. Curious, I headed over to see what he'd just been looking at. The poor guy almost had a heart attack when he looked up long enough to see me stop in front of the shelf he'd just left. He couldn't get out of the door fast enough. I could almost smell the burning rubber of his shoes. He was hauling ass.

My own heart skipped a beat when I saw the titles. I can't remember any specifically, but several had "nude" and "children" in them.

I'd just discovered a treasure trove and would spend hours exploring its contents. All the while, I couldn't help but wonder why those men acted so strangely whenever I tried talking to them. Looking back, I can see how weird it would have seemed for them to try to strike up s conversation with an awkward teen boy with a spiky Mohawk, when they were old enough to be his grandfather and were looking at naked pictures of young boys. They probably thought I was with an undercover sting operation targeting men who solicit sex from minors or part of a TV show like "To Catch A Predator." But back then I just wanted to have someone to talk to about my budding sexuality. Someone who wouldn't think I was a sick perverted fuck for liking little boys.

The first days in prison

The next morning, I woke up to the sound of a commotion out in the hallway. I wedged myself against the wall and prepared for the worst. Had a riot broken out? Were the other prisoners coming for me? The guards? My questions were answered when a guard appeared at the door and slammed open the slot.

"Breakfast," he shouted, shoving a tray through. I raced over just in time to grab the tray before it went clattering to the floor. As he slammed and locked the slot behind him, I carried the tray over to the desk and inventoried my meager breakfast: a carton of milk, a

single-serve box of corn flakes, and a bagel so hard it could be used as a weapon.

I ate the cereal and drank the milk and picked at the bagel without even tasting them before placing the tray by the door. The guard came back about an hour later to collect the tray. I passed it back through, then went over to look out the long window, but it was blacked out.

That first day set the tone for the next few weeks, which seemed to stretch on endlessly. To break the monotony, I would pace the concrete floor of the ten-by-twelve cell and toss and turn on the steel bunk, staring at the cinder block walls until they seemed to close in around me. The unanswerable questions and morbid thoughts that crowded my mind made me feel even more claustrophobic. Life was almost unendurable without dope and booze to dull my mind and mute my thoughts.

I mostly thought about my family, especially my mom and sister. How were they holding up? Were they okay? What had the Feds told them? Whatever it was, had it turned them against me? Did they know where I was? If so, would I ever see them again?

And I thought about my boys. Did they miss me as much as I missed them? What did they think was going on? What were the Feds saying to them? I hoped the boys didn't think they'd gotten me in trouble. Not having the answers to those questions hurt. I wished I could comfort them with hugs and kisses – at the very least call to check up on them. But I was sure the Feds wouldn't allow me to do either since the boys were now my "victims." The label "victim" made me cringe. It was never my intention to victimize them in any way.

I also thought about my friends from on-line. Although I'd alienated many of them by distancing myself from BoyChat, I still hoped to hear from those I remained loyal to, specifically Sheesh and the guys I'd invited to my gatherings. Surely I'd hear from someone. After all, I'd been a fixture of the on-line BL community since I was a boy myself. The least I could ask for was an occasional letter from one of my comrades. When I didn't receive any, at first I thought it was because my on-line friends didn't know what had happened to me or where I was. But the more I thought about it, that didn't make any sense. Word travels quickly in the on-line BL community and its members are very computer savvy, so they wouldn't have had any trouble finding me if they had wanted to.

The realization that I'd been abandoned by the only community I'd ever felt like I belonged to hurt. I'd given my entire life to the BL movement, but at what cost? My future hung in legal limbo, but I knew that the end result would likely land me behind bars for decades with vicious criminals who hated me.

 భ

I raced to the counselor's office and waited outside until he came in for the day. It was about 7:30 by the time he came in and got situated.

He dialed my mom's cell-phone number and handed me the phone. My mom picked up after only two rings. "Hello?" she said.

"Hey mom, it's me," I said, fighting back tears.

"Rosen! It's so good to hear from you again," she said, trying to sound cheerful, but the tone of her voice gave away the stress and worry she'd been experiencing over the course of the past few weeks. "How've you been?"

"Good to hear from you again too, Mom," I said, my own voice cracking as I forced the words past the lump in my throat.

"I'm fine. How have you been?"

"I'm glad to hear that," she said. "I was worried about you. I'm doing a lot better now that I know that you're okay."

I went on to tell her about Carter and my new friends and what I'd been up to and she told me about what my sister was up to and what was going on around the house and brought me up to date with what was going on with my family and all. We'd been talking about twenty minutes when my counselor interrupted me by saying, "Okay, Rosen, wrap it up. I've got other inmates waiting to see me."

"I'll call you again as soon as I can," I said.

"Good. Keep your head up," my mom said. "I love you." I cried when I heard my mom say those last three words because they were so rare. My mom had never been an affectionate or emotionally expressive person, so hugs, kisses and I-love-you's were few and far between.

"I love you too," I said before hanging up.

The counselor gave me visitation and phone forms, and I went back to my room to fill them out. My mom sent me some money, so I was able to go to commissary and buy a radio, cigarettes, toiletries,

sweat shorts, snacks and other necessities.

And that weekend, I got my first visit from my mom and sister. It was a joyous reunion filled with lots of hugs and physical affection and I-love-you's and tears of joy. My only complaint was that it was too short – since I was a pre-trial detainee, my visits were limited to only two hours. But that was okay because they would be back the following Saturday and every chance they got after that. Eventually, they'd be joined by other family members.

Visions of murder and mayhem

Waiting to find out what prison I'd be designated to was psychological hell. Would I be sent to a penitentiary? The other inmates on my unit had me convinced that I would since I had so much time to do and because of my charges. They told me horror stories about what happened to sex offenders in pens. Since I had no idea how the prison system worked, I believed what they told me.

My cellie Vince tried to console me by reassuring me that the Bureau of Prisons wouldn't intentionally put me in danger, that the designation committee would take all of the factors of my situation into consideration. I hoped so, but I couldn't be sure. I worried myself sick with visions of the murder and mayhem that awaited me at the pen. It got to the point where I couldn't eat without shitting or puking.

Unable to hold anything down, I survived on cigarettes and coffee. That holiday season was not a happy one. Christmas and New Year's passed barely noticed, under a dark veil of fear and uncertainty. Shortly after Martin Luther King Day, I was told to pack my property because I'd be transferred soon. When I asked the property officer what prison I was going to, he told me that he didn't know, that he was just told to pack me out.

Now I was sure that I was headed to the pen. Why else wouldn't they tell me where I was going? I know now that it's standard procedure not to tell inmates where they are headed for security reasons – the reason being that if inmates know where they're headed, it'd be easier for them to plan escapes. But back then, I was convinced that the feds were conspiring against me.

About a week later, I was ripped out of my sleep by a guard pounding on the door with a flashlight. "You got fifteen minutes to get ready. I'll be back to let you out for breakfast." I was shaking so

violently, I could barely keep my balance as I brushed my teeth and washed my face.

"It was nice to know ya," I said to Vince.

"Nice knowing you too," Vince said. "Keep in touch." If I live, I thought. I fought back tears as we shook hands and hugged goodbye.

"Keep your head up!" Vince shouted as I headed down into the day room. I wasn't the only one who was being transferred: there were about fifteen or so inmates waiting in line to get their breakfast trays. I was so sick, and nervous, I didn't even bother to get in line and just sat at an empty table instead and hoped none of the other inmates were going my way.

I felt like I was suffocating. I couldn't catch my breath no matter how hard I tried. Time seemed to stand still as I watched the clock. My vision went blurry, I felt sluggish, and my legs went to jelly while my jaw chattered like I was freezing. By the time we left the unit, I'd gone completely numb. Things get fuzzy after that. All I remember is shuffling down to Receiving and Discharge and waiting in one of the holding cells. The transfer team came and handcuffed, chained and shackled us. When it came my turn, one of the guards scowled at me and said, "Box him," to another guard. I didn't know what that meant, but quickly found out when the guard clamped a pair of handcuffs tightly around my wrists and covered them with a black steel box, which he fastened to the belly chain with a padlock. The cuffs cut into my flesh and caused my ankles to bleed and the chain was so short, I could barely walk. When I asked the guard to loosen them, he told me "Shut the fuck up and deal with it."

The other inmates and I were lined up single-file, then led into the parking lot toward a bus that reminded me of the ones tour groups rent for road trips. Before I could get on, the guards surrounded me, crowding me in with their beefy bodies.

"What are you in prison for?" one of them growled, his hot breath smelling like stale coffee and sour mint chewing tobacco.

"Child pornography," I whispered.

"What was that? Speak up? I can't hear you." I cleared my throat and said, "Child pornography" a little louder. The guards scowled and pushed closer in on me. "You piece of shit. You make me sick," the biggest of the group snarled. "Get out of my face," he continued, shoving me toward the bus.

Before I could get on, he yanked me back down the steps and

said, "If I hear one word out of you, I'm comin' for ya. Better yet, I'll tell the other inmates what you're in for and let them take care of you for me." I took a seat as far away from the guards as possible.

"Those guards look pretty pissed at you. What'd you do?" the inmate I sat next to asked. I just shrugged and stared out the window. We headed out of the city and hit the expressway, heading west toward parts still unknown. I fell into a trance as I watched other vehicles zoom by in blurs.

We were on the road for about three hours, before we pulled into the Harrisburg International Airport. What were we doing at the airport? I wondered. Were we about to be flown somewhere? I asked a few of the other inmates, but they were just as clueless as I was. And since I'd been warned not to talk to the guards, I couldn't ask them. So I sat in solemn silence and waited to see what would happen next. I held my breath and tried to think happy thoughts as I watched inmates get off. I breathed a sigh of relief when my name wasn't called to join them.

After other inmates got on, the guards handed out sack lunches containing a bag of juice, a wormy apple, a soggy oatmeal cookie and two sandwiches with unidentifiable meat on them. I almost puked when I smelled the "meat." We hit the freeway again and headed into the Allegheny mountains.

About twenty minutes later, we pulled up to the front gates of Lewisburg United States Penitentiary, an imposing castle-like fortress surrounded by a tall concrete wall. Violence hung in the air as I and the other inmates were shuffled off the bus one by one and escorted into the Receiving and Discharge building under the watchful eyes of guards bearing shotguns and automatic rifles. The Receiving and Discharge building was just as imposing as the outside facade with its dark and musky dungeon-like holding cells. I've blocked out most of what happened next. All I can remember is being more afraid than I'd ever been in my life.

The next thing I remember is being given a bedroll and told to get in line behind a group of inmates. We followed the guard out of R&D, back through the main concourse. Our voices and footsteps echoed as the guard led us down a long hallway, lined with columns that supported the high-arched ceiling. Hardened convicts glared at us from behind iron gates. We made a sharp turn and headed toward the infirmary. The infirmary was an old dilapidated building. The smell of

death hit me as soon as we walked through the door. I could almost hear the mournful wails of all of the inmates who'd died there.

Rusty radiators clanked in the background and the narrow hallway smelled like old piss as the guard led us past dozens of rooms with rows of bunks stacked three high, toward his office. He flipped through a steel binder to find empty bunks and assigned me and the other inmates bunks. I followed the other inmates into the common area, which was already overcrowded. A cloud of stale body odor hung over the maze of bunks as I made my way to my assigned spot.

The mattress was as thin as a maxi-pad and sallow with years of piss and sweat stains. The flip side was just as bad. So I just closed my eyes and made my bed, wrapping both sheets and blankets around the mattress the same way I'd lay down a nest of toilet paper before sitting on a public toilet.

After making my bed, I followed the sound of a blaring TV toward the back of the unit. The day room was crammed with inmates screaming over board games and cards or staring blankly at the fuzzy TV screen. I knew better than to go in: overcrowding often leads to tension, which then leads to violence. I can't even count how many fights I've witnessed over the TV. So I spent my days reading the trash novels I found in the shabby library and sleeping.

About the only good thing about my stay was the food. Compared to the food at FDC Philly, Lewisburg's food was gourmet dining. Since penitentiary inmates are generally serving lengthy sentences and are more prone to violence, they are fed better than most lower security inmates – the reason being that well-fed inmates are less likely to riot. Unfortunately, I didn't get to enjoy most of Lewisburg's offerings because I was still so sick and nervous, I still puked and shit whenever I ate or drank anything.

I still had no idea where I was going when the guard woke me up one morning and told me that I was leaving. The bus pulled out and headed north on the Interstate. I wondered where were we going. I became more and more bewildered every time we stopped to pick up or drop off inmates. On and on we drove into upstate New York, until we were almost at the Canadian border.

We pulled off the Interstate into a tiny town called Ray Brook, which is right outside Au Sable. With the Adirondack mountains towering over us, we sped past ski resorts and hunting lodges. The change in atmospheric pressure made me dizzy and I had to hobble

to the bathroom in the back of the bus to puke. Since I hadn't eaten much since leaving FDC Philly, my stomach didn't contain much but bile. I had an acidy taste in my mouth that I couldn't get rid of for the rest of the day.

We eventually reached our destination: a medium-security prison surrounded by tall fences and gleaming razor wire on the grounds of the 1980 Winter Olympics Village. I was shocked by the contrast between the beautiful landscape and the ugliness of all of that concrete and steel. A prison seemed so out of place.

Since my paperwork hadn't arrived yet, I was sent to the Special Housing Unit overnight. My cell-mate was a black dude not much older than me who'd been in prison for almost a decade. He told me he'd been transferred from the low security facility he was at for stabbing another inmate. And I believed him because he had a dangerous aura about him that made me uneasy. Luckily, he took a liking to me and gave me advice on how to do my time, which basically boiled down to the same advice Carter had given me about not borrowing, not gambling and not talking to the guards.

What happened to Lokni

The next morning, the Special Investigation Services (SIS) lieutenant pulled me out to discuss my paperwork. He took one look at my file and said, "With these charges you shouldn't even be here. If the other inmates find out, you're gonna have a tough time."

"Then what should I do?" I asked nervously.

"Keep your mouth shut and try your best to stay out of the way," he replied. He closed my file and stared sympathetically across the desk at me as I trembled in fear.

A few weeks later, I met a guy named Marvin, who lived a few cells down from me. Marvin, a Native American with tattoos all over his muscular body, talked tough and fancied himself a "convict." Marvin took an immediate liking to me because I was one of only a few young white guys on the unit and I stayed to myself. I liked Marvin because he oozed self-confidence and other inmates seemed to respect him. He eventually asked me to move in with him. I jumped at the opportunity.

Our friendship started out great. Since his family also sent him money for commissary, we always cooked and ate together. I also followed him wherever he went. People got so used to seeing us togeth-

er, they called me his "little brother." And since he was a member of the Native American Community, which was basically a gang, nobody ever fucked with me.

Eventually Marvin convinced me to have money sent to his commissary account since he didn't have to worry about his account being hit to pay any fines as I did. I agreed to have my mom send money to him – sometimes three to four hundred bucks at a time. With that kind of money, we could buy whatever we wanted. Since guards often brought in drugs and other contraband items, we smoked weed, popped pills and got pretty much whatever else we wanted. And since so many hillbillies are doing time at Memphis, moonshine flowed like water and Marvin and I got drunk most weekends. I also arranged for my family to come visit him, and we'd get called out to the visiting room together.

And come Christmas, I had my mom use her company's "Toys for Tots" donation money to buy his six-year-old son a Play Station 2 and video games. But that didn't mean I could let my guard down and relax. I constantly feared that he'd find out my charges, especially when we'd get drunk and he'd demand to see my paperwork. One night I put him off by saying that I'd asked my mom to send it but that it was intercepted by the mail-room staff, which was entirely possible since B.O.P. policy prohibits inmates from having their PSI and other official court documents. He must've have bought my story because he never asked to see them again.

Whenever he asked what I was in for, I told him I had a conspiracy charge without going into any details. Since I was young and white, he automatically assumed it was drug-related. And I never bothered to correct him. That worked for me just fine.

I shutter to think about what he'd do if he ever found out the truth, because he was constantly raging against child molesters and bragging about how he'd extorted them at other prisons. I'd always nod quietly and pray that I'd never experience his wrath. I still wonder what he would've done if he had found out. Would he have given me a pass because he'd gotten to know me? I doubt it. I'd seen what he and his Native American "brothers" did to one of their own when they found out that "Lokni" was a sex offender. He was gay, so the other Natives didn't want anything to do with him.

Like me, all Lokni wanted to do was be left alone to do his time as peacefully as possible. But all that changed when another guy from

the same reservation showed up and told the other Natives about Lokni's charges. Since the Natives "took care of their own," they saw it as their personal responsibility to get rid of Lokni. Although Lokni was a scrawny little man, five much bigger, stronger guys felt the need to gang up on him. After they beat him to a bloody pulp, Lokni went back to his unit and slit his own wrists. His cell-mate found him and called for a guard, who then rushed Lokni to medical where he was sewn up before being placed into protective custody. I never saw him again. I don't know where he wound up. I hope he turned out okay.

That incident haunted me. I felt so bad for Lokni. He didn't deserve to be treated like that because he didn't bother anybody. But whenever I brought it up to Marvin, he'd say, "Fuck Lokni. He's a no-good fagot chomo. He got what he had coming." So, after a while, I stopped bringing it up.

Lokni wasn't the only sex-offender or homosexual Marvin targeted. Whenever he found out that somebody fit into one or both of those categories, he immediately turned on them and started harassing them. Although I never witnessed it myself, I've heard that he'd been extorting several of my friends. I guess I shouldn't have been as shocked as I was to hear that, because whenever Marvin saw me with one of them, he'd say, "Stay away from that guy. He ain't no good." But at the time, I thought he was just jealous that I was hanging out with people other than him and his friends.

All the while, I put on a bad-ass front and did whatever I could to just be "one of the guys" – getting more tattoos, intentionally scarring my body with cigarette burns and razorblades and, though I hate to admit it now, joining in on the "chomo" and "homo" hating that ran rampant among Marvin and his friends. I also lied my ass off – so much so I had to keep track of my lies in a journal to keep from forgetting what I'd said and to whom.

Meanwhile, I'd been seeing Dr. Ennis, the prison psychologist. With his help, I began to deal with the many psychological issues I have, specifically my self-hatred and trouble coping with prison life. The main thing I took away from these sessions was that, in order to find peace within my environment, I first had to find peace within myself, and that the only way to find that was by forgiving and accepting myself first.

He did his best to discourage me from signing up for Axis II [*a program for men who were presumably "character disordered"*] by

telling me horror stories about how difficult it was there, but I'd already made up my mind to go. Eventually, I was able to convince him that I would be able to handle it and he turned in my application in November 2006.

When I didn't hear back from Dr. Ennis right away, I thought it was because I'd been turned down. But then a few weeks before Christmas, he called me into his office to tell me that I'd been selected for consideration and that he'd set up a closed-circuit TV interview with Dr. Weiner, the director of Axis II. He also went on to tell me that if I completed Axis II, which would take approximately twelve months, I'd be awarded with a "management variable," which would allow me to transfer to a lower security institution of my choosing. Now I couldn't wait to get to Axis II.

Of course, everyone didn't share my enthusiasm. I had plenty of "friends" tell me that I'd make a big mistake if I went into the program because the shrink at Springfield would pump me full of psych drugs and make me a zombie. They also told me stories about people they knew who knew people who'd met similar fates. But those stories seemed more like urban legends than facts, so I dismissed them as bullshit. Marvin was my biggest detractor.

"You've let those shrinks brainwash you. You've got it made here. You don't work, you got plenty of money coming in, dope and booze – and if you ain't a chomo or snitch, like you claim you ain't, then nobody will fuck with you – especially while I'm here. So why are you in such a rush to leave?"

That (the chomo part) was exactly the reason why I wanted to leave, I felt like telling him. But I'd come so close to accomplishing my goal of staying out of trouble for a year, I wasn't about to risk fucking it all up now. So I bit my tongue and let him believe whatever he wanted about me. If I was lucky, I'd be away from him before the new year.

But man, was it tough! Since his mom had died "of a pill overdose," Marvin had become an even bigger asshole, taking all of his pain and sorrow out on me. He'd criticize me about everything, until I began to feel like I couldn't do anything right. In many ways, he was more difficult to live with than my mom, Mellisa, and all of my worst cellies combined.

At first, I tried to overlook his insults and support him. After all, he'd just lost his mom and I couldn't even imagine how that felt. I

knew I'd be devastated if my mom died while I was in prison. I comforted him with food, booze and dope and hung out with him as often as possible. But no matter what I did, it was never enough. It got to the point where we were both spending our commissary limits every month and getting drunk and high almost every day. Whenever I protested or showed the slightest bit of independence, Marvin would call me an inconsiderate and selfish asshole, which always made me feel guilty and I'd go along with whatever he wanted to do.

After about three months of being treated like shit, I'd had enough and couldn't wait to get away from him. Axis II would be my ticket. A few days later, Dr. Ennis put me on call-out for the closed circuit TV interview with Dr. Weiner, which worked the same way as a web-chat with a tiny camera and microphone and our images in large and small boxes on a TV monitor. Dr. Weiner was a tall, thin blonde woman dressed like a kindergarten teacher who had a very soothing, but commanding voice. She asked me the same questions that I'd answered on my application – why I was interested in Axis II, what I hoped to get out of it, and if I thought I could handle the intense and emotionally challenging environment.

She then went on to tell me about some of the difficult situations I'd surely find myself in – like living in a dorm setting, someone invading my personal space by sitting on my bed or touching my property without my permission, fist-fights, etc. – and asked how I'd handle them. I told her the truth: that I'd have to see when that happened but that I didn't think I'd have too much difficulty adjusting because I'd put up with similar situations at Memphis.

She wrote down my answers as I gave them while I tried to figure out what she was thinking, which was impossible because she had a blank expression on her face. After she finished, she said, "Okay. From your answers, I think you're a good candidate for the Axis II program. I'm going to start the paper work for the transfer. Good luck. I'll see you in a few weeks." The TV screen went blank.

Dr. Ennis smiled at me and shook my hand. "Congratulations, Mr. Rosen. You're on your way." I thanked him and practically skipped back to the unit, smiling all along the way. I didn't tell Marvin or anyone else the good news until I was called down a few days later to pack out.

The night before I left, Marvin threw me a going away party – using my own money, of course. We got drunk and stoned and ate like

slobs, while reminiscing about all of the "good" times we had during the fifteen months I'd been at Memphis.

The next morning, December 16, 2006, Marvin walked me to R&D to see me off. "I'll call your mom tonight to let her know you left." "Thanks."

"Keep in touch," he said and we shook hands.

"You bet," I replied, although I had no intention of ever talking to him again. And I haven't, though he continues to correspond with my mom and ask about me. My mom says he speaks highly of me, but, like I tell her, that's only because he believes I'm somebody else. I don't know who to hate more for that – him or myself, for living the lie for so long.

Unlike in the past, where I had to take buses, layover in places like Oklahoma City and Lewisburg, I got a personal escort to the airport and a direct flight on a private jet with only one other inmate, a guy with one leg who was going to Springfield to get fitted for a new prosthetic. And without a blackbox, I was able to lay back and actually enjoy the ride.

I would go on to spend thirteen months at Springfield – a period that was both the best and the worst times of my life with all of the chaos, violence and surreal antics that ensued. But I wouldn't trade that experience for anything because I learned so much about myself and life as a result.

The biggest difference between being in the Axis II unit and any other place I'd been during my incarceration was that I felt accepted despite my charges and sexual orientation. And there were countless hilarious incidents, such as naked aerobics, late-night orgies in the TV room, even a gay wedding. Of course, there's always a trade-off. Here everyone had one or more personality disorders which often led to violent emotional outbursts.

The program helped me accept myself and my situation without judgment, to move forward without self-harm or self-sabotaging behaviors, and to eliminate the codependency that hurt me so badly in Memphis. And just like Dr. Ennis had promised, I got a management variable and my choice of lower-security prisons. I chose the low-security correctional institution at the federal correctional center in North Carolina because of its reputation as a laid-back place.

My time here at the federal correctional center hasn't always been easy. During the almost five years I've been here, an article from

a vigilante website called evil-unveiled.com – containing inaccurate facts about my case and written in incendiary language – was circulated all around the compound. As a result, I've suffered more derision and scorn than ever before. And since I have so much time left to do, I know my suffering is far from over. But at least now I can rely on the gift of hindsight and the lessons I've learned along the way to guide me through.

Lessons learned

I used to think that the story of Peter Pan was romantic, but now I see it as a tragedy. There's a scene at the end of the book, when John, Michael and Wendy go back home to their parents and grow up while Peter Pan is forced to watch on, alone, from outside the window. I can really relate to that scene now that I'm in prison. It's hard to believe that C, Cody, Mini-P, J-Dogg, M, and Nathan are all young adults and teenagers now because I will always remember them as the little boys they were the last time I saw them. My sister has also grown up and, like Wendy, is now a mother herself. Even I, the boy who refused to grow up, am now in my thirties and have begun to show signs of aging with hair loss and aching joints. I know that this shouldn't come as a big surprise, since everybody grows up. But for someone like me, who never thought he would, it came as a shock comparable to finding out that Santa Claus and the Easter Bunny don't really exist.

Since I've been in prison, a part of me has died. I'm no longer the wide-eyed, naive and innocent boy I once was. I've become someone I barely recognize – a bitter, hateful person who's angry at the world. I miss my younger self. I wish I could be that man-child again. But Peter Pan is dead. I often wonder: if it were possible to travel back in time and warn my younger self of the fate that awaited him, would he listen and stop doing what he was doing? Probably not. Knowing what I know now about that boy, he would've probably flipped me off and told me that I didn't know what I was talking about. After all, that was the way he responded to anyone who questioned his lifestyle.

But then again, he didn't know what I know now. For example, after years of being lied to and taken advantage of, I no longer believe that I can take people at their word or that everyone has my best interest in mind. In fact, I've become hyper-vigilant and don't let many people get close to me, which leads to loneliness, but at least I don't have to worry about getting fucked over.

ℭℨ

What hurts even worse than the loss of my own innocence is that of my Lost Boys' innocence. Unlike Peter Pan, who protected his Lost Boys from the evils of the adult world that Captain Hook and his pirates represented, I led my Lost Boys straight into the black lagoon. Since they are listed as my victims, I am not allowed to contact them. But I have been able to follow Nathan through my mom, who is still in contact with my grandmother with whom Nathan lives. If any of the boys turned out anything like him they couldn't have had an easy time. Since I've been in prison, Nathan has become a juvenile delinquent: he was kicked out of school for fighting and bringing in weapons. His behavior got even worse after he found the body of his mom (my Aunt Sara) after she died of a drug overdose. He is now in therapy and attending classes at a disciplinary school.

I can't help but feel responsible for all of his suffering. Did my actions contribute to his mom's drug abuse? Since my Aunt Sara is dead, I can't ask her directly, so I'm left with nothing but uncertainty. And it's that uncertainty that festers in my conscience. My mom assures me that my Aunt Sara's problems started long before Nathan was even born and that my Aunt Sara did far more damage to Nathan by forcing him to witness her total deterioration than I did. Even if what my mom says is true, that doesn't ease the pain.

ℭℨ

In the prologue, I asked myself the following questions:
• When did all of this start?
• What happened?
• Where did I go wrong?
• Why did I do what I did?
• Who had I become?

I've had plenty of time to think up answers. What I've come up with is this:

My dad's death left a void that I've spent my entire life trying to fill. When Ted came along, I thought I'd found a man who would love me and protect me. But he had his own demons to fight and was unable to provide those things. And the violence he rained down on my mother traumatized me.

I still have mixed feelings about Ted. Part of me still hates him for putting me, my mom and sister through so much trauma. But there's also a part of me that feels sorry for him. Since I've been in prison, Ted has had his own share of problems: he has been in rehab several times and has a long list of medical issues, including trouble with his liver that doctors attribute to hepatitis C. My mom tells me that he's also been experiencing regret and remorse and constantly talks about how differently he'd do things if he had the chance to do it all over again. And I can believe that – the last time he visited me, I barely recognized him. He looked so withered and pitiful.

I just wish he could have had that epiphany twenty years ago. If he had, I may not have landed in prison. Who knows? But I've learned that dwelling on such things is a waste of time. There is no going back. Life plods on at its own brutish pace. It's better to let go of past hurt and hatred and move on. Besides, if I want people to forgive me, I need to forgive others.

Zen Buddhism has helped me learn to cope with my anger and other overpowering emotions and realize that nothing is permanent. No matter how bad things seem, they will soon pass. Through meditation and mindfulness, I've learned to identify my emotions and think about the consequences of my actions before doing anything. I just wish I had the same self discipline back when I was a teenager. Maybe if I had, I wouldn't have gotten into all of the trouble that I have.

I also wonder if my life would've turned out differently if I were born into a different set of circumstances. What if I'd had grown up in a more stable household and had the same privileges as most middle class teenagers? If so, who and what could I have become? If only, if only ...

But like with everything else, it's too late to wonder about all of that and I need to make the best of my current circumstances. I always knew that I was "different" from my same-age friends, but never knew how or why. Not knowing made me feel anxious and isolated. And since I couldn't express myself freely to my family and friends, I withdrew and sought companionship elsewhere.

Part of the problem, I now realize, is that I was gay before I knew what being gay meant. This was likely further complicated by my "daddy" issues, which manifested themselves in my desire to seek the companionship of older men who I could look up to and love

and who'd love me back. What made things even harder was the homophobic environment that surrounded me. Out of fear of being ridiculed and abused by family and friends, I tried to keep my confusion about my sexuality to myself.

To mask my pain, I recreated myself as a larger-than-life, asexual character. By doing so, I was able to avoid questions about my sexual proclivities and to also gain the acceptance and admiration of my peers. But at the same time, I wanted to prevent other young boys from having to go through what I had to go through due to my lack of a positive male role model. I now realize that I had an ulterior motive: by befriending younger boys, I could also get them to admire and love me. In other words, I could become the hero I always wanted to have. Also, since I was a big kid myself, I could relate to younger boys so much better than my same-age friends. Little boys didn't care about how "weird" I was, nor did they care about the color or style of my hair, nor what kind of clothes I wore or how much money I made. All that mattered to them was that I loved and paid attention to them.

I couldn't believe my luck when I found BoyChat and the on-line boy-love community: here were the older men I'd been looking to befriend for so long. I loved all of the attention they gave. Best of all, they also loved younger boys and had young friends of their own and lived lifestyles I'd only previously imagined. Since they obviously felt the same way I did about boys, I gladly did whatever they asked me to do even if those things sometimes went against my morals and values. I would've done anything to stay in their good graces because at least they loved and accepted me which was more than I could say about my "real" friends.

Although I couldn't have cared less about what people thought about my lifestyle, I realized that in order to live the way I wanted to I needed to appear as normal as possible. Since I'd already failed at finding a gay lover my own age or older, and my family and friends weren't ready to accept me as an openly gay man, I went through a series of girlfriends before settling on Mellisa. It's ironic how drastically my family's and friends outlooks have changed since I've been in prison. Several friends and family members – including my Aunt Kathy – have since come out of the closet and been accepted without ridicule and scorn – most surprisingly by my mom, who stays in contact with several of them. The reason this comes as such a shock is because my mom was once a raging homophobe – so much so that

she threatened to disown me if I ever "decided" to become gay.

Mellisa was a perfect match. Not only was she a fat chick, which made it highly unlikely that she'd leave me, but she was also a sexual freak who promised to make my wildest fantasies come true. And she did, as the Bonnie to my Clyde. She was also the only person in real life who knew all there was to know about me. Back then, I considered myself lucky. Little did I know that the things I most appreciated about Mellisa would lead to my downfall. I used to joke with Mellisa and my BL friends by rating a boy by how many years I'd be willing to do in prison for the chance to do whatever I wanted with him. My legal drama has taught me that nobody and nothing is worth spending time behind bars.

But the real lessons I've learned have all come since I've been in prison. Since I've been in prison, I've lost all of the control I'd worked so hard to gain. I can no longer do what I want, come and go as I please, dress, act, or express myself as I see fit. Worst of all, I cannot be around those that I love most: boys. I've never felt so lonely and out of place.

Prison is such a cold, harsh and hostile environment, where people do what is necessary to survive – especially younger men. I know this all too well because I've been forced to act in ways that are contrary to my true nature. I've done many, many things that I'm not proud of – like lying, bullying, talking shit about people and betraying people's confidence in order to win the acceptance of the "in-crowd."

I've learned these lessons the hard way, after years of suffering shame and self-hatred. Writing this memoir has forced me to come face to face with these character flaws that hurt so badly. I'd masked them with bravado, swagger and posturing, and punished myself by cutting myself with razor blades. I guess that by doing so, I hoped to fool myself and others. But not any more. I refuse now to avoid my issues and have chosen to take them head-on instead.

Now that I've identified my flaws, I vow to do whatever is necessary to fix them. I don't just owe this to myself, but also to my mom, sister and friends who've stood by me throughout this ordeal. I can only hope to replace their shame and disappointment over my criminal behavior with pride for my accomplishments.

ʒ

I know that I'll offend some people by telling my truth. I already have. While I was writing this memoir, another inmate dropped an anonymous note expressing concern about the content of my manuscript – specifically that it was some kind of "how-to" manual on molesting children.

α

I just hope that readers take something away from my story – specifically that not all sex offenders are as evil as they are portrayed. In many cases, they are deeply troubled and haunted individuals with traumatic pasts who behave in ways that even they can't understand. I also hope that my story serves as a warning to parents. Perhaps I can prevent future abuse by making people aware of how a sex offender thinks and how one goes about choosing victims and the grooming process that goes along with it.

Advice

Perhaps I can also deter pedophiles from acting out on their desires by giving them a glimpse into the troubles that await them if they do. I have the following advice for anyone who finds himself sexually attracted to children: stay far away from the underworld of child pornography, Nothing positive can come out of venturing into its dark and dangerous territory. Sure, the videos and pictures you'll find there are alluring. But what they don't show is what's happening on the other side of the camera. I know now that the children in those images were threatened, beaten, drugged or worse before and afterward. I also know that, in many cases, the children who were used in those pictures and videos went on to live troubled lives – many becoming victimizers themselves. Furthermore, viewing child pornography is a lot like using drugs: once you get a taste, you want more and more until you find yourself doing things you never would have before you used or viewed the product. Before you realize it, it's already too late and you're hooked. People who truly love children don't do things that put children in harm's way. They do whatever they can to protect and nurture them.

In a perfect world, children would be free to grow up free of harm and worry, and be able to make their own decisions without coercion, fear or manipulation. But this isn't a perfect world. Unfortu-

nately, there are people who take advantage of children. Even those who don't take advantage of them, and enter into relationships with children that are consensual and equally desired, risk harming them in the eyes of society, due to its current views regarding sex with children. Too often, the justice system does more damage to child victims than their abusers did by forcing victims to relive their abuse over and over again during the process of investigation and prosecution of their abusers. And since, in a majority of cases, the victimizer is a family member or close friend, the legal process tears families and communities apart. All of this is separate from the media attention that usually surrounds sex-abuse cases. Although the courts and media try to protect victims' identities by not naming them directly, their presence in the courtroom makes it easy for the public to identify them. As a result, victims of childhood sexual abuse often feel responsible for the acts committed against them.

In the end, it's just not worth the risk of causing so much suffering. I urge people who find themselves attracted to children to use their passion in more positive and constructive ways – such as working as social workers, psychologists, counselors, mentors, pediatricians and other fields where they can help and not harm children.

If you find yourself in a situation where you feel like you can't control your sexual urges, I urge you to seek professional help. Sure, you may have to undergo therapy or psychological treatment, but at least you'll avoid hurting those you truly love.

I know that many people will read this and accuse me of being a hypocrite because I didn't heed my own advice. I know that I wouldn't have back when I was in the process of committing my crimes. But that was before I experienced all of the hardships that I have, and gained the insight that I have now. In hindsight, if I had had a book like this [*his reference is to the book he wrote, from which this is just an excerpt*] back then, I think I would've thought twice about going as far as I did. But again, it's too late to ponder that now. I must live with the consequences of my actions. If I can prevent one person from starting down the misguided path I took or prevent one child from being abused, and from suffering what I put my victims through, then it's been well worth all the trouble.

Chapter 3 – My Childhood and Adolescence

by G.D.

I was born in Maplesville, Mississippi, on Jan. 18, 1962. My parents were carnies. I was born premature. I had to stay in a premature chamber for nine weeks before I could live on my own. I was not able to have milk or egg products as a baby, so they put me on a special formula.

When I was three years old my family was staying in a motel down in New Mexico. My mom told me there was nothing I was afraid of as a child. She said I climbed on top of the two-story hotel, looked down at my dad and jumped off the roof into his arms, laughing.

One day, I was downtown Minneapolis, with my mom and dad. They purchased a five-cent coke bottle, 6 oz. Walking around, and I dropped my soda and tried to grab it, but it hit the ground and cut my left thumb off. My dad wrapped my hand and took me to the hospital in a cab. I was only five, but I remember my mom's face looking really concerned. My dad said that five cent coke turned into a five thousand dollar hospital bill. But the doctors did a very good job repairing my thumb. If you didn't know it was hurt, you would never know it today.

Being a carny was very fun, always visiting new towns, meeting new people. The Carnies were a family. If the police tried to take one away, they would get stopped by the rest. They protected each other. My mom ran a game and my dad did the electric and repaired the rides. I had to watch my younger brother, who was two years younger. When we wanted something to eat, we just went to the stand that sold food and they just gave us food or drink. We always hid in differ-

ent places. The adults never paid any mind to us at all.

Once when my brother and I were walking around the place, we found a dead body. At first I was thinking that he was only asleep. I tried waking him up. I was only seven at the time. I found an envelope full of money under the body. We put it in our pocket, and then ran and got help. Looking back at it, there was only $30 in ones. But to a seven and five year old, it was a lot of money. We were wrong for taking it. I don't know what happened to him, except that he was dead.

When I was a little bit older, about 8 years old, my mom and dad decided to settle down in Louisiana to give us kids an education. I was still shy around people. I figured the carnival would have made me be more open, but it didn't. I do remember that my brother and me missed it very much.

We lived in a trailer park right by the cemetery. It was a very good place to hide in to get away from everyone. I would get flowers from the graves to give to the teachers until one asked where I got the flowers and I told them. They told my parents. Mom and Dad said that people put it on the graves for their dead family member. At eight, I didn't see anything wrong, but didn't do it again because I was asked not to.

Then my family purchased some land near Marian and put a house on it. So I had to change schools again.

By now I had two younger brothers. When we moved over there, I started going to church on the church bus every Sunday. They would give us candy and food after the church services, but we had to sing songs. I really didn't have a lot of friends at the time. I enjoyed my Saturday cartoons and weekday cartoons, plus looking at the stars in the sky.

I was not very good in reading and writing. I didn't wish to let anyone know about it; even my mom and dad. But I could remember anything I heard or saw. I stayed by myself, mostly having a book, so everyone thought I was reading.

But when I was about nine years old, one of my teachers asked me to stay after class for a few minutes. She then started to ask me some questions that I answered without having to think about them. Then she asked me why I answered them wrong on the test. I felt really scared and just didn't answer, and I just ran out of the room.

Over the next few weeks, she told my parents. They acted sur-

prised by what she had told them. They gave permission for me to be tested. The test showed I was dyslexic and ADHD. The teacher called me into her office and said, "Your tests show you have a learning problem, but that you're very smart. That's how you've been able to fool all the people; only a very smart child could do that!"

"But I don't want any of the other kids to find out because they would tease me," I said.

"They don't have to know anything," she replied. They set up a special time for me to get help with my homework.

I still liked to go to the woods after school to get away and be by myself. I enjoyed the peace and quiet, away from my brothers and sisters. The school also had put me on medication. They said it would help me concentrate in school. It was Ritalin.

I asked my mom and dad to let me take Karate when I was ten years old. They told me no, because of my temper, fearing I would harm my brothers and sister. I was very mad at them and broke a window, then took off on my bike, to be alone. I thought they were wrong for not allowing me to take it. I still, to this day, think it would have changed my life, but I guess I'll never know.

I had a big book collection on science and space, plus a rock and stamp collection that I would not share with my brothers and sister. I would help them, and be there for them if they asked, but I didn't just go out and play with them. I enjoyed my own world where I could become whatever I wished to become. I had a very good fantasy life that I kept to myself.

My mom stayed home and my dad was a merchant marine. My dad always made sure that we did the work around the house, and if he was working on a car, electric, plumbing, framing, roofing, he always made us boys help him, even if we didn't want to! But we got to go every weekend to the movies. We never did without, at any time, and it taught us the value of hard work.

My parents were not the emotional type of people and my dad got upset if you showed too much emotion, saying that it was for women, not men. Men didn't show their emotions, so we would hide it if we were crying, because Dad gave you a reason to cry.

I remember a man called The Snake Man that came to our school. He allowed me to hold all the different snakes and allowed me to help him for his show. It made me very happy to be doing it. I stayed after to put up all the snakes. He invited me to go for a summer to help

him catch snakes and gators. He gave me his card and gave me a ride home. I told my mom and dad about it, but they would not allow me to do it. They would not even give me a reason why! I was mad at them for weeks for not allowing me to go. It would have been my first job, and something I would have enjoyed.

My dad also taught us that if we give our word, do it, and if our brothers or sisters did something wrong, don't tell on them because if you did, you would get more of an ass-whooping than the person who did the wrong. But if dad asked you if you did something, you didn't lie, you told the truth. Whether you did right or wrong, you still told the truth.

I still have a hard time, even today, if I'm asked (by Mom, police, Dad, etc.) if I did something, I have to answer with the truth. That's why I try not to allow them or anyone to ask a direct question. I try to get away. I prefer not to answer them with a lie.

I tried to get into Cub Scouts, but because I was ten years old, they wouldn't allow me in. They told my parents to get me into Boy Scouts, so they set it up for us to meet the scout master and he told them he could not accept me until I was ten and a half years old. He took the application and money to become a member, then dated it for them, and sent paperwork to Central Scout Office for approval.

I was so excited when my card came in the mail. My dad took me to Sears to purchase all my scout gear. I was so happy, I read the scout Handbook a few times – with some help; but I learned the oath and Creed. I still know them today! I appreciated all the survival training from the scouts. Every shy boy, or girl should spend a few years in the scouts to teach them team work and survival lessons, plus how to read a map and compass.

My mom, during the summer, would take us to the public pool. When I was ten – and not able to swim very good – I always hung out in the shallow end of the pool. But one day, one of the other children asked me why did I not get into the deeper end with the bigger kids and jump off the high board? I said I just played over here. He then called me a sissy and chicken. So I got out of the pool, walked down to the other end, and climbed up on the high diving board and jumped in.

The life guard jumped in and pulled me to the side. She said "If you can't swim, don't be doing that." I got out and went back to the high-dive board, climbed back up, and jumped off again. The life

guard shook her head. When I hit the water I pushed myself off the bottom and dog-paddled back to the side.

I said to the older boy "Now who is the chicken?" The older boy and I stayed in the deep end, playing until it was time to go home.

He said "I hope to see you here tomorrow" and he gave me a little hug – it freaked me out.

I said "I hope so!" The whole week, we saw each other at the pool and played. It was a lot of fun.

Everyday he went with me to the locker room to shower and change clothing; but at first I didn't like changing in front of him, nor did I enjoy it at school. I was always the last one out of the locker room. But he said "I promise it is nothing to worry about. I'm your friend." Each day it was easier to shower and change with him. I washed his back and he washed my back. After we were done showering and no one was in the locker room, he gave me a hug before we were dressed. He pulled me really close to him. He said thanks for everything. I did not say a word, but only smiled at him. The next few weeks we met at the pool to swim. His face always seemed excited to see me, and I enjoyed our friendship too. Every day he gave me a hug before we got dressed but it stopped bothering me and I started hugging him back because it was feeling real good to be appreciated.

But after I started scouts, I didn't go to the pool, except for on the weekend, one time a month. I didn't see him anymore, and he never told me where he lived. Even today I wish I could see his face, wish I would have known where he lived. I would like to know what happened to him. He was my first friend. Thinking about it today, he always had a hard-on after he hugged me, but at the time I didn't think anything of it since I was only ten at the time and he was thirteen at the time. But even today I miss the swimming, talks, snow cones, and hugs from him. My family didn't hug me, tuck me into bed, or read bedtime stories. He even called me his little brother, when people saw us hugging.

I remember one day when we were swimming, my brother kept following us around. I asked my brother to stop but he kept on. My friend swam under water and pulled off my brother's swimsuit and tossed it on the ground. He said "Now he will not follow us." I was laughing about it but my brother was in the water crying. I got out of the water and tossed him his suit back. We grabbed our towels and went to the locker room to take our shower and change.

Then we went outside to get a snow cone with all the flavors on it – called Rainbow. We sat outside talking and watching everyone swimming. He put his arm around me and said "You know I love you like a brother, right?"

"Yes," I said. He told me about his love of making model cars and ships; he had a big collection all over his room. My mom showed up and I had to go. I introduced him to my mom. He was 4'6", slim, lightly tan, brown hair, and brown eyes with a nice smile.

When we were traveling with the carnival somewhere in Kansas, when I was around 7 years old, we ran into a tornado. Everyone pulled to the side of the road. My dad told me to crack the windows in the back seat and my mom did in the front. My dad got out of the truck to get to the small trailer to open windows. He came back to the truck. I saw the tornado across the field, it looked as big as a football stadium; it was only about 100 yards from the truck. I was very amazed at it – I never saw anything like it – watching it going across the field and over the road a little ahead of where we were parked. Then we watched it just disappear into the sky. I asked my dad "What was that?" and he told me it was a tornado. I could see that my mom was very worried over it, but not my dad; it didn't seem to bother him at all. This was the first of the three times we had a close contact with a tornado! My dad told me later that it's nothing to worry about; you just have to take precautions, and hope it does not come your way. But you'll be safe as long as you take the precautions to save everyone. Property can always be replaced, but not your life or your family.

Early adolescence

When I was twelve years old, my group of friends and I were going out for a bike ride. They wished to take me to an old rock quarry that had been closed down for years. It was a very clear sky, the sun was very hot; we had to bring our canteens with us for the ride. When we got to the rock quarry, we parked our bikes. Signs were posted everywhere saying Private Property, No Swimming. My friends said, "We come here all the time, just didn't think you'd like to come." I felt bad that they never invited me before now.

They were undressing. I asked "What are y'all doing?"

"We're going swimming, join us!" they said.

I shook my head, no. They ran and jumped off the forty-foot drop into the water. On the other side of the quarry was a landing where you could walk back up the hill about 100 yards away. They kept yell-

ing "Chicken!" and "Sissy!" They knew that it would bother me. I took everything off except my underwear. They started laughing at me. "We have seen everything that you have," they said.

I said "But what if someone comes by?"

They said "So what! They get to see us in our birthday suit! We have nothing to hide, right?" I then took off my underwear and jumped into the water with them. We swam for a few hours before we got done for the day. We were laying out on the big rock sunning ourselves. Wilson, the youngest, said, "I bet I can jack off quicker than y'all." Everybody laughed. He said, "OK, everybody race me." So we all started jacking off. Joe won. He was the oldest of us.

He said "No one stops until everyone gets off. Ron was second Aidan was third. William was fourth. I was last. William was glad he wasn't last.

We jumped back in the water, walked back up the hill. By the time we got there, we were all dry except for our hair. We got dressed, got on our bikes, and rode to our hideout in the woods. It was not much; a little wood shack we built. We only had two rules: there was no clothing and no girls inside the hideout. We didn't even tell our other friends about it. We considered it our place to leave the world behind. We could talk about anything with each other, or do anything with each other, and no one was going to judge us. We kept a few Playboy magazines around, and some beer, when we could sneak it from our parents. We laid in the hideout in our birthday suits playing music, and looking at Playboy magazines.

But it was getting dark. We got dressed and hid the magazines and radio. We kissed each other goodbye and took off towards our homes. Later that night, after I got home, Joe called and said to meet everyone in the morning at 7 AM. We were going on a bike ride to the pond.

The next morning, I got up early to eat some cereal and juice and watch my cartoons. My mom came into the room and said "Dylan, you have to take your brother with you today," she said.

"But mom!" I said.

"I have to take your brother and sister to the doctor for shots for school. Take him with you!" mom said.

"OK, but he has to keep up with us on his bike," I replied. My brother was only nine at the time. I told Jeffrey, "Where we go or what we do today is our secret because my friends don't like tattletale

people, and you know dad doesn't either."

He replied, "I understand."

When I showed up with my little brother, they all asked "what's up?!"

"Mom told me to bring him along," I replied.

They asked, "Can he be trusted?"

"Yeah!" I replied. Then Ron said "What's your name?"

"Jeffrey," he replied.

"Ok, here's the deal. You have to keep up with us, do as we request, and never say anything to anyone about what you see, hear, do, or anything else. Do you agree?"

Jeffrey replied "Yes!" We got onto our bikes and rode for about forty-five minutes, then took a trail off into the woods for another ten minutes. My little brother had been complaining that he was tired, but William had been talking to him the whole way. Everyone pulled me to the side.

"Since your brother is new, he needs to go first," said Ron.

I walked over to my brother, looked at him, and said "Since you're new to the group today, they'd like you to get undressed first for the swim."

He replied "I didn't bring anything to swim in."

"Yes you did," I replied. "We're going to swim in our birthday suits. You always have it." Everyone laughed when I said that. I turned to the boys and said, "He does not wish to, so we'll all go swimming and let him stay here by himself." We all got undressed. Everyone was in the water except for my brother and William, but he was ready to go. I was not much older than him. Then my brother got undressed and got into the water with him. We swam out to the raft in the middle of the lake. It was made of wood. We were jumping and swimming around for a few hours. Ron had gone back to the shore to bring back a bag that had our lunch and goods. William asked my brother if he was having fun. My brother's eyes got big and he shook his head yes with a big smile. After eating we just laid on the deck. We fell asleep and woke up with sunburns on our bodies. So we swam back and dried off; my brother and I used the same towel. By the time we got back, it was getting late and everyone went home.

Before Aidan and Joe left they told me, "Don't forget we have our Scout Summer Camp we have to go to on Friday. We'll see you at the scout leader's house then, since we won't see you tomorrow. We

won't see you tomorrow since we have to get ready for it."

"I have not forgotten," I replied. "I know it's a two-week trip to work as a group and compete against the other troops in the state."

I got home with my brother. Mom asked him, "Did you have a good day with your brother?"

My heart started to beat hard when I heard the question, but he just said, "I liked spending the day with him and his friends. We had a lot of fun. Hope I can go again some time." He looked at me with a smile.

After supper and my shower, I was in my room, my brother came in and laid beside me. Then he looked at me with his brown eyes and asked, "Can I come along with you and your friends again? I had a lot of fun."

"We will see," I said. He laid there for a minute, gave me a hug, and then left the room. This was the first time my brother gave me a hug. I felt kinda bad for not wanting him to come along. But I didn't want him to experience some of the things I have in my life — I consider it protecting him by not allowing him to be a part of it. I talked him out of becoming a scout. Now looking back, I was wrong, because every boy should have the enjoyment of the scouts in their life.

On Friday morning, my dad said, "Do you have everything you need packed in your backpack? Have you been taking the sulfur tablets?"

"Yes," I replied. He then handed me some money.

"You're going to need this for the canteen store."

"Thanks, dad," I said.

"If you need me, just call and I'll come out and get you."

"Okay, Dad," I replied.

I tried to hug him, but he said, "You get things in the truck so we don't be late." I loaded everything into the truck and he drove me to the scout leader's house. Most of the other scouts were already there. Then he came up to the truck and told me to put my things in the trailer. I got out, grabbed my things, and put them into the trailer. I saw my dad and him talking for a few minutes, then my dad drove off.

Joe came up and said, "Hi! Glad you made it!"

"Me too!" I said. "I'm looking forward to earning more badges to be able to become First Class."

"If we work hard on them, it will be possible for us both to get what we are after," he replied.

The rest of the Scouts showed up, and we got into the trucks and cars for the trip. Since it was going to be a long trip (about five hours), and it was hot, we stopped at McDonald's to rest, use the restroom, and get something to eat and drink. The sun was just coming up in the sky, about 7AM. We ate and got everyone back in the vehicles.

The scout master said, "Everyone use the restroom? Because we will not be stopping until we get to the campsite." No one said anything, so we hit the road. We reached the campgrounds about noon. We were told to put everything away. The scout master then told everyone," We have some free time until the opening meeting tonight. Everyone can get their swim suits, go down to the lake, and have some fun. But be back by 5 PM. Does everyone understand?"

"Yes sir!" everyone replied. We all got our swimsuits on, grabbed our towels and ran down to the lake. When everyone returned, we hit the showers and got our uniforms on for the meeting. The scout leaders had chili and hamburgers ready for us to eat. A few of us volunteered to do the dishes. That night, at the bonfire, the state scout leader addressed everyone, explaining the events of the troops plus what badges we could get. Then he led everyone into the main building and did a skit for everyone to watch. Then he said, "Breakfast is at 5 AM, so get some sleep." Then everyone headed for their bed. I know I was tired from the events of the day. I got into bed in my underwear and t-shirt, falling right to sleep.

It didn't seem like I was asleep very long when I was awoken by the assistant scout master. He had his hand over my mouth, motioning to come with him. I put my flip-flops on. When we got outside where no one could hear, he said, "I will not keep you up too long. I missed you very much, you have not been coming around me at the scout meeting much. Are you mad at me?"

"No," I replied.

"Do you still care and love me?"

"Yes."

"Great! I just wish to spend a little time."

He motioned me to follow him. We went into the showers. It was a big building with lots of showerheads and benches. Next to that building was the restroom with sinks toilets and urinals. Everything was open. He turned two showers on with very warm water. He looked at me and said, "Get undressed and get in the shower, he said. I looked down at the floor, and then took off my t-shirt and under-

wear and placed them on the bench. I got under the water and closed my eyes. The water was warm and felt real good. I felt a hand on my shoulder and opened my eyes. He pulled me close to him and gave me a hug. At first I didn't hug back. Then I hugged him back with water running over us. My head rested on his chest. Then he let me go. I looked up, and he leaned over and gave me a kiss. Then he motioned for me to turn around. I did. He took some shampoo and put it on my head, scrubbing with both hands. It felt good. Then he pulled me back under the shower head to get the shampoo out of my hair. Then he took the bar of soap and washed my back – then my right arm and fingers – my left arm and fingers – my butt – right leg and foot – left leg and foot. Then he turned me around and washed my face. I closed my eyes till he was done. Then my chest – stomach – and dick and balls. He got on his knees and sucked me off, and then smiled up at me.

"Did that feel good?"

"Yes!" I said with a smile.

He stood up, looked down on my eyes, leaned forward and kissed me with much feeling. He asked me to wash his back. I took the bar of soap and washed his back. He asked for the soap back. He grabbed my hands and led me out of the shower. He grabbed a towel, drying off my hair and the rest of my body. Then he helped me put on my underwear and T-shirt. He then gave me a kiss and told me to go back to bed. He stayed in the shower!

I got into my bed, laying there thinking how sweet he was to me tonight. I fell asleep with a very happy feeling and fully relaxed.

Next morning, I got up, got dressed, and headed to breakfast. They gave us toast, jelly, eggs (scrambled), bacon, cold cereal, milk, and juice. After you eat, you turn your tray in with your glass and silverware. Then we went and signed up for what we were going to participate in. I signed up for archery, musketry, life guard, first-aid, canoe, plus survival courses – I can't remember the names of the badges.

Let me explain the different survival courses I took. In one, they gave a group of five a map and a compass and told them to hike about ten miles to a given point on the map. Second, they taught us the different types of plants and trees by the leaves and plant make-up. Third, they taught us to build traps, snares, lean-tos, teepees, fire (without matches), bows and arrows, fishing poles, sweat lodges,

breach-cloths, and moccasins. We ran around the whole time for this course in a breach-cloth and moccasins, with a pocket knife.

Next thing I knew, it was lunch time. They rang the bell. We had pizza, salad, and fries, with bug juice – don't laugh. Bug juice is very good. After lunch we had to see where we had to go for what we signed up for. They gave me a schedule for the next nine days. Toward the end, there were events where troop took on troop for the Troop of the Year Award. After supper, everyone took their shower and then went to meet by the campfire to sing songs, tell stories, and hear the scout master talk about the day's events. Then everyone went to bed.

The assistant scout master woke me up again as the night before. We went to the shower and he did everything the same as the night before, but when I was leaving and heading back to bed, I saw an older scout heading for the showers. I was hoping he didn't see me, but I didn't know him.

A few days went by with only the normal activities of the camp, without being awoken by the assistant scout master. I was having a lot of fun doing the different activities and learning the information they were teaching me.

The next day was the Indian Day training. After breakfast I had to change into my breach cloth and moccasins. When teaching us about the woods and snares, he taught us how to track the animals, then showed us where to place the snares to catch the animals. We caught a rabbit, and he taught us how to skin it and clean it, then cook it on our open fire. Then we built a sweat lodge with a tepee, and we all sat in it for an hour to enjoy the sweating. I really didn't like it very much at first, it was hot. But it did relax me very much. The other boys were smiling, so I think they enjoyed it too. A few of the boys took their breach cloth off. The teacher just smiled and didn't say a word. One of them had a hard-on and legs wide open, eyes closed. I was trying to figure out what he was thinking about but never did.

After we got done, everyone went down to the lake and jumped in it in only our birthday suits, because the teacher told everyone that's what the Indians did to clean and close their pores. I was still shy about running around naked, so I was the last one in the water, but I had fun. Then he taught us an Indian dance to do at the end of the closing festival. We took a shower and went to bed. I was tired but full of energy, it took me a little time to get to sleep. I was woken up by the Assistant Scout Master again and we went to the shower.

I got undressed without him saying a word to me. But this time was a little different. He held me and told me he loved me and cared for me giving me really emotional kisses with fire behind them. Then he had me wash him from head to toe and then he did me from head to toe. He then sucked me off. It always feels really good!

Then he turned me around with me up on the wall. Having me put my legs apart a little, he started kissing my neck, rubbing his fingers between the crack of my butt. Then he put his dick there. It was a little painful but nothing that bothered me that much. I was just allowing him to enjoy himself to show him I loved him and cared about his needs. He had his arm around my chest rubbing my nipples and kissing my neck. I hear a noise and he gets off of me. There was that older Scout standing there. I'm wondering, did he see anything? I grabbed my towel and went to the bench and got dressed and went back to bed.

I laid there thinking I'm gonna be in trouble because everyone's going to know what happened. I fell asleep.

When I woke up the next morning, I was still concerned about that night, but the boy was good-looking. I was thinking he was about 16 or 17, blond hair, green eyes, and slim. He had a very nice smile too. I hoped he didn't see anything.

Joe and I got permission to go hiking for the day. We went to where the waterfall was located. We brought blankets and towels with us. When we got there, we got undressed and got under the waterfall, giving each other a massage on our shoulders and back. Then we held each other looking into each other's eyes while we were in each other's arms. Then we went swimming for about an hour, and then laid back on our towels on the blanket. I explained to him what happened last night, and about the other Scout coming in on us. He said, "If anyone asks, just say you were in your bed asleep. There are hundreds of scouts here for this event. He didn't know you, so it's nothing to be concerned about. He's been getting me up too!" He looked at me. We laid there holding hands, watching the clouds and the birds, not saying a word for a long time. We knew we missed lunch, but didn't care, since we got to spend a little time together. Both of us were at peace, with no cares. Joe rolled on top of me, and put his arms around me and kissed me. Then he said, "We have to get back."

"OK," I replied. We got up, got dressed, and cleaned up the site. On the way back we saw a deer drinking some water. We stood there

enjoying the deer and then it left. We got back to the camp and went to the stand to get soda and chips. We then went back to our place to put away the gear we had taken with us. When the sun was going down, we went to supper, then to the meeting of the night. We sang songs. When it was time for bed, I could not sleep, so I sat outside watching the moon and stars in the clear sky. It was very peaceful. I heard the owls, crickets, and other noises of the animals, but it was still very relaxing. I went to bed and went to sleep.

Next morning, at breakfast, the assistant scout master pulled me aside. He said, "Don't worry about the other night, I took care of it. Now go eat your breakfast." So the daily events were fun. We had canoe races and swimming races, each troop competing for ribbons and trophies. That night I laid on my bed thinking about what he meant when he said he took care of it. I went to sleep and did not get woken up.

The last day of camp, I ran into the scout from the shower. Well, really, he ran into me at the restroom. I was brushing my teeth. He tapped me on the shoulder. I looked back and he was smiling at me. "Hi, I'm Bill! Can we talk for a few minutes?"

"Sure," I said. We walked a little bit away from there and sat on a log. My heart was racing and my mouth was dry. He looked down, then turned to me.

He said "I saw what he was doing to you in the shower." He didn't say a word for a few minutes. Then he said, "You didn't have to run off." I just sat there not saying a word. "He told me you were willing. Is that true?"

I nodded and looked at the ground.

"Okay," he said. "I'd like for you to know that he and I have been in the shower every night same as I saw you all." I turned to him gave him and hug and said, "Thanks."

He said, "After breakfast, I'd like to take a walk and talk with you in the woods, if you don't mind."

"OK," I replied. We agreed to meet outside the chow hall. I showed up first, then he showed up with his backpack. He patted me on the back and then smiled at me, then we took off down a trail. We didn't say a word for the whole walk. We got to a place that had a big flat rock that overlooked for miles. He said, "No one will walk up on us up here." He laid out a sleeping back and unzipped it. "Take off your shoes and sit down," he said. We sat down on the sleeping bag

just looking at each other. Then he said, "I'm an Eagle Scout. I've been helping out here for the last two years since I became an Eagle Scout. You're very good looking. No one knows I have these feelings, not even my parents. They'd kill me. I knew you would understand." I nodded. "If you don't mind, I would like to give you a massage."

I nod and take off all my clothing except my underwear. I lay on my stomach. I always love to get a massage because it makes me feel relaxed and at peace. And he undressed himself completely. He had hair around his dick and was hard. He noticed I was looking.

"You make me feel that way!" He said smiling. He got himself across my legs, and I felt his dick on my butt. He started massaging my shoulders, neck, then right arm and fingers, left arm and fingers, then my back (very slowly). I said "You're good at this. You've done it with other boys."

"No, my girlfriend taught me, but you're more enjoyable to me than my girlfriend," he said. I gave a big smile, but was thinking: was he telling me the truth or just telling me this? I didn't care! He got down to my butt, started pulling down my underwear.

"Is this okay with you?" he said. I didn't say a word but allowed him. He massaged my butt, legs, and feet. Then he turned me over and started massaging my face, chest and stomach. I had a boner. He said "You're the only boy I have done anything with except for your Assistant Scout Master. I have always felt that way. But what would people say? I know you won't say a word and we won't see each other after tomorrow." Then he played with my dick. He's never done this before, I was thinking. I got off a few times. He got off and laid beside me. He then grabbed a towel and cleaned me up. Then he got down and sucked me until I got off. He lay back looking at me. "Did you enjoy everything?" He asked.

I said, "Yes very much, thanks!"

He said, "All I ask is you jack me off, please."

I sat beside him and grabbed his big dick, and played with it and his balls until he got off. I cleaned him up. I lay back down beside him. He moved the hair away from my face, and then put his arm around me and gave me kisses on my cheek.

Then we laid there. I fell asleep. When I woke up he was watching me. "You're very beautiful when you're asleep," he said. I just smiled. I sat up, laid back on his chest, and he put his arms around me. "Thank you for this day with me," he said, "I felt at peace with

you, and could be myself for a day." He kissed me on top of my head.

"Thanks for liking me," I replied.

He said, "We have to get back, it's almost supper time. They're going to be looking for us. If anyone asks, I'll tell them I was teaching you more about nature." I laughed. We got dressed and hiked back to camp; but before we got there, he stopped me and gave me a big kiss on the lips.

"I have been wishing to do that all day; I just got the nerve up to," he said. I hugged him back and kissed him and we went back to camp. I went to supper, took a shower, and went to bed. I was thinking about how the assistant scout master has not been around because he found himself some new fun. But I'm glad he left Joe and me alone for most of the camp. Our troop got a few first-place ribbons, and each scout got their badges.

After breakfast, I ran into Bill and asked him back to where I was packing. I gave him a hug and a long kiss. His eyes got big! I just smiled. "Thanks for your help, on this trip, with nature. I learned a lot from your teachings," I said. He looked around the area, but no one was around. Then he let himself relax.

He said, "I'm still confused about everything, but I would not trade it for anything. I hope you're here next year." I shrugged my shoulders. He gave me a hug and left.

I grabbed all my items and put them in the vehicles. On the trip back, I didn't say anything to anyone. My dad was there to pick me up. On the way to our house he said, "Did you have fun?"

"Yes! Lots of fun!" I replied.

"Good. You have to cut the grass and help me with a few things around the house for the next few days, so don't make any plans," he said.

"Fine," I said, thinking, boy, he really knows how to bring a person down. But I got home, put everything away, cut the grass, ate supper, took a bath, and laid back and relaxed. That night in bed, I could not get Bill out of my head, but I decided not to tell anyone about him until now.

For the next few days, I helped my dad around the house. I talked with Joe and William on the phone and we set up plans to go to the rock quarry to swim. William asked me to get my brother to come along for the day. He said that since school was to be starting up again in two weeks, we should let him have some fun too. So I asked him.

His eyes got big, he was very happy, jumping up and down. I told him to ask Mom if he could go with me. She said "Fine, take care of him!"

"We're going at 6 AM," I said. "Turn in at 9 PM so you can get you up in the morning."

The next morning, I packed some food, water, sunscreen lotion, and mosquito spray. I knew I'd been taking the sulfur tablets, but my brother had not, so the mosquitoes would eat him up if I didn't bring the spray! I put it all in my backpack with towels and blankets. I wanted to be more prepared than generally when we went there to swim.

My brother and me got on our bikes and met up with everyone else. We took off for the rock quarry. William hung back with my brother. I told everyone else, "Let's be careful what we do around my brother." They knew I meant the sexual things.

When we got there, we put our books down, then everyone got into their birthday suits. My brother was the last. Before I let him go, I got out the sunscreen and mosquito spray.

He said, "I'm not a baby. I don't need it."

"Humor me, OK!" I said. Then he let me put the sun screen on his back, butt, and legs. I told him to do the front everywhere. "Close your eyes and put your arms out," I said. I sprayed his whole body head to toes. I walked with the backpack down to the landing. My brother took a few minutes before he jumped into the water. I got in, swimming with everyone else. We were racing, jumping off rocks and climbing back up to the top to jump off again. After a couple of hours I sat on a rock and Joe joined me.

"Looks like your brother is having fun with William," he said.

I looked at him, shaking my head. They were laughing and playing tag in the water. I jumped back in and Joe followed me to the shore. I got a soda out for us and put out the blankets. I handed him a towel. He dried off. I did the same and then sat down on the blanket watching everyone else playing.

"How about we go to the movies Friday night and get a pizza afterwards?" he said.

"Fine by me!" I replied.

"My mom will drop us off and pick us up after we call her," he said.

We saw my brother and William on the big rock talking.

I could not hear what William was saying to him, but saw him

playing with himself. I shook my head. Then my brother lay back on the rock playing with himself. But William left him alone on the rock. He swam over by us. He said "I explained how to jack off, then told him to lay back and close his eyes and do it until his body felt relaxed." I looked at him, shaking my head. But my brother didn't stop doing it for a long time. It seemed like a half hour or more.

William got back in and swam with Ron and Aiden. When my brother stood up, everyone clapped for him like he'd just won an award. He took a bow a few times, then jumped into the water. Joe and I got back in and went swimming again. My brother swam over to me.

"See what I did?" he asked me.

"What did you do?" I replied. I knew what he'd done, but he seemed like he wanted to tell me.

He explained what he'd done ... And how it made him feel. Then he said, "You know how to do it."

"Yes, I've done it once or twice," I replied ... not wanting it to seem like a big deal. An hour later we stopped for lunch. Everyone dried off and my brother put more sunscreen on. He didn't really want to, so William put some on too. Then my brother had no problem. After eating, we cleaned up the trash and put it in the backpack. We laid back for the next hour, talking about going back to school. My brother, Ron, and Aidan fell asleep. I woke them up so they could go swimming again.

My brother said to me, "Can I show everyone what I learned?" His face looked so excited. I looked at everyone else. They shook their heads OK.

"One condition," I said. "You never say anything to anyone about what you did in front of us." He did not say a word but lay back on the blanket, closed his eyes and started playing with himself as everyone watched him. I was very concerned. My dad would beat my ass if he knew I allowed this to happen. What is done is done. There was nothing I could do to change it. When my brother got done nothing came out but he enjoyed himself. Everyone patted him on the back when he sat up.

Then everyone went swimming again. After a few more hours of swimming, everyone got out, dried off, drank the last of the soda, and got dressed. Then we all rode off for home.

When we got close to my house, I told Joe, "I'm looking forward

to the movie: *Close Encounters of the Third Kind*." Then my brother and I went home for the day. When we got home, I put the towels and blankets in the washer. Then mom had supper done. We sat down to eat. Dad was still at work. Mom said, "Did you have fun today with your brother?"

"Yes! Swimming was very fun!" he replied and then went back to eating. After dinner, we washed the dishes. When Mom gave my other brother and sister their baths, he said to me, "Don't worry about me, I won't say anything about today!" He smiled at me.

That night he was in the bathroom taking a bath and I walked in to take a pee. He was playing with himself again. He stopped, opened his eyes, and saw it was only me.

"I'm sorry to disturb you," I said. "But you should lock the door if you're going to be doing that. You don't want Mom or Dad or our brother and sister to walk in on you. They may start asking questions." On the way out of the door I turned the knob to lock it behind me, thinking to myself, I'm glad William did not ask to do it for him. I would be in a real mess now!

After he got out, I took my bath and then watched Star Trek. Then I went to bed so I could get up to watch my cartoons in the morning and mow the grass, so I'd be able to go to the movies on Friday, with Joe.

Joe's mom and Joe came and picked me up at 5 PM. We sat in the back seat of the station wagon. It was a four door, dark blue Dodge. His mom was playing some country music. We didn't like country music, so we just sat and talked about what we were going to do tonight. The theater was ten miles from my house in Gonzales. When we got to the theater, we got out and thanked his mom. He let her know we'd call later. There were about 30 people in line to purchase tickets, so we went to the back of the line.

"When we get inside, we'll pick where we're going to sit after we get our refreshments," he said. But he knew I always sat front row, center of the big screen. I didn't like people in front of me for the movie. We got a big popcorn, a large candy bar, and two large sodas. We went down to the front to sit down. He laughed. "You're predictable," he said.

We never talked during the movie, just sat there staring at the screen. When it was over, we got up and headed for the front door, talking about the movie. We went across the street and down a few

blocks, to the Pizza Hut. We ordered a large pizza, salad bar, and a pitcher of Pepsi. We put a few coins in the juke box and picked some songs and sat back down. He said, "How about you spend the night!" I sat there for a few minutes thinking about if my mom would OK it, if his mom would OK it too.

"I have to ask my mom," I said. I got up and called her on the pay-phone.

She answered, "Hello!"

"Mom, can I spend the night? His mom will have me home tomorrow by 6 PM."

"If it's OK with his mom."

"Thanks, Mom." I went back to the table. "Mom said it's fine, as long as your mom doesn't care," I told him.

"You know my mom would let you stay every night if you wish, fool." We both smiled with a laugh to ourselves. After we were done eating, we called his mom to pick us up. It was eleven o'clock. His mom showed up.

"Mom, he's going to stay the night with me!" His mom just nodded her head. We get to his house, and go to his room and turn on the TV. We take off our clothing except underwear. We then lay back in the bed. He puts his arm around me. I just look into his eyes and he mine. We kiss. "Thank you for inviting me here," I say.

"No. Thank you! I've been bored being by myself." He says. He turns the TV off and takes off his underwear and I did too. We get under the covers. I roll over on my side and he pulls me back and kisses me. "Sleep well," he says. I roll back over and he put his arm around me and pulled me close. I can feel the warmth of his body on my body. I fall right to sleep.

When I wake up, he is still sleeping. He looks so peaceful. I turn the TV on to watch my cartoons. I put my underwear back on. I lay back on the bed. An hour later I had to go take a pee and brush my teeth. He was awake. I got back in bed and lay back on his chest. We laid there until noon watching cartoons.

"Ok," he said, "we'll go ride the go-cart now! My turn first!" First we ate some Captain Crunch and had some juice. Then we got dressed and drove his go-cart for a few hours. Then we went back into his house.

"We have to get a bath before you go home," he said. So we went to the bathroom and get undressed. He ran the water in the bath tub.

It was a real big, cast-iron tub. It was very warm, almost too hot; but I got in and laid back. He got in and lay back on my chest. I put my arms around him, thinking this feels good and peaceful. I don't know how long we lay there but the water started to get cold. He turned the hot water back on to warm it back up. He turned around in the tub facing me with the shampoo. He put some on his hair and my hair. He started doing my hair so I did his hair. Each taking turns going underwater to get the shampoo out of our hair. Then he had me stand up so he could wash me from head to toe. Front and back. I sat down to get the soap off, and then he stood up and I washed him every inch. He sat down. He pulled me close and kissed me. Then we got out taking turns drying each other off. We then hugged each other and kissed again before getting dressed.

He said, "Spend tonight too."

I said I would love to but have to go to church camp-out. He looked sad. "But next weekend I will stay with you," I said. He smiled.

Then we got dressed. His mom fixed us a late lunch. She didn't want me to go home until I ate lunch. On the way to my house, he asked his mom, "Can he stay next Friday and Saturday, since it's the last weekend before school?"

She said, "OK!" They dropped me off at home.

I asked my mom if I could stay the next weekend at his house, and told her that his mom already said it was OK.

"If you get your chores done around the house, then you can go," she said.

The next morning I caught the bus to church. We sang different songs on the way. When we got there, I entered the church and saw a new boy. He was very magnetic. I looked at him for a few seconds, but it seemed like minutes. Everyone was gone and it was only him and I in the church. I walked up to him and said, "My name is Dylan."

He said, "Mickey is my name. This is my first time. My dad made me come."

"Can I show you around?" I said. He shook his head. He was wearing black jeans, a red dress shirt, a blue t-shirt under it, and tennis shoes. He was about 4 foot tall, 85 lbs., had hazel eyes, and light brown hair to his shoulder, rosy lips, and light complexion. He was very small. "How old are you?" I said.

"11," he said.

"I'm 12. You're very beautiful," I said.

"Thanks," he said, and smiled. We spent most of the day together, and only when he went to the restroom were we not together. In the afternoon I took him up to the attic where the church stores clothing and other supplies. We sat on a big bean bag chair. We sat and talked for a little bit. I wanted to kiss him, but I was nervous. I leaned over and kissed him on the cheek.

Then I kissed him on the lips. I kissed him again on the lips and he kissed me back. So I gave him a real long kiss. I said, "Thanks."

He said, "Does this make me gay because I like this with you?"

I was surprised by the question. "Why do you ask?" I said.

"I have had those kind of feelings since I was eight years old and never told anyone. I never had the nerve to do what you have done," he said.

"No, you're not gay. You're just going through a phase as I am," I said. I kissed him again and rubbed my hand under his shirt. I unbuttoned his pants. Kissing him some more I put my hand down his pants. Then I pulled them down and his underwear, looking right into his eyes. He looked at peace. I then sucked on his dick until he got off. Then I pulled his pants all the way down, undid my pants and pulled them down, and my underwear. He reached for my dick, playing with it. I stopped him. I had him lay on his stomach. I slowly stuck it in him. "Are you okay with this?" I asked.

He shook his head and said it was fine. When I got done I pulled out and rolled him on his back laying beside him. Looking into his eyes, I said, "So what do you think? Did you enjoy yourself? Have you done this before?"

"I did enjoy every very much. I've never done anything like this before. Can we do everything again?" He replied.

"Yes we can. We have all night to sneak off to do things together," I replied.

"His eyes lit up and like he was getting the best Christmas gift. I pulled him close and let him take the lead for kissing. I had my left hand on his butt. I rolled him on top of me, with him looking down on my eyes. I said, "We better get back before they start looking for us."

He stood up, still with a hard-on, so I sucked him again. I looked up at him. He had a big smile. We got dressed, spent time around so everyone will see us and we ate some food. He grabbed my hand to take me back up to the room. It was 6 PM. As soon as we got into the room he took off all his clothing. So I did too. This time he started

sucking me.

"I hope I'm doing it right," he said. I shook my head. Then he turned me over and stuck his dick into me. I had to explain what to do, but he got it down real quick. He was done. He was very joyful. He said, "I'm gay. I'm gay."

I said "No you're not. This is just for us to have a little fun and share love." We kissed some more and I held him. Then we got dressed and went back where everyone was eating and singing some songs.

The next morning, after breakfast, he pulled me into the restroom and gave me a hug and kissed and said he loved me, with tears in his eyes.

"I love you too," I said. I really hated to see him go. He told me where he lived. I promised I would see him on Wednesday.

On Wednesday, I got on my bike. He lived five miles from my house. When I got to his house, his mom answered the door. I asked for him, but she said, "He's not here."

I said, "He promised he'd be here!"

She then said that he told his dad he was gay, and that he's felt that way since he was eight. When he was at church camp, he figured it out, and he accepts it. His dad beat him real bad, saying "No son of mine is going to be gay!" She said that after she took him to the hospital, and then she took him to her sister's to live until his dad calmed down. I started crying.

She asked, "Are you the boy he fell in love with?" I shook my head. "I will let him know you came by for him. I'll tell him you love him and miss him," she said.

"Thanks," I replied. She gave me a hug. I got on my bike, but I only got a few blocks away when I pulled into the woods. I sat there and cried. I knew it was all my fault. I hoped he was going to be OK. When I got home I took a shower and went to bed. I didn't feel like eating. I had my mom call Joe to spend the next few days with me. I didn't have a TV or go-cart, but I did have a radio in my room. I knew we could sleep in our underwear at my house, but not nude, and no taking showers together. But I locked my door, turned the music on low, and explained what I had done at the church camp with Mickey.

He did not say a word for a long time, then he said, "It's not your fault. It's his dad's because he could not accept his son for what he is." Even him holding me didn't make me feel better. I never could tell my dad anything like that, I kept thinking to myself.

I asked my dad to see if he could get the phone number to call him. My dad took me by the house. I asked his mom would she give me the number to call him, to check on him and see how he's doing. But she would not give it to me because her husband would beat her if she did. I gave her my number and told her to give it to her son. She said she would. But he never called.

My dad said, "He was a friend of yours?" I shook my head. He put his arm around me. Dad did not say a word to me. But I tried not to cry, because dad would have gotten mad at me for crying.

Chapter 4 – **An Old Friend**

by O.R.

Here at the prison where I am incarcerated we have an RMU (Regional Medical Unit) instead of an Infirmary. We share it with 17 prisons. I was there getting x-rays when I saw this young correctional officer (C.O.) His face looked so familiar. He looked like he was 16 at most. He was trying to point me in the right direction when he noticed my white and red cane and realized I'm legally blind. So he took my hand and walked me to where I was going. He kept staring at my name tag, trying to say my name. So I corrected him and I enjoyed myself: although he was 29, he looked much younger.

I went back a week later and there he was again. He looked at me and said "Mr. R____, you're here for results. I'll take you in to the doctor in a few minutes. Sit down and relax."

One of the other inmates said to me, "Wow, you rated a Mister!"

I said, "He is a kid. Sometimes the gray hair gets some respect." A few minutes later, he came, took my hand and led me to an office. He said, "You're Mr. R____, ain't ya?"

I said, "I was once but you are way too young to have any way of knowing that."

He said "I am Robert Urban Jr. My father is Peewee."

I said, "I don't recognize the nickname."

He said, "You always called him Robby because you knew he hated that nickname."

Then the face came back to me. He could be his father whom I haven't seen in 30+ years.

Robby Sr. was a 11-year-old in my friend's troop. They lived in

a poor neighborhood. I would bring some of their boys to summer camp with my troop for free. Robby was one of those boys. He was short – even tiny – and shy. His mom sent him to camp with three socks, underpants, and tee shirts in a day pack, and a sleeping bag. No bathing suit or sneakers or spending money. To top it off, he was a bed wetter. The other boys in his troop called him Peewee because of his size and nocturnal habit.

On the first day of camp I had to deal with a wet sleeping bag. I asked him in private if he had done this before or was this a rare accident. The tears in his eyes told me all I needed to know. I cleaned the sleeping bag, and brought him some camp clothes, a bathing suit and a pair of over-sized sweat pants and diapers. I gave him the clothes and put the diapers in my tent. Every night he would put on the over-sized sweat pants and go to the latrine where I would bring him a diaper, and nobody was the wiser. But everyone noticed he stopped wetting his bunk (as far as they knew). I also put spending money in his camp store account so he could buy snacks like the other kids. He was very appreciative and physically affectionate over it.

After that summer he came on several trips with my troop and to camp two more summers. Then he moved up-state.

When we were at his last summer camp, his parents, who were poor, took his sister to Great Adventure while he was at camp, and then rubbed his nose in it on the phone, making him really depressed. So later that summer I took him on a trip to Disney with my family. Later that year he moved and we lost touch. Well, his family moved around NY and ended up in Buffalo where he is a hospital cop. His son is a correctional officer. Not much improvement but a better pension.

Robert Jr. mentioned my long name to his dad the night he first met me. His father had him look up my case and told him no matter what anyone said I could never have hurt any child, and if anything I had to have been screwed. He told Robert Jr. to tell me he has never forgotten how well I took care of him.

I don't remember doing anything all that special. There were several boys over the years that I brought clothes and helped in other ways. According to Robby, somehow I saved his life. He moved away with his parents but he went the foster care route after running away. He said I showed him there were people in the world who really cared for people.

It is almost a high feeling hearing from someone other then my son that I am a good person and I did good. All I ever hear in prison is how much I hurt people, how I should kill myself, and so on. Hearing Robby's son tell it, I must have been superman. If I could get one second off my time for every hour I spent fighting with a school, or parent, or social services to help some one else's child, my 20-year sentence would have been done before it started. But all that was forgotten. All they remember is I am an S.O. and, as such, not worthy of breathing the same air as anyone else.

Since then, the C.O. Robby has brought me in an envelope with a letter and pictures from his father. He sent me pictures of him from when he was a young teen so I would recognize him, and pictures now, and several pictures of his son, the C.O., growing up, showing me his son is his mirror image.

He has also passed the word that I am an okay guy so basically I only have four haters here – much better then anywhere else I have been. But Robby Jr. is here on training so he will be gone in a month or so, but I will accept any good that comes of him being here. Robby Sr. claims he will come visit me. But over the last 10 years I have had several former scouts promise to visit me, and only once did that happen. But I will accept anything that come my way and accept it as a great gift. His words have helped me so much already if nothing more comes I can't complain.

It may sound funny but just the human contact from Robby Jr. was a great gift. The simple act of holding my hand and not just grabbing my arm and tugging me along made my day on those days. I showed him the correct way to escort a low-vision person by offering his elbow. I have seen him escort others from my unit and he gives them his elbow but he still takes my hand. One of the other C.O.'s commented to him about that and he told them to mind their business.

Then last night his son brought me in a meatball hero to my cell. It was in an x-ray envelope and he complained to the other C.O.s about being made an errand boy for the doctors, all the way down the corridor to my cell. I thought it was paperwork until I got it open and he was gone by then. He just handed it to me and told me to have a good night. I had a great night. If it ever happens again I will try to chew it instead of inhaling it.

Chapter 5 – **A Six-Century Sentence**

by H.D.

I used to just live. Now I don't live at all, and I am endlessly treading water just trying to keep people from forgetting that I ever did, and that they used to care that I did. Actually, there is a part in the book *A Galaxy of No Stars* that keeps barking at me for attention. In chapter two of part two the book relates how Christopher's father "was curious about everybody." Since most people love being asked questions about themselves, his household was generally full of "conversation." He was gregarious with an odd assortment of guests. That spoke to me. I used to have so many friends, and I think that was partly because I was interested in people. I got called a "good listener" a lot. I feel like such a douche these days, when everything, for me, is about me. When I read that little bit I realize that's at least part of what's happened to me. Vincent Lorenzo [*Christopher's father*] (and tons of others) could focus all their attention on others because he/they can take themselves for granted. I know I did. I took myself for granted, and why not? How not?

I was happy, healthy, and stable. Safe, liked, loved, wanted, respected, enjoyed. So I would feel all of those things for others easily. The opposite of a "vicious" cycle. I can't take myself for granted anymore. I barely even exist now, and to the extent I do, for others, it's in a wildly degraded, eroded way. It's basically a fictional version that's all in their heads because I'm not in their lives. The well has been thoroughly poisoned – what little of it that hasn't has been drained by the pigs who never knew me at all but managed to convince even

many of those closest to me that they knew "the truth."

[In a previous letter I mentioned to you] my personal acquaintance who surprised himself by being so moved by *Marcus and Me*, (a novel that depicts boy/love in a positive manner)... Well, I may give him *No Stars* next (another novel with a positive image of boy/love), but I do wonder how long-lasting the shift in his views were. I'm continually shocked (so it shouldn't be so shocking anymore, right?) by how little effect anything ever has on anyone's long-term views. I've got a half-dozen examples off the top of my head, but they don't matter. I just notice that almost no matter how apparently thoroughly someone "gets" some new idea that contradicts an old idea, the new wears off – mind-blowingly quickly, it wears off – and all that's left is the old. In fact, my experience is that when a person is reminded that there was a "new" view that shook their "old" view to the core, or even demolished it, and they acknowledged it, they never are so moved again. The reminder doesn't do it, your conversation doesn't do it, and they generally resist revisiting the original source of the new idea, and will try to minimize it in any case. It's super-demoralizing.

So I expect to find that my buddy—who spoke to me at the time as if he experienced a kind of epiphany and had tears in his eyes and promised never to think in such simple, dogmatic ways again— has fully recovered by now, and perhaps even erected new barriers to infection by similarly disruptive ideas in the future. I'm not saying he did, I just think it's likely. Sad. Sad that I'm such a pessimist these days.

Life before my first arrest

I was prosecuted and imprisoned twice. First time I was 20. I had then two brothers, my parents, and a huge extended family. I was the youngest and grew up with no siblings in the house, but we were very very close. I believed family was inviolable, unbreakable. All my sibs treated me great and each other too. Many lived out of state and I often spent weeks or months with them, especially in summers. My parents raised me differently from all of them, giving me a lot of autonomy, privacy, and respect. I never felt like a "kid" per se. I always just felt like me. I didn't always get my way, but I did get coherent reasons for whatever my parents did, and generally speaking, if there was no reason, there was no "no." I felt valued, and I was at first baffled, then outraged, when I began noticing that not all my friends

were treated the same. My friends often look like chattel to me, more property than people in their own homes. I resented it. Predictably, I resented school too because there, as with all adults, they were trying to treat me as less than a full person. I dropped out, eventually.

I had lots of friends, and good friends – the kind who rally for you when you need help. When I got arrested I needed help, and my friends were there, apart from my younger friends, I'm talking about those who were high school or early college age, like me. Some offered to hide me and whisk me away to safety. Others gave me places to stay and ran interference when enemies came around. They banged on the surveillance van, hassled the under-covers who came around, and spoke strongly in my defense to both the big interrogators and others who were on the "other side." The "other side"—what was that?

Before the arrest, I had lots of younger friends. Long, complex story. In short, I had one friend in particular who would be closer to me than anyone in my life, from the time he was 11 and I was six. We were beyond close – I loved him deeply. I believe he loved me too. He moved, and I was lost. I made another great friend, and we were close too, but he never felt the way the other had felt. He may have actually loved me even more.

I dropped out of high school, but I went to college. I had a great family, tons of great friends, and nothing but hope for the future. I felt I could do nearly anything I wanted to do since I was young, healthy, reasonably intelligent, and interested in people and life. Basically I was a happy kid, and I had no enemies. People who met me liked me, and I liked most people I met too, except for bullies. My reputation was kind of goodie-goodie in that everyone knew I never drank, smoked, did drugs, swore etc. Truth is, I didn't even jaywalk. I was an anarchist-in-waiting who never broke laws. Well... I liked to speed a lot. Most people assumed I had a bright future, and into my teens, other kids' parents often used me as an example, which was absurd because I often thought those parents were schmucks.

Life before my being arrested the first time was good – I was happy and so were the people I knew.

Life between the first and second prison sentence

When I was released from my first imprisonment, and on parole, life was inhuman. I was expected to live like an animal, and I had to

keep that act up vigilantly or I'd be put back in a cage. This was my second life (the first was murdered), and I intended to live it as well as I could. I was pretty successful, making dozens of new friends, some very good ones, and going back to college for a degree in philosophy and one in psychology which were made a good pre-law foundation. I planned to become a lawyer doing criminal defense and civil rights work. I had excellent credit, work when I needed it, and my family was still very supportive, with a couple of exceptions. Many of my old friends welcomed me back with open hearts and arms, and right up to the night I was arrested the second time, I was someone people liked having around. I made people laugh in supermarket checkouts. I gave money to homeless guys at freeway off-ramps. I stopped to help people with flat tires and car troubles. And no one ever ever thought I was on parole after some years in prison. My professors loved me, and most of my classmates liked me, at least once they got to know me. I was very vocal in class, and many disliked my views, which I didn't then recognize as essentially anarchist-humanist. And once again, young people took to me fast. I clearly looked and seemed younger than what my birth certificate would have led one to believe, because I was younger. I was 19 or 20 at most. I rode bikes and skated with people from 8 to 28. Then many of my friends were from 10 to 15. My best friend, best new friend anyway, was 13 when we met and 14 when we became as close as brothers. Again, I was happy, reasonably successful, and well-liked. I was, I think beyond question, an asset to society. Even the cops who met me and didn't know my "parole status" liked me, never suspecting I felt any disgust toward them. People saw me as honest and fair and helpful. Before I was arrested again.

I never came out to anyone, unless I was attracted to him and made a decision to pursue the possibility of a relationship. Never. I never saw my sexuality as anyone else's business. Not one person ever came to me and said, *"Listen bro, I gotta tell you something, and I hope it won't mess up our friendship, but you have a right to know and I need to tell you man, I like girls. Just gotta get that out there between us."* Nobody. And why would they? Unless they were into me, their sexual attractions were not my business. And to the extent I cared, I could just look for the clues on my own. Others would figure me out too, if they really wanted. Plus, I didn't want to "be gay"... I just wanted to be me. If you're "gay," it's the same as being the kid

with cancer or having one leg, or no eyesight, or having the wrong skin color in your area... It defines you first for everyone. You're the black kid, or the handicapped kid, or the gay kid, not "Mike" or "Danny" or "Zachery." Plus I fit almost no stereotypes. I'm all boy, masculine, athletic, "normal," and kind of elfish., Even though I'm totally sexually submissive and 100% homosexually attracted, no bi-this-or-that at all, and no interest in being that typically "male" partner. I tried not to let it affect my social relationships, but sure, when friends would get "girl crazy," I wouldn't, some started to wonder. More than one here and there suspected or accused.

I guess I first realized I was attracted to guys younger than me when I was about 14. I also discovered the word "pedophile" in the dictionary around that time, and I thought it was great! I found a word that recognized my sexual orientation (I thought). How cool! LOL! I didn't know how totally pejorative it was. But as I got older... I don't know. I never at all felt personally "less than" for my attractions to any age. I knew from the start that I was "normal... How could I not be? I just liked who I liked. There was some friction between my older and younger friends. It was mainly due to some friends feeling jealous or envious of newcomers getting so much of my attention. Once or twice a friend commented on the "little kids" I knew. It wasn't meant to be insulting. It was just me, and I had lots of younger friends. All but one (for years) had no idea I was even gay, let alone interested in them. I sometimes wonder if a couple of boys figured me out though, because two in particular really came on to me in unsubtle ways, and I was too afraid to respond well. What if they were just messing with me? My fear of being "outed" trumped all. Dummy.

In my second life (my life on parole), I was much more "adult," and my attractions affected my social relationships a lot more. I had to be very careful not to raise suspicion, but I was lucky to be perceived by nearly everyone as "normal." Parents of my younger friends tended to like me a lot, all but one, and he was afraid I posed a threat to him, I think, since he wasn't the world's best father and he knew I knew it. My self-image was affected by my sexual orientation primarily in how it caused me to remain young, and true to myself, and on the side of youth instead of feeling graduated from, apart from, and superior to it. When they are kids, everyone says children shouldn't "have to ask," or "kids should get to ask." When they "grow up" they change their minds. It's like the final version of that age/grade chau-

vinism most kids indulge in. In third grade they hate the fourth graders who were making fun of them, and then in the fourth grade they may make fun of the third grade while resenting the fifth graders were mocking them. I saw the absurdity of that in first grade, the very first time I saw a friend taunting the kindergartners on the playground below. It just made no sense at all to me... And I never lost that perspective. I think it's all interrelated, somehow, those mental habits and my sexuality.

౪

The boys
All in all, I've been convicted or accused of "abusing" six times. The relationships with them were, in a word, all GOOD. The first might be the most dramatic.

Roger
At 20 I was convicted of "molesting" my friend Roger, who was 10 then. We were not best friends at all. Few of my friends, younger or older, liked him at all because he could be so obnoxious and often was. We didn't have much in common. I liked him, and I tried to make my other friends at least be civil to him. But we didn't have a very dynamic friendship. We did have fun though. I was his first real friend when he moved to my neighborhood. When he was six he introduced me to sex. He showed me his, and asked to see mine. A day or two later, he was showing me how he could "eat the muscles" (flexing his erection). Then, out of the blue, he asked me if I had "ever had sex with a little boy." I said, "No. Come on."

Then he said I "should try it. It's fun." So I asked what he had done. He described how his friends in LA lay on top of each other. Of course I was intrigued but also scared shitless. I didn't want to be outed as gay. I eventually asked if anyone ever put their mouth on his penis. He said "No! Eww!" Or something like that. I guess he thought about it though and soon he wanted me to try.

He almost let the cat out of the bag many times over the years, often on purpose, often to freak me out – and maybe that helped keep some distance between us too. He was one of two people I was accused of "abusing" the first time. He moved across town, and then I moved. One day, while I was picking up the son of the lady whose

house I lived in (never had even remotely intimate contact with him), the demon snuck up to my window and scared me. He wanted my new phone number and told me where he lived. He wanted to hang out, and he called me that weekend and we spent a day together. Nothing extra special happened but we did talk about it. The next time I saw him was as I driving and passed him and his mom in the opposite lane. He climbed out of the window of her (slow) moving SUV, really waving at me from the roof. She was tugging at his leg to pull him back in. I laughed and waved to both of them. The next night, cops came to where I lived, and took the owners of the building to the station for a few hours. When they got back, I was kicked out at 2 AM, due to "accusations." That was how my relationship was with Roger.

Rolando

The second one was a kid named Rolando. He was Roger's friend, and I was never charged for him. When Roger brought him around, he grabbed me through my sweatpants and said to Rolando, "See, I told him he was gay!" Rolando turned out to be what some might call a sociopath. (I don't accept the term myself). Too bad. He could have been a lot of fun. Although he started off extremely sweet and shy and sort of submissive (I don't mean sexually I mean his whole personality), the "rough boy" came out with familiarity and it was such a turn-on to me! But it went nowhere, since he stole from my mother, which I couldn't prove, but I also wouldn't forgive. Actually Roger and Rolando discovered each other when, one day at Roger's house, Rolando just thrust his hand down Roger's pants, uninvited, and Roger got hard in "like two seconds." So they made a good match. But I got the impression Rolando didn't really care if Roger responded favorably or not. Roger was about five years younger than Rolando at the time (though Rolando was very small for his age). I hope he didn't become a rapist.

Danny

I met Danny when he was 11. We were skating. We became best friends and he was the first person some of my older friends became jealous of . Long story short (very long story) – I totally fell in love with him, and told him, after debating almost a year whether I really wanted to, I told him that I was gay, and that I liked him that way. He replied, "Yeah, I know that already." After that, I asked him to do sex-

ual things with me pretty often, and he said no, but maybe someday. I stopped asking because I felt like a jerk. Then he started asking me to keep him company while he showered and eventually let me see him in the shower (before that, we just talked through the curtain). I was 17; he was 12. He started letting me see him pretty often, changing clothes and such and one day, showing me up close, he said I could do what I wanted to do. I guess stopping asking him made him take the initiative.

Actually there was one incident just before that, after a shower when he let me dry him off, then "play" a little before school. We played a bit too much. That caused a reaction, and he got super pissed at me. He didn't want to discuss it again for about a day. The pigs called him about Roger and Brent (I'll tell about them soon). He adamantly defended me, as did his mom. They teamed up against the cops on the phone. I had the recording. She knew I was gay, and I believe she knew about her son and me for years. He flew from New York to support me at sentencing, spending a month with me, and pissed off the prosecutor to no end. He stayed in close touch with me in prison for 3 ½ years, then one day... very suddenly... no more. One really vicious letter, and that was the end. He said, "I finally came to my senses." He had many girlfriends... many many, in New York. I had talked with most of them. He always felt obliged to share his past with me with them, for some reason, and it always hurt him in the end. Breakups, falling-out, angry words, and out came the claws, drawing his blood in front of all the friends he didn't want to know. Every time. I think it broke him down. I called him one day, from prison, and he wasn't there, but some friends were. His friend, who I didn't know, accepted my call and we chatted. No drama. I never spoke to Danny after that again. Not till he talked to me one last time, after sending me that awful heart-smashing letter, a couple of months after his friend talked to me. He told me it had happened again, another angry cat used his openness against him, calling him a fag with a boyfriend in prison in Cali. Again he cleared it up with his friends, explaining it all away. Just a day or so later, I called. One of those friends answered, and I messed up his cleanup. I think this has a lot to do with his rejection of me. Also, his latest girlfriend was an incest abuse victim, apparently a legitimate one, as it was her little brother, and it seems like maybe this became some sort of intimacy for him and her... both "childhood sex abuse survivors." Maybe. It all adds up, but I've never gotten the

story from him, just the schlock about "realizing it was wrong." Other than the new girlfriend with her experiences, no explanation for how he came to this dramatic "realization" that contradicted all his personal experience and prior beliefs. He was contacted in the current case and agreed to testify, reluctantly, and only after the persecutor insisted she "needed" him to "tell his story" because it meant my "not doing the same thing" to "another little boy," and she never knows how those things are going to shake out (especially when she has no actual case). It could help her get her life sentence. That's what my relationship was like with Danny.

Nolan

I met Nolan shortly before they moved to New York. I won't say much about him, but he really went to bat for me the first time, when they dragged him into the DA's office and tried pressuring him to accuse me. Instead he went psycho and threw their phone across the room. All the more remarkable because before I was arrested, we had a real falling out, and I was less than the best friend to him. He wasn't so cool to me, either. But when I was in trouble, he acted like we never had a moment of friction between us and he defended me all the way. I love him for that.

When I got home, I tried to contact him as a first priority. He'd written and sent me pictures in prison. His stepbrother finally told me though, that Nolan didn't want me to call. I could write him if I wanted to. This scared me. I don't really know what happened with him, either, except sometime before I got out he saw a psychologist for various reasons, and he told her about me. It doesn't seem like any of it was ever about me, but I came up. The psychologist told him he couldn't keep that confidential, and she called the cops with him there. I don't believe he'd ever wanted that, but I don't know. I was already in prison, and as it turns out, Nolan always had believed I was sent there in part because of him in the first place, so this deal with the psychologist years later struck him as weird. Nothing came of it, but apparently all that caused him to feel the same urge to tell his mom one day in the car that yes, as many had suspected at the time, he and I did have some sexual contact before the Roger/Brent arrest. And from that day on, he hadn't written me anymore, and didn't take my calls when I got home. The saddest part of all... they dragged him in, very unwillingly, with the same bullshit they hooked Danny with,

making him feel like he wasn't testifying for himself, but for this poor little defenseless waif I had manhandled and mauled in San Diego. To ensure I got a life sentence for what I "had done" to this new kid. He said some really mean things in his phone interrogation with the pigs this time, really letting me have it at times, but then also talking about how much good he remembered about our friendship too. I thought he'd be vicious at trial. Hadn't seen him in a decade. He was big, lots of tattoos. And when we caught each other's eyes, we held the gaze, and I saw him cry a bit. Not obviously, but clearly, to me. And when he spoke, almost every single thing he said was enthusiastically positive. Almost like he wanted to tell me how much good stuff he remembered. And then he even said he had loved me. But he told that there was some sexual contact, so all the rest was irrelevant. I was to be punished. That's all the jury needed. And that's the relationship we had.

Brent

He was part of the first conviction. He is why I'm here now, but he's a victim too. They all are. I met Brent after Nolan and I fought. I was smitten – tall skinny, blond, 14, tons of fun. I told him about me after a while; he said it was okay. He might or might not want to fool around, but either way he didn't hold it against me. He told me he had a male cousin he slept with a few times. Brent's dad was crazy and abusive, in every way except sexually. He beat the shit out of Brent, and at his house, I saw the lock on the outside of his bedroom door. I saw hair brushes too, and the tears. Brent was on probation, and was seeing counselors, etc. One day at the bowling alley, Brent and I were hanging out in the arcade and Roger showed up. Turned out Brent knew Roger, but none of us ever realized we knew each other. Now we did. Roger was... indiscreet. He asked me, in a loud whisper, if Brent liked "sucking dicks" too. Then he asked Brent directly, and then moved a bunch of video-games away from the wall so we could all three go behind them. I played like Roger was a not bad kid, Brent uncomfortably accepted whatever, and Roger went cackling off on his merry way. I had to explain, so I did. I told Brent that Roger and I had some history. No big deal. A few days later I got a message from the older brother in the house I lived at, who was Brent's friend too, that Brent gave him an urgent message for me: that I had to meet him the next day at the bus stop after school. Blake (Brent's older brother)

had been delivering many over-sized notes between Brent and me for about a month, so this was a shock to him. Brent was forced to stay away from me for six weeks by his dad, after his dad saw me pick him up one morning at the bus stop, and then followed us to the mall which was right across the street from his school. He wasn't bitching, but it was still upsetting to his dad who already didn't like me because I was a wrench in his control machine. That was also the night, it turned out, when the pigs came at midnight and I got kicked out later. Clearly this was all related, somehow. When I showed up the next day, as instructed, and Brent didn't get off the bus, I was 100% certain that something was very wrong. Next thing I knew I was accused of "molesting" both Brent and Roger. It had all stemmed from the report made by a mandated counselor at Brent's school (on the day I got the urgent message to meet him the next day) and soon I even heard the recordings of Roger, in tears, being questioned by ruthless pigs who wouldn't accept his answer that we were just friends. Then I heard Brent telling some DA that, "yeah, he's a pedophile and he'll probably just get what he deserves in prison." Nice words to hear from a friend. Yet I never stop believing Brent was my friend, not even after I was already sentenced and in jail, waiting to go to prison. When the Santa Barbara homicide detectives came to question me about the high-profile murder of a girl who lived about halfway between my house and Brent's. I learned that Brent gave them my name. What was he trying to do to me?

When I got out, I wanted to find Brent but I was also afraid to. He could lie and get me in a ton of trouble on parole, and he'd already lied like crazy when I was on bail. He claimed that my friend and I went to his house, looked at him and laughed, and then kicked the jack out from under my dad's truck in the driveway (which actually had been knocked down). He also said that he'd seen my friend vandalize his dad's truck in the parking lot (when it really had been spray-painted). We did none of that. Turns out he had done it all himself. I know because, after I was arrested this time, the cops contacted him... He was in prison in Montana, doing life for murder. He said he'd gladly come testify against me now.

I finally just had to write to him and lay it out on the table and just ask... WTF?

He replied. He apologized. He told me how everything had gone down, how scared he'd been, how much pressure he was under, how

he learned he could do crazy shit to mess up his dad, who he hated, and then just blame it on me, and all his dad's anger would go toward me instead. A card played often, too often. Then he got caught in a lie about me once, and his dad broke several of his ribs. He said he'd always thought of me as a friend, a true friend, one of the few he ever had. A person who came into his crappy life, and for little while, made it better. He said he often remembered fun things that we'd done together, and that I had always been nice to him. We never had sex of any kind, not even a touch on the shoulder or anything. I had told him flat out one day that he knew my feelings, and if he ever wanted, all he had to do was let me know. And he never did. But anyway, I'd been exactly right... He never meant to get me in trouble.

They told him everything he said to the mandatory counselor was private, and he believed them. So he told about the Roger incident, and, after that, he lost all control of the avalanche. He wanted to warn me about that. That was the message from Blake, but his dad didn't let him ride the bus the next day, so the window was closed forever. He just accepted his role and played along. He apologized, didn't expect forgiveness, but hoped we can now, all these years later be friends. I told him of course... We are friends. That's the relationship I had with that "victim."

Glenn

I met Glenn about a year after I was released from my first imprisonment. He lived around the corner from my parents' house. Again I was smitten. He was gorgeous. Tall, blond, 13. We became close, and I eventually told him I was on parole, and even why. I told him because it explained why I acted so weird so often, like refraining to go anywhere public with him, and always leaving him by 6 PM. I had a 7 PM curfew. He said he knew me. Who cared about that other stuff? Soon I told him more, and that I was gay. He was very surprised, never would've guessed, he said but... so what? "We're friends, that changes nothing." I never told him I liked him. He could give me a sign if he had any interest, and he didn't. So, it never came up, at least not for a year or so. He started making jokes about me looking at his ass as we rode bikes. It was a safe acknowledgment of things we both knew, but never talked about. We were supposed to be brothers, shared laughs and tears and hopes and fears... When he started having sex with his girlfriend, he sometimes asked me for ad-

vice. Like they were considering anal, but both were little nervous to try. I told him he could practice on me all he wanted, lots of love! He laughed and blushed, but, of course, never took me up on it. Glenn was the one person in the world who knew me better than anyone else, besides Danny, years before.

When the shit hit the fan, Glenn was 100% in my corner. He knew and had met the person I was accused of "abusing" in San Diego. The pigs got to him, pushed him into a corner, scared the shit out of him. I was in jail, They had listened to all our phone calls. They cornered him in school, threatened him, and ultimately got, not only his cooperation, but apparently even his heart and mind. They told him they had photos of me "molesting" a kid down the street (they didn't, because it never happened). They told him he didn't know the real me, but they did. He had 3 ½ years of almost daily contact with me, they just heard of me a month earlier and never spoke to me, but they knew me better than he did. Right. They told him I would for sure throw him under the bus the first time I could, and that I would sacrifice him to get myself the smallest break. He said that it didn't sound to him like me, but after everything else they told him, he didn't know what I was capable of. We've had very little contact since then. It's really upsetting. I don't know what he thinks ... what he believes about me. It hurts. I'd really like my friend back.

Oh, and they told him, over and over, that they "know more happened" between him and me, so when he's ready to talk about it, he can call them. He kept telling them no, nothing happened. They just rolled their eyes and said "okay." If only he could see that they did the same thing to others. The others cracked and gave the answers they were told to give.

Conrad

He's ground zero for the second persecution. We met when I got off parole and was riding in Huntington Park beach. He and his friend Morris were there, and we all got to talking. I lived very far, like two hours away, but my school was part way there, so I often went from school on the last day of my week to his county to stay with my friend, or sleep in my car, plus spend the weekend with Conrad. We communicated mostly through My Space when I wasn't there, or sometimes he would call me. I never called him. His dad and stepmom liked me a lot. We rode bikes, snuck into movies, hung out at fast food places,

got chased out of the mall for playing on the escalators, went swimming and to the beach, hung out at his house doing nothing, dropped into the river, climbed trees and cliffs, built very illegal fires on the cliffs, and talked for hours. I helped him learn a lot of bike-handling technique, and once, when he pulled something very cleanly, I told him he was a fast learner, and he said, "Maybe that's because I've got a good teacher." The first day we met, he told me he had a scar on his penis. The second time we hung out, he showed it to me. In between there were some chat conversations on-line. I was never actually sure where he stood, but he sure seemed to be telling me he wanted to fool around, especially on My Space. I won't go into detail but I was sure he was telling me, not very subtly, that it was on when I came back. But in person ... it wasn't that way. I felt I had to tell him I was gay because it seemed like he knew, and was saying he was into it, but then, nothing. He told me he knew nothing all along. Later I told him I liked him a lot in case he didn't know. He said he knew all along. I asked how he knew. He said it was always in how I looked at him. Still nothing happened, so he'd show me his scar pretty much whenever, and he hugged me a lot, often with a butt squeeze.

Well, the story ends with us going for a weekend beach camp-out, a long way from home, at a nude beach. On our last night together, he finally told me he would mess around with me, like he and Morris had done before. He had a boner a lot that day, and he even jacked off on the beach before we left, with the water near his feet, as he said he'd always wanted to do. He wanted me to watch, but that was it. No touch, not even to help him cleanup when he was finished. He was twelve and nine months, five foot two, dark hair, Mohawk. On the way back, dressed, he said he wanted to get naked again, so I said okay, but I had a boner now and sort of hid it. He said, "Just let me see," so I did and he smacked it, hard, painfully actually, then he laughed. He had one again, too. And that was it.

We got dressed again. Soon after, we walked to the car, and I let him drive. I let him drive because the parking lot was empty and well lit, and we were in no hurry. He just did circles inside the lot, about two miles from the exit. Conrad had the biggest smile on his face I'd ever seen as he "gunned it" in my manual transmission BMW 10 to 20 mph in two seconds.

Then we got pulled over on the way out of the parking lot. No crime, except him driving, but we had four or five cop cars there,

Morris

When I first knew him, Morris was 11 and 10 months, blond, maybe 4 foot 11. I don't think anyone ever seriously accused me of "abusing" him, and certainly I was never charged. But, he's worth mentioning anyway. He was Conrad's best friend, and Conrad later created those elaborately dramatic lies, like the time I supposedly tried to "touch" him in our underground hangout (a real place). He said he left, but then heard Morris screaming, and came back to find me sexually assaulting his friend. So he beat me with a stick and they both escaped, me in hot pursuit but never catching them. He was clearly a "person of interest" for the pigs. Morris never knew Conrad's stories though, so his statements were... well, they were gold for me. They totally undermined Conrad's lies.

One day Morris asked me, out of the blue, with Conrad there too, "Did Conrad ever tell you how I'm curious?" One day when we were by ourselves, he asked me, again totally out of the blue, "Do you like me in a gay way?"

I said, "Dude! No! Why the hell would you ask that?" (He caught me very off guard).

He grinned and said, with a certain edge to his voice, "It's okay if you do. I know I'm hot." I told him to shut up.

Another time, his sister, who had a major crush on me, invited me over when we talked on My-Space. Since I was going to Conrad's house anyway, almost next door, I said okay. When I got there, I asked if Morris was home. She said he was inside and being pissy because I came to see her. She said when she told him I was coming over, he threw a fit and yelled, "Why is he coming to see you? He's my friend!" Before that I'd actually thought he didn't like me. He was pretty standoffish and a little insulting when we first met. Well, he finally came out – wearing jean shorts, nothing else – and we all talked a while in front of their apartment.

Then he just looked at me with a grin, like he was about to show his winning hand in a poker game, and he blurted out, "Would you want to be my boyfriend?"

I was shocked. His sister was horrified, and he just laughed. She told him to go put a shirt on because he was "half naked." When he left, she just shook her head at me and said something like "I don't know what's wrong with that kid." The last time I ever saw him, before trial, he begged me to stay the night at his house. It was weird

because, like I said, we had become pretty good friends, yet I always had this feeling he didn't really like me 100%. Like, sometimes he would be a little rude, and he seemed to look down on me somehow. But other times, he was just super cool, and even sweet. In the end, I think Conrad is basically straight and was just open to experiment, but Morris I think was/is gay. Conrad has a daughter now at 19! And Morris... No sign of a girlfriend, and he grew up to look like an Abercrombie and Fitch model.

Arrest and prosecution

A few days after I was arrested they jacked up my bail ($250,000 to $500,000), due to a "change of circumstances." So I was back in jail, with no way out, and the pictures of Brent were still at my house in some form. Roger had turned over all my electronics – drives, cards, phone, etc. – after they threatened him at school. He'd been holding a lot of my stuff that was in my room. So Brent was tracked down through pig visits to local schools, and they took him to a little room, with no warning or parent's notice. The recording of that is heartbreaking. He hadn't seen me in months by then. He had no idea what it was about. He was like a happy puppy – just a little confused by the situation. Then the pointed questions came. He denied any bad things happening, said I was a nice friend he met a while back. They hit him with the pictures and it all got very dark. It was all so insignificant in the real life version of events, I think he had assumed all were deleted and he forgot about them once I evaporated. But now he was faced with such shame – naked photos! The pig was predictably somber and serious, like a cache of severed heads or dead cats and been found in his drawer, so Brent took it seriously too. Was he in trouble? He probably heard of kids getting in trouble for similar things. For sure, at least he was "wrong," since he'd no doubt seen many stern warnings about such "dangerous" behavior. At least ... at least ... he looked like a weirdo, doing naked pictures with another guy. What was wrong with him?

I felt beyond awful when I heard Brent had been dragged into all this. He was the most "innocent" of anyone. He hardly knew me, had no idea what kind of mess he was in now, and was stuck there because I'd been slow/lazy about doing the only thing he asked of me... Delete any pictures showing his balls. I said I would. I didn't (not fully anyway) and now he was suffering. I felt like shit. Now this

perfectly happy kid was a "victim." I was largely responsible for him getting a life long label and involuntary identity. THAT is the worst thing about all of this, maybe. I mean, we were barely even friends! He sure as fuck didn't deserve all the life disruption he experienced.

Conrad was similar by the way. He stood by me too... Until the pigs showed him pictures of his naked body at the beach. Super innocuous. Everybody's type of photos, but nude. And only three short videos: one of him throwing a stick in the ocean; one of him sitting, ankles crossed, weaving at the camera; and one he took himself between his legs, looking at the ocean and islands. But with these pics, he couldn't deny so much. And how could he just stand on the truth? It had been a happy day of naked romping on the beach with his older gay friend? What would his dad think, or his friends?

Abandonment and new friends

After my first arrest, there was no abandonment. After the second time, only one sister speaks to me regularly. Another has certainly not abandoned me, it's just a pain to communicate. One brother stopped communicating, and the other won't say a word to me. Rumor is he experienced some sort of sexual abuse as a kid. Five sisters pretty much disowned me. Parents stood by me – especially Mom, but Mom died recently and Dad has fallen apart. He supports me, but also blames me. Says he's not convinced I did anything "harmful," but everyone else is very convinced, so he is also not convinced I didn't. At any rate, he thinks I was unfathomably stupid. One old friend who I deemed unshakable then... almost no word for three years. Another friend, with whom I was very close, finally wrote me and said, more or less, he can't understand or forgive any of this. I was selfish and stupid at best, and his work with abused kids has made him totally unfit to be around those who "exploit" them. He doesn't believe a young person has the confidence to "safely" enjoy sex, yet he is torn by some of our long, late-night conversations on the subject after the first arrest, but before the second. At that time, he didn't believe I had ever actually "done it." All my young friends, many of whom are described above, are incommunicado, and at least one was simply hostile the last time I checked. Yes, all in all, this time I was abandoned by nearly everyone, and if not for my mom's influence before she died, it might have been everyone. Almost no one said why.

I wrote to a handful of anarchist Black Cross organizations, and

sometimes found kind, responsive people there, but not exactly "pen pals." I did have extensive correspondence with one person from Chicago. I also wrote a few pen-pal organizations and had little luck. I put an ad in the Radical Faerie Digest, and got a number of replies, but all from other prisoners wanting to "hookup" after release and talk dirty now. That didn't work for me. I did get a pen-pal from the Center for Inquiry, in New York. She was super cool, with interesting and lengthy letters. But it's been many months now and two or three unanswered letters, so... is she still a pen-pal? I don't know. My best "pen-pals" are guys I met in county jail who became two of my closest friends. I never thought I'd be able to, or would want to, say that, but here it is. They write often and I'm close with their families, too.

And there is Brent, the one who started all this, and ruined my life. We reconnected our old friendship. I hope to have similar luck with a lot more people from my past, but it requires constant, reliable, competent help from someone in the real world who can and will use Facebook and other social media, send emails and get replies back in a reasonable time, and even make phone calls. People out there can help people in here reconnect with their lives, or even never fully lose them, if they start helping early enough. Also as far as pure pen-pals, I bet I might get a few more if someone would post and monitor something like a Craigslist ad for a week or so. Not sure.

I never did and never will accept life in prison, and I don't think "adapting" is a smart choice. I want to maintain my integrity, dignity, and self-image. I have thought through every aspect of this horror show with every fiber of my being, every minute I've been in a cage. I'll never call a cell "my house," and I try never to adopt prisoner language habits, or any of their other habits. It's not easy, but neither is holding your breath underwater for a long time. If you stop working at it, you'll drown. Or maybe, there's some easy out, like growing gills. Adapting. But... what happens to the gill grower when he finally reaches the surface? Fish boy is a monster now. He's great underwater, but an ill-functioning freak on land. Maybe he can adapt again, maybe not, but either way, at minimum, he knows he is changed. He has melded with his environment. I'd rather hold my breath and breathe DEEP, with great relief and joy when I break the surface... or die trying. To me, either way is death, whether you just collapse and expire, or kill yourself off for the sake of adaptation. What is melding with one's environment if that environment is a cesspool? You be-

come a piece of shit, along with all the rest of the shit. I can't accept that, and I can't ask the people who care about me to accept it, either.

Incarcerated life

My typical day starts at 11 AM or so, and ends 2 AM or so. Similar to my real-life hours. No one else here does that, but the less time I spend in this sewer in daytime, the less chance there is of running into all the miseries of prison, or of their running into me. Inmates and pigs populate this place all day. I don't care much for either, so I avoid them. At night, it's quiet and stable... I can read, write, and think. I tried to maximize all of those positives.

I don't go to breakfast. It's too early and I end up eating again a few hours later anyway. I'm lucky to get a few things from other inmates though, extra bread and such. Ideally, I get to a place where I can cheaply buy kitchen food like dry pasta or powdered milk, two staples I can thrive on. A little dry cheese or dry potatoes are good too. Powdered milk gives protein, so I can never have too much. Personally, I spend a ton of time doing legal work, 90% for myself, as my court adventures are far from over. I help others when I can, and I never charge them. I'll accept gifts, but they aren't necessary – if I can help, I will, and I hope others will follow my lead. I don't have much material support from the real world, so I do try to make beneficial trades of commodities, but for the most part, I try to give what I can where it's needed or wanted. My many books and magazines are always free. I try to live up to my ideals. I try to exercise regularly, and the more food I have the harder I work out. I expect to maintain my body and mind in as near the condition they were when I was put here, for as long as I can. I seek intelligent conversation, but it's mostly futile. I find some, occasionally, through correspondence (like this), but locally... It's almost inevitable that however promising a relationship starts, the crazy comes out if you open the right door. Institutionalization is the norm and it's depressing every time.

I cope with inner feelings by staying in as much real world contact as possible (not much, lately), and by staying in my own head the rest of the time. I write a lot, even just journals, and I read voraciously. All of this helps keep me sane. As for external threats... They come from the scum in blue and the scum in green, roughly equally, but different. I don't set out to antagonize either, but I tend not to let either just roll over me, either. I'll file grievances and pur-

sue them to lawsuits when necessary, and I encourage others to do the same, for everyone's sake. But I try to treat all pigs civilly: there's no need to manufacture conflict. As for inmates, sure, the threats are ever present. Some people hide themselves, and I've done that too, but I am much more open these days. There are so many people with sex-related convictions, it's obvious to everyone that if we just do it together we'll be safe rather than individually scurrying around like cockroaches hoping not to be stepped on. Individuals are targeted over and over, one at a time. Then all the temporarily non-targeted individuals breathe a sigh of relief that it isn't them outed this time. So they spend another week or month or year pretending to be a drug dealer or murderer or tax evader. I know not everyone can do what I'm doing about this, but paradoxically, everyone could do it exactly the same, much better even, if everyone just did it. Anyway, I found that an indignant attitude in response to the "what are you in for?" questions often gets more respect. Then again, I don't have to lie to say I'm truly innocent of what I've been convicted of, and I don't have a moral monkey on my conscience either, like some who actually hurt others might have to deal with.

There are, of course, real rapists here, and people who genuinely did take advantage of young people, maybe family, for sex the other person really didn't want. I guess they can't take the blameless-victim-of-cultural-stupidity role as easily as I can... though they still can, I suspect. These dudes who murdered kids after some kind of sexual contact, usually forced but sometimes not, would they have done such a terrible thing if they didn't feel so desperate and fearful of a world that would hate and hurt them for their demonized sexual orientation? I'm thinking in most cases, no.

600+ years seems like a pretty reasonable sentence, all and all. Anything less would have posed an unacceptable risk to the community of....? I don't know. Again, society was just protecting itself, as well as sending an important message. Before I was locked away it's undeniable that there were just too many happy young people left in my way, some of whom even showed signs of self-efficacy and self-actualization. Something had to be done, and it was.

The real answer to why they gave me such an absurdly long sentence is, I think, simply this: they imposed the six-century sentence because they could. That's really it. I got what I got because it was possible. I didn't get more because more was not possible. I didn't

get less, because then more would have been possible, and that was impossible for a prosecutor, bent on maximum punishment, to allow. Every extra year was another candle on her psychotic cake. Shortly before the preliminary hearing, the first time live testimony would happen, the persecutor told my attorney bluntly that if I thought I might get out of this on account of uncooperative witnesses, I could abandon those hopes. She already set up the dominoes needed for taking Conrad into custody, and even Roger, Brent and Morris if necessary. Those people were going to come to court for her, no matter what she had to do. I thought that forcing a witness to testify might be counterproductive. But my lawyer reminded me that, at a preliminary hearing, there's no jury to be upset with an inquisition. Once the testimony she squeezed that out of them is recorded under oath, she didn't necessarily need the witnesses – my friends – anymore. She could have her jury show-trial with just their sworn statements. All those people, especially Conrad, were mere tools for the prosecution, never even realizing that their mouse-voiced little DA friend in San Diego had a metaphoric gun to their heads the whole time. And cuffs were just a hesitation away.

I like novels featuring revenge, like the Count of Monte Christi! No just kidding (mostly). I read almost anything and usually enjoy it. But favorites... books like *Marcus and Me* and *A Galaxy of No Stars* have a special place because they tell the truth and feel familiar. Plus I am very much into anarchist literature, whether theme fiction or books about the history of the philosophy of the ideas, and stuff by big thinkers of anarchism like Tolstoy. I like singularity-themed sci-fi a lot, especially when it's optimistic. I read tons of magazines many about sports. I love motocross, BMX, skateboarding and snowboarding. I am a huge fan of *Harper's*, which may be my single favorite magazine. I like *Reason* too except for their worship of all capitalism, even the soulless, destructive, cruel, corporate kind. I love Mary Renault novels... I wish we had these for texts in high school history! Up-to-date cognitive and social psychology is good too... Books on jealousy and love, or most things from an evolutionary-biology perspective. I love philosophy of all sorts. But if a motocross race or tennis match or the X games or Little League World Series is on TV, all reading goes on hold.

Chapter 6 – **Out from the Ashes**

by K.J.

After having served 24 years in prison, it looks like I am finally coming to the end of the line. My parole date is September 2017, three years away, providing I have a place to go. My TPM (tentative parole month) has already been approved by the parole board. If I were to max-out instead of parole-out, my date would be October 2030. I would be 79 years old, so with some years left of the two 20 year back-to-back sentences, along with 20 years probation, should I make parole I would still have some time left to enjoy the remaining years of my life. Back in December 1990 I was convicted of sexually molesting my eight-year-old nephew.

Did I do the crime that got me so many years? Psychologically yes, physically no, unless touching my nephew's penis while giving him a bath, something that I admitted to, is worth 20 years in prison, and sleeping with him on a bed in a motel room while taking him on a train to photograph an excursion train is worth another 20 years in prison.

What sealed my fate was the coerced statement made by my nephew. "My uncle David hurt my bottom but I don't want to talk about it!" It was something that I never did do. In two affidavits submitted later by my nephew, one when he was 10 and the other when he was 18, he admitted to making that one statement up because of constant pressure from the investigating authorities. But that did not help me get out of prison. During my motion for a new trial the same judge, despite my nephew's recantation, stated that, once convicted, you remain convicted even if the victim recants. This is especially true in cases of sexual abuse. That is the Georgia law. I was only sup-

posed to do 80 months according to my original grid sheet but those 80 months were turned into 240 months. My original TPM was set for September 1997, but a new commissioner, and the philosophy for the state to come down hard on crime that was prevalent during the 90s, changed that. My original TPM date was rescinded, and I was told that I would have to do 80% of my time, almost a life sentence.

I won't deny that I did have fantasies that involved my nephew.

೪

I was born in New Jersey in 1950. I have a brother who is two years older than me and a sister who is five years younger than me. My father was a World War II veteran who served under Gen. Patton during the Battle of the Bulge. During World War II my mother worked for Wright Brothers in New Jersey assembling airplanes to be used during the war. They were married in 1946. After the war both my father and mother had to work to make ends meet. My father worked as a grocery store clerk all his life, having only a high school education. My mother worked mainly as a waitress at various hotels and inns. She would talk fondly of meeting Pres. Eisenhower and serving him a dinner back in 1958. An alcoholic and chain smoker, my father passed away in 1984. My mother passed away a year later in 1985. She had become addicted to prescription and over-the-counter drugs. Both my mother and father were in their early 60s when they passed away. Their marriage was rocky to say the least.

My mother was verbally and sometimes physically abused by my father when he was intoxicated, which led to her emotional and mental stress. It got so bad that eventually they got a legal separation from 1973 to 1983 when finally, after therapy, they were able to get back together. But due to severe health problems from smoking drinking and drugs getting back together lasted for only one year. This is what me and my brother and sister and I grew up with. My childhood was rocky and confusing but somehow I survived.

Despite all their problems, my parents were able to send me to a religious-based camp called Sunrise Ranch for 2 to 3 weeks during the summer. It was a yearly tradition from the time I was six years old in 1957 to 1966 when I was 15 years old. In 1967 I put myself through camp using money I earned on weekends working as a veterinarian assistant in my hometown.

While at Sunrise Ranch I was a CIT (counselor in training). In 1968 after I graduated from high school, I worked the summer at Sunrise Ranch as a paid counselor, earning $200. I used that money to put me through junior-college. Prior to college I was able to land a full-time job as a psychological aide working with the mentally retarded kids at a state institution. In 1969 I left the state institution to work for a year for a railroad. I worked on the third shift as a switch power operator, which left my days free to attend junior-college.

I had a love for trains. Photography was also one of my hobbies, and I now have a collection of over 10,000 slides that I took of railroads in the United States, Canada, Mexico and even Cuba between 1968 and 1990, the year of my incarceration. I also developed a love for the out-of-doors that included backpacking, camping, fishing and canoeing that I would pursue actively during my adolescence and early adulthood years. In 1971 I graduated from junior-college with an AA degree in human services.

During my adolescent years I had an attraction for boys who were younger than me and had numerous experiences involving my friends. I wanted to go back to working with boys so while I continue to work the night shift on the railroad I took a part-time job working as a playground counselor with a local recreation facility. I worked both jobs during the summer of 1971. In 1972 I left the railroad to take on a full-time job as a group-home counselor working with boys 11 to 16 from a children's home in New York. I also became a youth leader with the Christian Boys' Brigade, an organization similar to the Boy Scouts affiliated with the church that I attended. We would do everything that the Boy Scouts would do including hiking, camping and working on badges. I saved the money that I earned during this time to put me through college since my parents could not afford to.

It was my grandmother who suggested that I move south to attend the University of Georgia in Athens, Georgia to continue my college education. She lived with my aunt and uncle in Decatur Georgia near Atlanta. She thought that, due to problems at home, this change would be good for me. In 1973 I left the group home and moved to Georgia so that I could attend the University of Georgia. I stayed with my grandmother, aunt and uncle on weekends, when I had no classes at the University in Athens. I needed to work to put me through college for the next three years. With my counseling and recreation-

al experiences I landed a job at a church-affiliated children's home where I would work part-time during the school year, and full-time during summer break. Between Athens and Decatur it was 61 miles so during the week I would live at a dorm on the college campus while attending classes then drive to Decatur for the weekend on Fridays to work as a house parent and recreational aid at the children's home. I also took a part-time job with the Athens YMCA working as a coach for three hours in the afternoon after the kids finished school.

Both of these jobs were in line with what I was studying in college. I also found time to become a volunteer for the University of Georgia's community program, becoming a Big Brother for an 8 year old retarded black youth. Not only did I end up being a Big Brother to him but to his two older brothers, one 10, and the other 13. All three boys were small for their age. I would take them out to eat, fishing, to the Athens zoo, and even to the University of Georgia swimming pool which was open to students when no classes were conducted. I would have taken them to the pool at the YMCA where I was currently working as a coach, but blacks weren't really welcomed there back then. In 1976, just prior to my graduation, I received a certificate of appreciation from Community for my volunteer work. In 1976 I graduated from the University of Georgia with a BA degree in outdoor and therapeutic recreation. I continued to work full time at the children's home where I met my future wife who worked at that same children's home as a house parent.

During the summer of 1976 I took my dream job. I became an outdoor therapeutic counselor at a private, but very exclusive outdoor therapy program located in northwest Georgia. This program was for boys that could not cope with their families, schools, and their peer groups. My schedule was rigid: six days on, 24 hours a day, with one day off, and one four day long weekend off each month.

I would live with the boys in shelters that they had built themselves on a camping site. The shelters included A-frame cabins, ordinary cabins, and tent sites. After I completed a three week orientation and training session I ended up working with a group of 12 ranging in ages from 9 to 14. The group was named Dakanda, which was an Indian word meaning "bonded together with friendship and love." We lived in small cabins which the boys themselves constructed.

Group meetings were required. We had one every day at sundown and additional ones whenever any problems would come up

within the group. The meetings lasted anywhere from one hour to three or four hours depending on how soon the problem was solved. I did everything with them. I would sleep in the cabin with them, eat with them, work on both vocational and recreational activities with them, and even shower with them. All those activities were in my job description.

Therapeutic outings and trips were in another part of therapy. Depending on how well the group was doing, therapeutic outings took place once a week. Those outings included a night out when the group could eat at McDonald's or another fast food chain and visit an historical or educational site. We also went on extended therapeutic outings which included backpacking, camping, a bicycling trip to Florida, horseback riding trips, and even sailing on the Gulf of Mexico. Along with the counselors, the group would take part in planning their trips.

I stayed with that program for seven years and left in 1982 to take a position at another private outdoor therapeutic program in northwest Georgia as resident director. Taking this position which wasn't as time-consuming as my previous job, enabled me to continue my college education. In 1984 I earned a degree in guidance and counseling from West Georgia College. In 1985 I married the girl who I met back at the children's home that I worked for while going to the University of Georgia. She had been a house parent at one of the other cottages. In 1986 I took a position with a state-owned outdoor therapeutic program in the north Georgia mountains nearby, where I remained until my incarceration in 1990.

In 1988 my sister was living near Oklahoma City. She was a single parent trying to raise five children by herself – three girls and two boys. She was having numerous problems with her eldest daughter who was 12 at the time. This daughter ended up in a youth development center in Oklahoma City. Because of the kids' living conditions, the Oklahoma Department of Family and Children's Services was about to take her remaining four kids away, for placement in foster homes.

After talking the situation over with my wife and relatives, I came to the decision to drive out to Oklahoma, pick up my sister and her children, and move them to Georgia where I could be closer to them and help them in case future problems were to emerge. We wanted to give her an opportunity to start a new life. Arriving in Georgia two

days later with the help of my family we were able to find a place for my sister and her four kids to live. Her eldest daughter remained in Oklahoma City for another couple of months, when she eventually came back to live with the family. Within a year problems arose again within my sister's family. After another talk with my wife and relatives, instead of allowing the children to be separated into foster homes, I decided to take the two boys in. My cousin would take the two younger girls in. The elder girl would remain with her mother. This arrangement once again was made to give my sister a chance to get back on her feet. Since my wife physically could not have children this would enable me to be a father for a little while. I was very close to both my nieces and nephews, taking them to places that my sister could not afford to take them.

Unfortunately that arrangement did not last very long. Little did my wife know that during the three years of our marriage I had become addicted to pornography. I was also attracted to boys which I had kept secret from her. I had a collection of triple x-rated adult books involving mostly boys with sexual relationships with other boys, men, and even women. I also had several photography books involving boys. Those books I had purchased during the late 60s and early 70s. They included, "The Boy: A Photographic Essay," "Boys Will be Boys," "A Certain Freedom," and "Show Me," a sex-education book for kids that included live children models, just to name a few. My sex life with my wife was unsatisfactory for me and my wife.

I also wrote several adult-oriented books for possible publication that would help me through a financial crisis that we were going through at the time if published. Writing has been one of my hobbies, along with art and photography. When we made the decision to take in my two nephews, I had my collection stored in a plastic bag in one of the closets of the house my wife and I lived in. Not wanting my two nephews to find the material, I took that trash bag of materials and put them into the trunk of my car out of their reach.

In March 1990 I was on a canoe trip with some boys in a state camping program, when my wife's car broke down. My sister drove my wife to the camp where I had my car so that during my absence she could use it until I returned from the trip. Opening up the trunk of my car they found my stashed materials. Finding that material blew her mind. Instead of talking to me about the material, fearing that I might be molesting my nephew, she turned the material over

to the Division of Family and Children's Services (DEFACS), who immediately turn the material over to the County Police Department. My two nephews were immediately removed from our custody and put into a children's shelter. The police department launched an investigation. I was arrested in April 1990. Made bail in June, and took my case to trial in December 1990. After a week long trial I was found guilty of three counts of child molestation involving my eight-year-old nephew. I was sentenced to two consecutive 20 year sentences and 20 years of probation. Not only that but I was given a $10,000 fine. So began my time in prison.

It was later found out that my nephew had been traumatized by the investigating authorities constantly questioning and harassing him concerning the relationship that I had with him. When he was 10 years old he told my lawyer about what had happened to him during my investigation. My lawyer decided to pursue a motion for a new trial based on what my nephew had told him. He had my nephew file an affidavit on my behalf.

The affidavit said:

I want to correct something I said in the trial last year. At the trial I said that my uncle David hurt my bottom and had done things to me. That was not true. I said that because everyone wanted me to say it was uncle David. Uncle David never did anything to me. What I said at the trial was not true and I am signing this paper and changing what I said because I want to tell the truth. I know that it is wrong to lie. No one told me to change what I said. I am making this statement without duress, threat of harassment, or promise of anything to my benefit.

When his first affidavit was brought up in my motion for a new trial, along with an appearance at the court room to answer questions, the judge denied my motion, stating that because I was already convicted, the victim of sexual abuse could not recant a statement that he made in order to change the decision of the court.

Eight years later when I was putting together my habeas corpus, my nephew, then 18, made another affidavit for my defense. In this affidavit he stated:

In 1990 when I was nine years old my uncle David was arrest-

ed and accused of sexually molesting me. He was later convicted of several charges related to that. During the police investigation of the charge the DEFACS people and two police investigators, including Detective K, intensely and repeatedly questioned me about uncle David molesting me. They did this at every place DEFACS placed my brother and me to live before the trial. Before my uncle's trial I never told the police, DEFACS, or anyone else that my uncle David molested me or touched me in any inappropriate way. That was and that is the truth. I would've told my uncle David's lawyer this truth before the trial but the DEFACS people never let me contact him or him to contact me. Right before my uncle David's trial I was told by the lady DEFACS worker that the police would continue to repeatedly question me unless I said at his trial that he had hurt me. Their questions all the time had become unbearable and I wanted them to stop. The police also said if I did this they would get help for him so at the trial I did not need to tell them the truth, and I said that my uncle David had hurt my bottom. After that I found that my uncle David had been sent to prison and that the police had not helped him like they promised. I was scared and really ashamed that what I had said had probably caused this. Several months later when my mom came to visit me at DEFACS I told her what I had done because of the police pressuring me and lying to me. She said that she would talk to his lawyer. When my mom got custody of W again my uncle David's lawyer called me into his office and we talked privately about what uncle David had done to me, whether he had molested me or not. My mom was not present but she did tell me to tell the truth. I told my uncle David's lawyer that I had not told the truth and why. I wanted the police and DEFACS workers to stop harassing me and bothering me. In January 1992 at a court hearing I told the trial judge under oath that I had not told the truth. I swore the truth that uncle David did not molest me. In August 1998 I went to the parole board after my uncle had been convicted and again told the truth. My uncle David did not molest me and I asked them to let him go.

And he finished by saying in his affidavit, "under the penalty of perjury of the laws of the United States I swear that this statement is true."

My habeas corpus hearing took place in 1999. After reviewing

my case and the affidavits that my nephew had submitted, the judge said that my request looked favorable and he needed some time to consider it. Unfortunately during that time the judge passed away and in November a new judge was brought in to review my request. That judge denied my habeas corpus, stating that because he had not been there during my ABS hearing, he could not render a decision on my behalf that would be favorable to my cause.

That was 16 years ago. My nephew is now 32 years old with a boy of his own. He has been with me through this time giving me the support that I needed to make it through prison. Both my wife and sister have been supporting me as well. My wife passed away in 2009. My feelings were that she had died of a broken heart, letting her health deteriorate because of what she did. At least that was what her last letter to me indicated. Had we talked the situation over prior to her turning the materials in to the DEFACS, she probably never would have done what she did. She had no idea that I would be convicted and given as much time as the judge gave me.

This is not to say I am completely innocent of such charges. I am guilty of the feelings and fantasies that I had involving him that I never acted on it except for that one touch while helping him bathe. I could have acted out my feelings and fantasies involving him as time progressed. For a variety of reasons, I have come to the conclusion now that my sentence, as harsh as it was, was justified. This is what I will be dealing with over the next three months in the classes that the parole board is requiring me to take two years prior to my release.

Hopefully these two classes will help me to set my mind straight so that when I finally do get out I will be able to lead a productive life in what years I have remaining. I know that I will never offend again, but still I need to go through with this to gain a better understanding of my life and the reasons that got me where I am now.

Chapter 7 – In Defense of Intergenerational Love

by R.R.

This section contains two excerpts from a longer work: a part of the introduction and one chapter. In this work, the author theorizes about his relationship with a boy he loved. The second section – "Becoming Your Big Brother" – is taken out of the middle of the book, and that may create some confusion to the reader. At this point in the narrative, R.R. had already formed a relationship with a boy who is referred to as "A.J."

Introduction

It has been referred to as "the love that dares not speak its name." We are speaking, of course, about intergenerational love relationships – particular, those between adult men and boys. A society's acceptance of these relationships varies greatly over time, and from place to place, but usually corresponds with the degree to which a culture is "open" and its people enjoy personal freedoms in general. Human societies undergo slow but continuous change over time. Advancing or retreating, like a giant pendulum, they swing toward one extreme or the other – sometimes in the direction of greater trust in human nature and innate goodness – an increase in personal freedom and prosperity for all – only to retreat once more into an era of fear and mistrust: of the future, of government, of one's fellow man. It is at this end of the social spectrum that things formerly allowed become taboo. The state seeks greater control over its people in uncertain times. Any minority, including any sexual minority, becomes

increasingly suspect and vulnerable to prosecution. Intergeneration-al love is highly sensitive to these changes in a society's belief system over time. Contrast the difference between how the practice is treat-ed in modern-day America with that of ancient Greece, where love relationships between men and boys were celebrated as "love on an elevated plane."

Yet despite various attempts to eradicate the practice, it has al-ways steadfastly remained as if it were a necessary part of the way human civilization has formed. Throughout recorded history, until the present day, examples of highly regarded intergenerational love relationships can be found in every country and corner of the world – and amongst every racial and ethnic group of people on the planet! Why should this be?

One answer is to look at how humans have organized themselves into extended family and social groups over the centuries. Alliances of like-minded people with a common objective were often formed to address a particular problem or meet some need within the commu-nity that had been going unmet. If they were was successful in this ef-fort, their solutions would eventually become a permanent part of the culture and, through tradition, be handed down from one generation to the next. The "alliance" persisted because it advanced the group's survival prospects by providing somehow for the common good of its individual members. It is precisely in this way, that intergenerational love relationships evolved to become an integral part of nearly all hu-man societies: they are an ideal solution to meet an important need within a community – and thereby advance the cause of the greater society.

The main purpose of intergenerational relationships is to catch, and provide one-on-one mentoring to the lost, unsupervised, dis-enfranchised, and self-destructive youths that exist within every culture. These relationships are the safety net of last resort to give companionship and guidance to troubled and delinquent boys whose parents are unable or unwilling to do so. Intergenerational love re-lationships don't depend upon "referrals," some distant bureaucra-cy, or state funding to do what they do. They're available to a boy in the neighborhood where he lives and sometimes struggles to survive from day to day – an immediate help in times of trouble. They work through the natural "affinity" that exists between a man and a boy. Such relationships have elements of student/teacher, father/son, big

brother/little brother relationships, and they build a road from childhood to adulthood that the boy can then travel successfully.

These relationships aren't designed to meet the needs or address the problems of every boy, and they may not be the best solution in every situation. But occasionally they can be the most cost-effective, workable, and practical alternative to more conventional forms of help. Certainly no one is suggesting there aren't other ways to help the boy to achieve the same objectives – only that the intergenerational love method may be the most natural way, and the option a boy would choose for himself if given a choice. To allow such relationships to flourish, especially when other forms of help are unavailable, only makes good sense.

Even in today's climate of fear and mistrust, the potential benefit of intergenerational relationships is acknowledged and recognized – hence, the existence of such organizations as Big Brothers/Big Sisters, Boy Scouts and Cub Scouts, and other similar mentoring programs. The main objection to "boy love" relationships is not simply the inclusion of the word "love" – but that these relationships often also include some type of sexual intimacy between the two. So I will address the issue of sex in an upcoming chapter, and try to show why there may be a legitimate purpose and place for sex within some of these relationships – and why it probably isn't as harmful as is commonly believed.

How then does one go about proving that an intergenerational love relationship is capable of having a healthy, positive influence on a boy's growth and development – and isn't simply another form of abuse heaped on top of whatever he may have already suffered? It is difficult since it is possible to make a case either way! It just depends on which of these relationships you choose to hold up as examples of the practice – and focus all the media attention upon. As with all fallible human endeavors, there are good ones ... and some not so good. In today's society, only the most exploitive and abusing relationships are given media attention and coverage. As a result, there is no longer any distinction made between those that are clearly harmful, and those that arguably might have been beneficial in some way. The mainstream media outlets, increasingly ratings-driven and under pressure from the authorities, have been so successful in attempting to "socially-engineer" intergenerational love out of existence, that most people are unaware that positive examples of it even exist!

One can think of it in this way: each year in this country, there are children who suffer great harm, some even killed, at the hands of their parents. Now, if the media were to focus attention solely upon these examples of horrific parental abuse and neglect, without including any examples of responsible, loving parenting, then an outsider looking in, with no prior knowledge about the issue on the basis of which to form an opinion, might well conclude that the traditional family unit is an unsuitable way to raise a child! Well, it is mostly the same dynamic at work which is giving intergenerational love such a bad name.

In this article, I will take the role of a lawyer trying to defend a client everyone already assumes is guilty. I will present my case for why my "client" (intergenerational love) should be acquitted. I will try to show that it is a misunderstanding to characterize these relationships as simply the means by which an adult befriends a boy so that he can "groom" or manipulate him into a sexually abusive situation. Critics of such relationships frequently point to the "unequal balance of power" between the boy and the man. Yet the balance of power in an intergenerational relationships is not as lopsided as is claimed, for it is often the boy who calls the shots and has the real power! Any parent can tell you how perceptive and shrewd a kid can be in playing one parent off against the other to get his way. He is intuitive, and cannot easily be fooled. A boy will sense early on in the relationship if part of an adult's interest in befriending him includes a sexual interest in him. Yet this awareness seldom repels or frightens him away. Why? Because he senses an opportunity to gain from this situation. To have an adult "wrapped around his little finger" gives him real bargaining power! So yes, he may be chosen by the adult ... but he also chooses for himself whether or not to enter into an intergenerational relationship with a particular adult.

◌ৱ

During the 1960s, and even into the 70s, intergenerational love seemed to be quietly gaining a wider acceptance in most societies. The practice was debated and discussed openly in academic circles, while surveys conducted by social researchers interested in the subject revealed a surprising finding: when thousands of college students from campuses across the country were questioned about their sexu-

al histories, of those who reported having had sexual encounters with adults while they were still children, the majority remembered these experiences fondly and considered them a positive influence over-all. Researchers began to consider such experiences mostly harmless as long as they weren't forced on an unwilling victim. In this era of great personal freedom, as long as adults could be trusted to act in a responsible manner toward children, and no real harm was done, many "unofficially" adopted a live-and-let-live attitude toward the practice. Papers were published which cited evidence that children were fundamentally sexual beings from birth, and should have rights over their own bodies and the freedom to satisfy their natural curiosity about such things if they wanted to.

Advocacy groups like NAMBLA were formed to educate the public and seek further legitimacy for intergenerational love relationships, by removing the veil of secrecy that had surrounded the practice for so long. In those days boy lovers were welcomed into the larger gay rights movement in general – and often brought up the rear in "Gay Pride" parades and marches. The "age of consent" was a mere 12 years old in some states, and just 14 in most others – for both males and females – and the world didn't come to an end! In fact anyone who is old enough to remember that era will tell you children were much safer back than. So what happened?

Beginning in the mid-1970s great social change, accompanied with uncertainty about the future, swept the land. This rapid change corresponded with a breakdown in civil society. In general there was an increase in all categories of crime. About this time there emerged a new kind of sexual predator who seemed to have no conscience, and who thought nothing of molesting scores of children, causing a great deal of harm. The kidnapping of a six-year-old boy, while on his way to school in New York, gained national attention and shook the country. This was followed soon after by news of another young boy taken from a South Florida shopping mall. A panicked public, unable to tell by looking who these monsters in their midst might be, simply began to mistrust all adults ... convinced now that many were intent on harming their children. The seeds were being planted for the backlash against intergenerational love that exists today. Even though boy-love relationships had nothing in common with these criminal acts, the practice nevertheless began to fall into disfavor through a kind of "guilt by association" factor. Furthermore, even though these

crimes were always relatively rare, the media did its part to fan the flames of hysteria by sensationalizing the few that did happen, and making it seem as if terrible danger awaited children around every corner!

Boy lovers with the means to do so fled the United States, with its increasingly draconian laws, for more enlightened places. Arthur C. Clarke, the noted science fiction writer who wrote "2001, A Space Odyssey," moved to Sri Lanka. There he lived out the rest of his life taking in homeless and destitute street boys and teens, giving them a safe, loving home and a college education. But even there he wasn't safe from the long arm of the United States law. They learned of his activities and became suspicious of his intentions with the boys he was helping. Authorities here pressured the Sri Lanka law enforcement officials to arrest and investigate him for his so-called "crimes." Little known is their response to this pressure: they told the US government that his work with youth was a helpful and important contribution to their society. He was a citizen of their country – and therefore under their protection. The US should butt out of the internal affairs of another sovereign nation! It is the good deeds of a man like Arthur C. Clarke that represent the true nature of intergenerational love – not the criminal acts of a few.

Becoming your Big Brother

Now, before we continue our look at the friendship AJ and I are developing, I'd like to say a word or two about how someone like myself becomes a boy lover. Since I am completely normal in every regard except that one, it is something of a mystery even to me. But I'll begin by debunking the claim most often cited by the authorities: that we ourselves were sexually abused as children. I'm not saying it doesn't happen, but I wasn't sexually abused growing up, and neither were most of the other boy lovers I've known. I think that theory was advanced to make intergenerational love seem as sordid and pathological as possible. So if it isn't because we are somehow pathologically compelled to inflict abuse upon some poor unwitting victim, because of some terrible ordeal we ourselves suffered through, then how does it come about?

We can be nearly certain that becoming a boy lover is rooted in some kind of childhood experience. I think everyone would agree on that. Everyone's childhood, boy lover or not, can be thought of as a

lengthy mathematical equation that contains several variables. Now, think of each variable as some childhood experience – good or bad. Each time you plug a different variable into the equation, the final result (or answer) will be different. So it is with how our childhood experiences help shape the kind of adult we eventually become.

I think there is evidence that physical abuse – harsh disciplinary methods such as severe spankings whippings and/or beatings – during one's childhood can produce the adult boy lover. Think of it in this way: if a boy is brutally disciplined growing up, he may well develop an anxious, fearful, hyper-vigilant approach to the world. This internalized timidity may make forming adult relationships with women difficult, and facilitate relationships with children who are seen as less threatening. Transitioning from childhood sexual expression, which for boys is primarily experimentation with same-sex peers, into heterosexuality, involves moving out of one's comfort zone and into the unknown. The traumatized boy becomes stranded in this childhood stage of sexual expression, unable to move on. Instead of transitioning into adult heterosexuality, he grows up still falling in love with the same-sex peers whose friendships had brought him such great comfort as a child – only now they are much younger than him.

If this adult befriends a boy who is undergoing similar bullying or physical abuse, he will be highly empathic and understanding of the boy's plight, because he has been there himself. If he reaches out to help the boy, he is only doing those things he wished someone would have done for him growing up. If he can succeed in helping the boy, and making a difference in his life, he has also begun the process of healing, and reconnecting with, his own wounded inner child. Because of his relationship with the boy, and in the process of helping him, a scenario is re-created through which his own inner child receives the healing and comfort it needed, but lacked growing up. This process is also known as "transference" – with the boy acting as the "stand-in." It occurs mostly at a subconscious level.

Now if you extend the same line of reasoning to include other boyhood plights such as poverty, neglect, poor self-esteem arising out of a struggle with sexual orientation issues, or whatever the case may be, then I think you will have found one of the main root causes of most intergenerational love relationships. There's something inside of the boy lover that is keenly responsive and sensitive to a boy's

plight or perceived needs.

With regard to any long-term damage or negative consequences resulting from sexual contact between the two in these relationships, let me say this: no one would deny that forcing unwanted sexual activity upon an unwilling victim causes long-term harm. But there is a big difference between that and the sexual intimacy that occurs within the confines of a relationship that is based on mutual love – where deep friendship and an emotional bond exist between the two. When the boy is a willing, even eager, partner, and finds pleasure in the sexual encounter he has with his adult friend, then the entire experience closely resembles that which he might normally have with another boy of his same age during a sleepover. In this instance, the sex issue really becomes a non-issue. It simply assumes its place as one experience among many others that the two share together, and it actually facilitates the bonding process between them by lending their relationship an air of exclusivity. The course their friendship takes closely resembles one a boy might enjoy it with a same-age buddy.

ೞ

As far back as I can remember I have, with few exceptions, been primarily attracted to other males. An incident in the fifth grade sums it up nicely. I fell in love with the boy in my class at school, and actually got up the nerve to write him a note telling him so. I still remember how amazed I was when he wrote me back, and essentially said we could get together after school and play at either his house or mine, and become friends. I was so thrilled. I held his note to my heart and even slept with it. Needless to say we did become friends. He was a tougher boy than I – good at several sports. So I let him call most of the shots. He got me into a lot of trouble, including skipping school the final two weeks before the summer break that year. But he was my best friend and I loved him dearly. I would've followed him anywhere.

Our sex play didn't amount to much. I will share with the reader one incident I recall vividly. During one of our adventures we had stumbled upon a vacant house in the neighborhood next to ours. Finding an unlocked window in back, we sneaked inside to have a look around. The former occupants had left behind clothing, pieces of furniture, and other belongings scattered around. In one bedroom

we found a bare mattress lying on the carpeted floor. We romped through the messy house that day like we owned the place, examining all their discarded personal property for anything of interest, and shedding our clothes along the way. We chased one another around completely naked from one room to the other, finally ending up on the mattress wrestling each other. He was the stronger, and succeeded in wrestling me over onto my back. He climbed on top of me, and stretched himself out full-length on me to hold me down, then pinned my arms back against the mattress by the wrists. "Now I've got you," he teased while trying to kiss me. I remember twisting my face away from his, pretending that a kiss from him would be the most disgusting thing in the world. Then after the briefest of struggles, giving up, and allowing myself to be kissed, secretly enjoying the feel of his mouth and lips on mine, the weight of him, the warmth and softness of his skin, on top of me.

But he was only practicing on me for what would come next, for by the time he hit sixth grade he was already "making out" with girls, and had girlfriends. So clearly, as nice as these childhood sexual experiences can be, they do not, in and of themselves, seem to predict adult sexual orientation.

I waited until I was 14 to decide I didn't want to be gay any longer. I started dating girls exclusively and had some success. I had my first child, a girl, at 16, when I accidentally got my girlfriend pregnant. I married in my early 20s and had my second child, a boy, with a woman in New Mexico. After my divorce from her, I moved back to Texas where I stumbled into my first intergenerational love relationship (since becoming an adult) with a boy. Here's how it happened.

I had rented an efficiency apartment inside of an old Victorian style home on the south side of Fort Worth. At one time the neighborhood had been one of the nicest in the city, but over the years the condition of the huge old stately homes had deteriorated. Many were subdivided into duplexes, small apartments, or rooms, and rented out cheaply, sometimes by the week. The area began to attract a lot of transients, and those down on their luck. The place I rented had a huge, wraparound, front porch, with chairs, an old couch, and concrete steps to sit on. It was a perfect place to relax after work.

However, I soon learned the porch had become a gathering place for nearby teens who, along with a few of my fellow renters, would sit out there at night to drink beer, or get high by sniffing paint if they

had some. I pretty much just kept to myself, and sat on the other end of the porch drinking my beer and just enjoying the night air. On one such night, while I sat there smoking a cigarette, a boy of only 12 approached me. Slurring his words he asked for a cigarette. He was carrying a plastic bag with silver paint sprayed inside, and had a ring of paint all around his mouth. I could see he was higher than a kite. I handed him a a cigarette, and invited him to sit and talk awhile. Over time, this boy and I developed a deep friendship that eventually became love, and I was able to make a big difference in his life. It was through this first intergenerational relationship with him that I discovered these relationships could accomplish a lot of good, and serve an important purpose in someone's life. I found that a boy was, in many ways, a perfect fit for me, and that mentoring one came natural. Whether I was taking him camping or fishing, to the zoo, museum, or amusement park, or to football games and WWE Wrestling at Rogers Coliseum, I was introducing him to things he had never experienced before and to a whole new way of living. I knew then I had found my niche in life.

Other intergenerational relationships would follow. Here then are a few ways I have met boys whom I would come to know and love: late at night, in front of a gay bar, a 13 year old looking to earn money by turning tricks; sitting behind a convenience store, a 12 year old, completely intoxicated on shoplifted wine; panhandling for spare change in front of a pool hall at only 11 years old, after running away from home to flee an abusive situation. All true – I swear! I befriended boys from every racial or ethnic categories you can imagine: White, Black, Hispanic, Indian, and Asian (Vietnamese to be exact). And I can tell you, at least up until a certain age they are remarkably alike. But this was not intentional by any means. I simply accepted any boy who needed me, and wanted me in his life without regard to skin color or any other consideration. Any boy that wanted me, could have me.

Now the authorities would have you believe that I callously took advantage of a boy's desperate situation, using the opportunity (under the pretense of helping him) to groom or manipulate him into some kind of sexual activity later on. Now if what you mean by "grooming" is bonding with the boy through shared experiences with him, then I admit I'm guilty of that. It is easy to pass judgment and assume to know another's motivations when you occupy a lofty, unassailable

position of moral authority and certainty in all matters. Unfortunately, in the real world where some must struggle to even survive, life isn't so pretty, nor exactly as we would have it to be. Idealistic thinking goes out the window, and issues of right and wrong are not always so obvious, or easily defined. Sometimes it simply becomes a matter of what works and gets a person from point A to point B.

These were often boys who walked the mean streets of the inner-city alone, in neighborhoods where people mistrust the police and authorities, and you would never consider calling Child Protective Services or some other state agency for help. It is in these places, where real danger and exploitation can find an unsupervised boy, that the true purpose and place of a boy lover in society becomes apparent.

ⳃ

Whenever you want to remove or eliminate a certain behavior from society (whether it be cigarette smoking, drug use, or what have you) you must first demonize the practice by making it seem as disgusting and loathsome as possible. In order to accomplish this, a steady stream of news articles and information must be released to support the particular viewpoint or mindset you're trying to create within the population. Any opinion or viewpoint that is contrary to that must be shouted down immediately lest it take hold and influence people in the wrong direction. These efforts to socially engineer the public through a system mostly based upon shame results in a very biased one-sided misrepresentation of the facts. However, some people, if they think something through for themselves and arrive at a different conclusion from others, will "stick to their guns" and defend their difference of opinion as long as they have good reason for believing as they do. So it is with me.

A few years back I ran into the boy (an adult now) that I mentioned earlier: the 12-year-old who was sitting behind the convenience store intoxicated on wine he had shoplifted from the store. At the time a barrage of negative publicity surrounding intergenerational love had me questioning myself: could the authorities be right? Am I just trying to rationalize and justify something that shouldn't be done? Am I really inflicting lifelong damage on boys that I profess to love and think I'm helping? I thought running into this man, with whom I had had a relationship when he was a boy, might help to an-

swer a new question. He had actually lived with me for some years, so I undoubtedly had an influence on him growing up. I remember the encounter well – including every word spoken.

He recognized me right away and we hugged for a long while. "Listen," I said to him, "I'm terribly sorry for being a bad influence on you when you were growing up, and for anything I did, or exposed you to, that I shouldn't have. If you are having problems now in your life, I take full responsibility."

I remember how he looked at me as if I had lost my mind. "Are you kidding?" He asked. "You were the best friend I had growing up. Don't think like that. I wouldn't trade the time I spent with you for anything. If you'll remember, both my parents were bad alcoholics, and the problems I've had were because of that." He went on: "I'm doing fine. Got into a little trouble with the law and did a few months in the county for breaking and entering, but I straightened up since then. I've got a job in an apartment now." And so that was that. He didn't blame me for anything. He was fine.

Unfortunately, there is no shortage of men and women who were victims of severe sexual abuse as children and are ready to be paraded out in front of the camera to tell their terrible tales. But this is not the whole story. Were they to interview the young man above about his experience as a boy in an intergenerational love relationship with an adult, his account of it, and its impact on his life, would differ greatly from what one normally hears. It's a side of the story seldom heard.

Ꮳ

I already missed A.J. and couldn't shake the feeling that he really needed me. I decided to go back over to the apartments after work that next afternoon, not knowing what I might find. I prepared myself for the worst but figured I could salvage the visit by apologizing to A.J.'s mother, then seeing if my friend was around. However, when I pulled into the parking area I was surprised to find A.J. sitting outside their door. As soon as he saw me, he broke into a smile and jumped up. He jogged over to my window and said excitedly "I knew you'd come back. Come inside. My mom wants to meet you." Then he lowered his voice and added, "She needs someone to watch after me while she goes out tonight. I told her you wouldn't mind. Please say yes so she'll let you. Okay?" I followed him to their apartment,

relieved that everything was all right.

"I'd be glad to watch him for you," I announced walking through the door. She was applying makeup in front of a mirror but shot me a relieved look.

"Thanks. He said you wouldn't mind, but he didn't know for sure if you would be coming back tonight. I hate to leave him alone in the apartment in this neighborhood. Know what I mean?" I could see packing boxes of various sizes scattered around, most only partially full. "I can't afford to pay you," she said. "But there is beer in the fridge, and cable TV here, so just make yourself at home." She was very pretty and I could see where A.J. got his blond hair and good looks now. But what really surprised me was how young she was. She must've had A.J. while just a teenager herself, I thought. She was rummaging around inside one of the boxes in search of something. "I guess he already told you we were moving. Right? We've got to be out of here by the end of the month."

A.J. spoke up: "Mom, I want Mike for my big brother. You said I could have one."

She gave me an exasperated look, and said, "Well, did it ever occur to you maybe Mike has better things to do with his time than hang out with you?"

It was my turn to help out: "I'd love to be a Big Brother to A.J.," I said. "He's a terrific boy."

She stopped darting around for a moment and took a deep breath before replying. "You don't know what you'd be getting yourself into. I was going to enroll him in the Big Brother's program at one time but he has so many behavioral problems, I didn't think anyone would be able to handle him. He has ADHD which is hyper-activity disorder, and he can be very difficult to control. You just haven't seen that side of him yet. I glanced over at A.J. who sat rigid. He had his arms crossed in front and was frowning at this disclosure. Clearly he had not wanted me to hear all that.

I spoke up in his defense: "He behaved very well for me last night."

"Well," she said, "it wouldn't be fair not to warn you ahead of time. They took him out of regular class at school because he was so disruptive, and put him into a special education class where I don't think he's learning anything at all. He's been diagnosed as being developmentally delayed which I don't understand at all. He can be re-

ally smart when he wants to be."

Hmmm, I thought. That would explain the feeling I had at first – that perhaps he was a little slow mentally for his age.

"I don't know," she said with a sigh. "Perhaps that's what he needs – a male role model in his life. Someone to talk to about his temper. He pulled a knife on me once and I told them if it happened again I would put him in the juvenile home.

A.J. who had been quiet up until then suddenly erupted in anger and yelled, "I did not!"

She ignored him and turned to me. "I've got to run. This guy I'm going out with doesn't even know I have kids yet. I'll try to be back by 11 PM or so. Is that okay with you?"

"That's fine," I assured her. "Go enjoy yourself and don't worry about a thing. I'll take good care of him." And with that she was gone.

The place was a mess, especially the kitchen. I went about straightening things up and throwing out trash, hoping to surprise her when she returned. "A.J., bring all the dirty dishes into the kitchen," I instructed, filling the sink with water. There was no food in the apartment so we walked down to the little store and bought milk, cans of spaghetti and ravioli, and a six-pack of beer. I fixed us both a light supper and then cleaned up afterwards.

We walked to my friend's apartment, and A.J. watched TV in the living room while my friend and I sat at the kitchen table and drank beer. He recognized A.J. but, as I suspected, didn't seem too fond of him. "Yeah, the kid's a brat," he whispered. "Seen him running out of their apartment one day, yelling at the top of his lungs. Needs a good whipping if you ask me. Mother is very pretty though." Then a thought suddenly occurred to him, and he grinned, slapping me on the shoulder. "Yeah, I know what you're up to. Trying to get in good with her through her kid. Hmmm. It just might work," he said thoughtfully I smiled and nodded, as if he had found out my secret. After a while we left.

Back at the apartment A.J. dug through one of the boxes and pulled out a game. "Play Monopoly with me," he begged. He set the board up on the floor in front of the TV. While I counted out the money both of us were to have, he checked to make sure all the property deeds were there. As we threw the dice and moved around the board buying properties, we joked and talked. A couple of times I caught him trying to distract me long enough to snatch an extra S500 bill

from the bank. "Look!" He said pointing at the TV area I glanced around at the screen, realizing an instant too late that it was a trick. I turned back just in time to catch them in the act.

"Put it back, A.J. I saw you," I warned.

He held the stolen bill high in the air and giggled. "Come take it from me. That is, if you think you're big enough." He challenged. I playfully tickled and wrestled him onto his back holding his arm by the wrists and working to pry the little fingers apart.

"Hey," he wailed. "Quit trying to hold my hand." I finally did manage to get the bill away from him, but only after an exhausting struggle. He was remarkably strong for his size, and nearly too squirmy for me to hang onto.

Later on I tried talking to him. "You pulled a knife on your mom, buddy?" I asked.

He immediately became defensive. "Because she was being a bitch," he blurted out. "I wasn't going to stab her or anything. I just wanted her to listen to me."

"A.J., listen," I said trying to make eye contact with him. "You have to try to behave okay? It sounds like she might let me become a Big Brother to you. That means we could start spending a lot of time together. But if she puts you in a juvenile home, we'll never get to see each other then."

He looked away. "Oh, you'll get tired of me. Just wait. No one can stand to have me around for very long," he said sadly.

I took him into my arms and hugged him against me then – for the very first time. "Listen, A.J., I care about you. There's no way I'm going to get tired of you. It just ain't going to happen. Okay? I'll be there for you as long as you want me to be"

He didn't seem completely convinced, but said "Okay."

We fell asleep at opposite ends of the couch, while watching a movie. I heard his mother's key in the door a little after 11 pm. She smiled when she saw us. "He really likes you. I can tell," she said in a quiet voice. "Did he behave himself?" We both glanced over at A.J. who was still sound asleep. He looked like a little angel lying there – so peaceful.

"Oh yeah," I said truthfully. "I've never had any problems at all with him."

"I'm surprised," she said quietly. "I've never seen him make friends with anyone so quickly. He would've run most people off by

now."

"He's a great boy," I told her. "I already think the world of him."

She talked me into spending the night with them. "It's too late to be driving back. I'll set the alarm. I know you have to get up for work in the morning," she said. "Do you smoke pot?" She retrieved her stash and rolled us a joint. We smoked it and talked in low voices while A.J. slept only a few feet away. "Don't worry about him waking up for anything," she said. "I allow him to smoke pot at home. It is the only thing I found that calms him down so he doesn't drive me crazy." We both had a quiet laugh at that.

Beginning with that night, details of their lives together slowly emerged. His father had deserted them shortly after A.J.'s birth and had little contact with them over the years. She had tried to keep a roof over their heads, but working only as a waitress, sometimes just part-time, it had been difficult to make ends meet. She was estranged from her family and parents, so they had had virtually no one to help them out all these years. When A.J. started developing behavioral problems, it had made matters worse. He had gotten kicked out of several places, once by setting a vacant lot across from the motel on fire. So they had been forced to move around a lot – sometimes staying a few days or weeks with friends, or one of her boyfriends, most of whom had little patience or time for A.J. "I guess you could say he's been through a lot," his mother admitted wearily. "I blame myself for most of his problems. I was doing a lot of drugs around the time I had him, so that's probably got something to do with it."

His home life has certainly been chaotic and uncertain to say the least, I thought. Still, my heart went out to his mother. It could not have been easy to raise him by herself, yet she had done her best under the circumstances. After our talk that first night she had shot me an exhausted look and confided, "He needs more supervision than I can give him. I wondered if it would be better for him," she nodded in A.J.'s direction, "to put him into one of those residential facilities for emotionally disturbed children, where he could at least receive some counseling or something."

I took a moment to gather my thoughts and then responded. "I understand how you feel. But sometimes those places can do more harm than good. Since you're going to let me be a big brother to him, why not give me a chance to see if I can't make a difference? I have some experience working with boys like A.J., and I might be able to

help." I was relieved when she agreed that giving me a chance was a far better solution.

So over the course of the next two weeks, I picked A.J. up for some kind of outing nearly every night, even if he only went with me to grocery shop and pay bills. I wanted to keep him out of his mother's hair as much as possible. I was determined to help out with him so that she would not send him away, or put him in some kind of home. He was generally better behaved with me than for just about anyone else, but I did catch occasional glimpses of what his mother was talking about. A.J. did have a terrible temper. If he was overstimulated or became agitated, he could be quite unpredictable – hyper and difficult to control. I remember once when we were in a store together, he got mad about something and just started walking home.

But I was already beginning to fall in love with my very spirited little companion, so I took such incidents in stride – never even raising my voice to him. Instead I would hug and stroke A.J. to calm him down, and then try to reason out what was going on. What did he need from me? I had a feeling he was dealing with a fear of abandonment in the only way he knew how. He was so certain I would dump him or lose interest that he was trying to run me off before he became too attached to me. It was a way for him to protect his feelings from being hurt. It would take time, I thought, to convince A.J. that I was in this thing for the long haul. That I really cared for him.

One Friday night, toward the end of the month, I had taken A.J. out to see a movie and eat at Burger King. By the time we arrived back at the apartment, his mother was in a good mood. Having him out of the way, she'd been able to finish packing the rest of their belongings. She rolled a couple of joints, and the three of us smoked them together. It was the first time I'd ever seen A.J. high, and I soon learned he loved to mess with people's minds when they were stoned. He sat on the arm of the chair where I was sitting and teased me relentlessly. He'd wrap his arms around my neck, then giggle and fall over into my lap, pulling me down at the same time – egging me on until I would finally tickle and wrestle him. I looked at his mom helplessly, wondering what she thought about us being so affectionate and touchy-feely with each other. She pretended to pay no attention but I could tell she was watching closely to see how we interacted together. What I didn't know then, was that his mother believed that when a person was "high" they couldn't hide their true nature or intentions.

Their real self would come out, or become apparent, so from that perspective I did okay that day because what she saw and cared most about was how happy and comfortable A.J. was with me, and how patient and good I was with him. I had passed her test that day even though, at the time, I was afraid we'd blown it.

Chapter 8 – I Am a Bit Like an Omnivore

By O.D.

tI had a decent childhood. I was loved and never truly needed anything. I had few friends though I played sports. I actually preferred to be with people older than myself.

I had figured out that I was a MAP at the age of 13. I had known that I had to keep the younger friends separated from older friends. In effect I was leading two different lives and in the few incidents where they crossed, they were easily explained. I remember a time when I was about 17 I had to explain away a pair of boys briefs in the hot tub filter. That was probably the toughest. I really never gave my own image much thought. My relationships were in two separate categories.

The relationships that I had in my teen years were more about having fun. We would go fishing or just break away from the others and play around; some touching, cuddling, and oral. I never had full-on relations unless we were much closer in age. For example one boy was two years younger and he and I were in full-on relations until just after high school.

I have two separate cases. The first one was brought about in 1991 while I was 19. Before my first charges, I had few friends and had started on my career path in sales. There were few girlfriends and few boyfriends. There were an abundance of younger friends to partake in. I knew I was more of a loner and thought differently than others, so I took what few friends that I had and kept them close. While it may have been a case of naïveté, I really did not feel like what I was

doing was wrong. It felt right, but others did not see it that way, and I had to keep hidden that part of my life.

Between my first and second conviction my relationships turned more into love. I loved the younger friends and would take care of them in any way that I could. I have even put a couple of them through school and started them along their chosen fields. Those relationships and others during my 20s and onwards were significantly more involved on the emotional side. I can truly say that I love them.

After my first conviction I was left out of my paternal family events. I had one friend that did stay with me, but all others I had were gone. It was a start over for me. Being in the car business then, I started building new relationships fairly quickly. I eventually became involved with a woman that had two children and we had one together. I was doing pretty well until this present case was brought against me.

I have to say the whole labeling thing does not work for me. I am a bit more like an omnivore. I really do go all over the board. I already knew I was not like anyone else I knew. The girlfriend I had lived about 50 miles from me, and we usually met at a skating rink. I had some relations with another boy two years younger than me so that part of my life worked out very well. When I was younger I seem to attract more than my fair share of older males. That seemed to drop off around the age of 12 which coincided with puberty. The few friends around my age were loners as well, but they were not MAPS. I preferred to hang around with adults. They seem to be more accepting. I guess that while I knew I was different I found ways to cope.

I've been locked up now for four years, and the only people I have regular communication with are my parents, one brother, his family, and one friend. All others have abandoned me. None has given a reason. They simply just quit talking. I do have a couple of contacts that I will write to on our email on occasion. I do not want to impose on anyone, so I have never tried to establish any ongoing relations with anyone on the outside. I do not know how to do this with like-minded people.

My daily routine in prison does not vary much. I try to look out for others that are SOs, and when new people arrive I will reach out to those to welcome them. I am usually in my unit, and if not I am painting. There is quite a bit of inner turmoil in my feelings. I get frustrated with people over what I perceive as ignorance. I am not like the

"standup" guys, but because I am an imposing person the SOs cannot see that I am here for the same charges and therefore I am put out into the middle by myself. I have been told many times that I am the last person they would suspect. While we are not looked upon in a favorable light, I will not brook any open disrespect to me or others that are here as SOs. I see some SOs attacking others just to remain in hiding. I have to take very small strides in my feelings about my family and friends as they often are too painful to delve into. My future is completely uncertain and any thought in that direction is just speculation. As for my personal safety, I think that most of what I see as a threat is just overactive imagination. As I said, I am a large guy who will get confused as the biker type by attitude and looks.

I do think I did receive an unusually long sentence. They used a 20-year-old charge against me and in this case (possession of child pornography) there was no direct victim. Even though I had that conviction before, they failed to realize that there was no Internet available in the middle 90s as it is today, so there was no way of working against the availability of pictures. I also feel like it was another outlet that was much safer for all those involved.

I feel like they took a contributing member of society and destroyed a family to set forth their brand of draconian justice. The pre-sentence investigator was more interested in trying to find new charges for me than finding out what kind of person I am. As the federal prosecutor so succinctly put it, "Mr. Walker made his bed. Now let him lay in it."

I enjoy reading fantasy, ancient history, and books on MAPs or like-minded people.

In the mid-90s I was giving speeches about community-based corrections instead of lengthy prison sentences for SOs. Many of these speeches were heard by the very same people who locked me up. It was a very sad day when I was informed that the Adam Walsh act was passed. I do agree that violent offenders do need to be locked up, but where's the line? I have never forced, coerced, or otherwise made a boy bend to my will in matters of our relation. I do truly love and appreciate every wonderful and special moment that I had with him and hope they feel the same.

Chapter 9 – **Two Loves**

by I.W.

My life as a boy

From the above title please do not think I am transgender, transsexual or trans-anything. I was born a male and always will be. I love the freedom of being able to pee standing up.

When I was eleven years old I was lucky enough to meet a man who treated me with great kindness and affection. I was out riding my bike one day when I saw him working on the old house he and his wife HAD just purchased. The house was located far enough from my parents' place where I lived as to not be considered a neighbor. I had seen the man before because my dad owned a small business that brought people to our house. The fact that I lived in a very small town in rural New England also made it easy to know the man's name. If you have never lived or visited a town like I just described, you may not understand how fast word of mouth can spread information.

As I rode my bike down his driveway he looked up and seemed to recognize me. When I got close enough he asked me what I was doing so far from home. I guess when you're "old," three or four miles on a bike is a long way to travel. My bike was my ticket to the wider world. I loved being on the road. The freedom that went along with a banana seat, two wheels and a sissy bar was like heaven to me. I told him I was hot and thirsty and was wondering if I could get a drink of water. He got down off his ladder and said he needed a break anyway so why not. He had a cooler on the back of his pickup truck and went and got us each an ice-cold drink.

He sat on the tailgate of his truck and I sat on my bike. We chatted about the nice weather and about the house he was working on. It

was a typical old farmhouse in need of much repair. After I finished my drink I just sat listening and talking with him. It was strange to me that he seemed to care about and listen to what I was saying. I felt awkward because I knew I had no real reason for being there yet I didn't want to leave either. He may have seen that I was uncomfortable because his next question was "Would you mind giving me a hand before you leave"?

I was just thrilled that he wanted my help. I jumped off my bike and said, "Sure what do you need me to do?"

He said he was putting up an eve board and needed me to hold one end while he got it nailed into place. I helped him for an hour or so then told him I had to get home for lunch.

The ride home was incredible. Never had my bike peddled so easily or gone so fast. I had no idea why I felt the way I did, I just knew it was a great day. I kept thinking about how he listened when I talked and he asked me for help. I felt useful and important. I wasn't just the kid up the street or so and so's little brother. I was a helper, I could do things that were useful to a man. Seldom since have I had such a feeling. Maybe it is because for the first time I felt someone needed me. What I do know is I changed that day. No longer was I just a kid, I grew up and I knew it. Life for me was not going to be the same; I had turned a corner and was more alive because of it.

From here on, out of respect and for protection, I will refer to my friend as James. For obvious reasons I can't use his real name.

I waited a few days, and then rode my bike back to his end of town. With only one road through town there was the north end of town and the south end. I lived in the north, James in the south. I was really disappointed when he wasn't outside. I had looked forward to helping him again and just thought he would be there building away. His truck was in the driveway but I couldn't see him. It took me a few minutes but after a while I got up the nerve to go knock on the door. When he opened the door he looked almost as happy as I felt. Any fear or apprehension left my mind and body without any haste. He grinned at me and asked if I needed another drink of water. I felt a little stupid then because I hadn't thought of a reason to be there. He had no way of knowing that being there made me happy. Nothing else was said as to why I was there, he just invited me in.

I knew from conversations he had had with my dad that he worked nights at the paper mill nearby. When he told me he had fin-

ished working on the house for the day my heart sank. All I wanted to do was hang out with him and help him repair something. From my first visit I knew he had a lot of knowledge about fixing things. That day was not going to be like the first day and I'm sure my sadness showed through. He told me he had to leave soon but that I could rest there until he left for work. I sat at the kitchen table watching him make his lunch pail up for the night shift. Trying to make conversation I asked him where his wife was and he told me she had a job too and was gone every day. I told him I thought it was strange that a man would have to make his own lunch. My mother always put up my dad's lunch. He smiled but didn't seem offended by what I had said.

If I thought my life had taken a turn three days ago it was about to make an about face. James told me he had started working on the bathroom and that he had no water in there so he was going to shave at the table. As he got a small basin of hot water ready along with the old fashioned lather brush and razor I started panting like a dog. I hid it the best I could but for some reason I was really excited about watching him shave.

At this point I must tell you about the "dirty magazines" as my mother called them. My grandfather had given some old issues to my dad and I found them hidden under my parent's mattress one day. After sneaking a few looks at them I realized I liked the ones that had pictures of men in them. There weren't many and it was always the girl parts that the photos were focused on, but there were one or two that showed men with erections. The pictures were up close and personal, and I liked them.

As I watched James lather up his face and get the razor ready (they were scary in those days), I started thinking what he would look like if he was in the dirty picture book. I tried not to think about it, but as he stroked the shave cream off his face my fantasies just took over. I was staring at him in utter fascination. I had never watched a man shave like that before and certainly never thought about what he would look like naked in a picture. I was too young to ejaculate but I'm pretty sure I came in my pants so to speak. My mind was going places it had never been before.

On the ride home I was really mad at myself. James had done nothing but be nice to me and I wanted to do bad things with him. It didn't seem fair. If he ever found out what I was thinking he would hate me. I didn't know much about the whole sex thing but being the

youngest of six children I had heard enough to know I was "one sick fucking child." With what I knew about adults at that time I was convinced James already knew what I was thinking. He knew my little penis got rock hard and that I had that funny tickle down there that happens when you and a friend monkey around in the tree house. I felt I could never go back to James' house again and I had ruined everything. I was going to hell and I knew it.

When I was watching him shave and having the thoughts it didn't seem bad. I didn't want to hurt James. As a matter of fact, while my mind was seeing naked pictures of him I felt it would be like loving him only different. What I also didn't understand was, if he knew what I was thinking, why did he say it was nice seeing me again? Why did he tell me he could use a hand the next day holding the copper pipe in position while he soldered it?

The next day my Mum was "going into town." At that point in time going into town was a big deal. It meant getting on your school clothes, washing your face and combing your hair – not the most important things to an eleven year old. I also had other plans. Things were different now. I was grown up and someone wanted my help. I don't know why my parents hadn't seen the changes that had taken place in their little boy, and I wasn't about to tell them.

I told my mother I was planning to go play baseball with Shirley. Shirley was the town tom boy, she was tough, and could spit better than any of the rest of the gang. As parents do, mother had to throw a monkey wrench into my plans. This included taking the trash to the dump. In those days you just picked a corner of your 70 acre farm and used it as a dump. There was no curbside pickup or recycling. I also had to get the lawn mowed. There was a small amount of whining but I didn't want her to say I had to go to town so I raced through my chores. Mum left before I finished the lawn. I knew I was going to be in trouble and have to re-mow the grass. You can't run with the lawn-mower and think you're going to get a good job done.

Needless to say I didn't stop at the ball diamond. I rode as fast and hard as I could to James's house. Any thoughts about how evil I must be disappeared overnight, and I was only a little concerned about him knowing what I had been thinking the day before. Just as I got to the driveway a car was pulling out. This nice lady stopped and told me she was James's wife and that I must be "Little Billy." (To this day I hate family nicknames). I said I was and she thanked me for

being such a big help to her and her husband.

The driveway seemed ten miles long that day. Meeting James's wife bought back a flood of yesterday's feelings. What was I going to do? How could I tell him I didn't mean to have those bad thoughts, they just happened? By the time I got done scuffing my feet and dawdling around, James was already at the door waiting for me. I hung my head and walked to the door. He greeted me as if things were just great, and there was no scolding me for thinking bad things. I was sure he was just waiting for the right time to yell at me and tell me he hated me and to never come near his house again. The longer I waited the worse it got. The strange thing is he never did yell at me.

Finally he took hold of my shoulders, squatted down so he could look me in the eye, and asked what was wrong with me. To this day I don't know how I kept from bursting into tears because that was all I wanted to do. Cry and run. I told him I was a bad kid and if he knew what I was really like he would hate me. At that point the smile went from his face and that serious adult look that I had seen a hundred times but still didn't understand replaced it. James took me to the kitchen table and we sat down. He told me that he didn't think I was old enough to be really bad and that he couldn't think of any reason that would ever make him hate me. It took a long time but I was able to tell him about my thoughts and that I wanted to touch him. I'm not sure where the "I want to touch you" part came from but I said it and I couldn't take it back.

All he said was, "That is serious stuff and I'll have to think about it." He got me a snack and went back to work. I sat at the table thinking that the world didn't come crashing down and he didn't yell at me.

Over the next two weeks James and I only got to see each other a few times. He had to work a shutdown at the mill and I had family stuff to do. His not freaking out did make me more brave. Every time we did get to see each other I would ask him if he had thought about it. His response was always the same: "That's serious stuff. I need to think about it."

My being the kid I was, my comeback was, "It's just for fun, it's no big deal or anything." Deep in my heart though I was a little hurt that he didn't feel the same way. Once I said it out loud the fear went away for me and was replaced by desire.

The big day came not unlike any of the other times I would ped-

dle my skinny little ass to his place. We were working under the house on some plumbing stuff. James was laying on his back working and I was holding the flashlight. At one point he had to spread his legs to get leverage on a piece of pipe he was trying to move. I just reached out and put my hand on his crotch. He stopped for a second but didn't pull away. After he got the pipe moved he looked at me. I started laughing and said, "I bet mine's bigger than yours." I already knew that wasn't true, but I didn't know what else to say. James just told me we'd see about that later but for now we needed to make sure the water in the bathroom worked.

For the first time I was really mad at James. I had been the one to tell about my secret thoughts. I was the one who wanted to cry when I couldn't see him. I was the one who held his stupid boards and pipes in position while he fixed them. Why was he more concerned about the water running than about my feelings? We were in a little secret hiding place where no one could see us and all he wanted to know was did the solder hold. I didn't hide my anger well, and when we got out from under the house and were dusting each other off, I hit him a lot harder than I needed to. I was mad and I wanted him to know it. My little tantrum continued into the house where I threw myself into a chair at the table and made a huffing noise. James proceeded to the bathroom to check the water flow. I was really pissed off then.

Because of the remodeling there was no door on the bathroom. When James walked out I knew he was there but I wouldn't look at him. I could tell he was just standing there looking at me and I was a little ashamed for being an ass to him. Again, all he had ever done was be nice to me. I was being the jerk and I knew it.

All James said to me at that time was, "Do you really know what your doing?" As I turned and looked at him I realized his pants were unbuttoned and the zipper was undone. His white briefs were showing a little and I could not take my eyes off them. I told him I did understand what was going on and that it was what I wanted. When he stepped closer to me I reached out and took hold of the elastic band around his waist and pulled it down. He was not erect and he did not look like the pictures I had seen in the magazine. He had, what he later explained to me, was a foreskin. I didn't have one of those and I found it wonderfully exciting.

As that first summer went on, James and I spent as much time together as we could. He worked hard at teaching me how to mea-

It was the end of that summer that I learned what real heartache felt like. Sex was never the dominating factor in my relationship with James. I wanted to fool around a lot more than he did, but I just liked being with him. He knew so much about construction and getting things to work that it was like being at school all the time except it was fun. Like any kid who hears his dad tell the same joke all the time, I got tired of hearing, "Plumbing's easy, boy. Just remember shit flows down hill." What I really didn't want to hear was the day James told me we couldn't do the sex thing anymore. I don't recall his exact words but something to the effect, "This just isn't right" or "This isn't normal." I was crushed. Our friendship seemed so normal and great to me that I didn't understand why he felt that way. My suffering didn't come from the hands of an abuser, my suffering came from the words of a man who feared for my wellbeing. I kept telling him I was okay with things and nothing needed to change. Change did come and even my begging wouldn't get him to monkey around with me. It happened once or twice after the big talk but it was never the same.

I grew up and moved away from my small New England town. I had boyfriends and girlfriends, long-term relationships and short-term flings. I had fun jobs, bad jobs and high-paying jobs. At the age of thirty I married a wonderful woman and a few years later had an even more wonderful son. We moved back to my hometown and I built a house with my own hands. During that period I thought many times about all the things James taught me – like "Do it right the first time" or "Remember that shit flows down hill" or "Plumbing sucks but it isn't hard." He was right about a lot of things.

There are ten thousand therapists out there who would still say I was a victim at the hands of an abuser. I was not. I have every reason in the world to give in to what I have been told, and put all my problems on James, but James was not the problem! I was there. I know what happened, and I know how I felt. Maybe I'm the only boy in the world that had a loving caring relationship with an adult man but I doubt it. This is a true story, and all I'm asking is for you to realize that you are being fed a bunch of crap when you are told intergenerational relationships are always bad. They are not always bad and I am living proof.

James is still married, has grown children and even grandchildren. I see him occasionally even though he has since sold the old

farmhouse and moved to a nearby town. Again rural New England life. We have only talked about our two summers together once as adults. I was going through some hardships a few years ago and wanted him to understand I in no way blamed him. He had given me something that no one can ever take away and I wanted him to know that.

Philip

I was born in January and by June I was sitting in the water either in my diaper or buck-ass naked. I drowned at the age of six and one of my sisters got me back to breathing. The most memorable things about that was my little purple titties. And the feeling of peace I had. I have never been afraid of being around water.

My dad didn't swim very well but he always taught us to respect not fear being on the lake. At one point in my life I had 21 Red Cross certificates from first responder, CPR, all of the swimming levels, and life guard training. By the age of twelve I would have my dad or one of my brothers drive me 2-3 hundred yards off shore in the boat in high waves and blowing wind and I would jump overboard and start swimming for shore.

I started working in my dad's business when I was 12 years old and school was just something that had to be done. The expectations of anyone in my family actually doing anything significant was pretty low. The problem for me was I did really well in school and for the most part I liked it. What I knew was the three months of "summer vacation" was hard work. It seemed so much easier to listen to what the teachers said and puke it out on a quiz or test than to carry lumber all summer.

It wasn't that everything in June, July and August was bad. I got one week off from work every year. The first summer I had the chance to guide my aunt and uncle and their two girls around the lake where my parents had a camp. I knew every reef and rock in the place. Plus I had been handling a boat on my own for the past two years.

Uncle Charlie was a good man. He worked hard to provide a nice home and living for the four of them. He and auntie could never have children of their own so they adopted two girls that really needed a stable environment. The problem was he was useless in the outdoors of Maine. That's where I came in as the boat driver/fire starter/hook baiter for their week at the lake.

The importance of that week lay in the fact it set the groundwork for many more summers with me in command of the boat. Starting the next year I was able to take the boat and one friend to camp for a week. My mum would help us with the food shopping and dad would go on and on about all the things I needed to watch out for. Every summer it was the same lecture from dad. Watch out for rocks and dead-heads (partially sunken logs), keep an eye on the wind, drive into the waves not across them, check your gas first then the spark plug if the motor doesn't start. The list went on and on and every year it was the same. Over the next five years of going to camp alone my friends and I did have technical, mechanical and "judgment" problems, But, we always fixed the issue and made it back to home shore on the right day at the right time to be retrieved by my parents, safe and sound.

Do you remember the first time you fell in love? As an eleven year old boy I had the great experience of loving an older man. But this was different. I was head over heels in love with Philip. It was my junior year in high school and he was a freshman.

I met Philip in the library at school. Sitting at the table next to me was a new face which meant he was a freshman. A very cute freshman in my eyes. Being seventeen and unsure of everything in life, my reaction was to throw a pencil at him. He stopped it as it skidded across the table and looked up at me. I got up and walked over and quietly said, "Sorry dude, lost control of my writing instrument." As he handed it back I asked if he was a freshman and he said yes. I told him he needed to carry my books to my next class. It was freshman initiation week so that was accepted. When we got upstairs to my physics class I took my books and said, "Thank you, but I'm only a junior not a senior." Even under his dark skin I could see him turn red knowing I had just fooled him. I said I was sorry and asked if I could give him a ride home after school. He got a big smile on his face and made a sigh of relief. I think for the first time he realized he'd make it through high school. He said, "Yeah, that would be cool." We made plans to meet after last class and off he went.

For a freshman Philip still had a bit of baby fat. By no means was he a chubby boy, he just had a coating under his skin that gave his body a nice shape. Plus it gave me something to pinch and tease about when we got into bed. I don't know if I have mentioned this before, but Philip and I were two grades apart in school but depending

on birthdays 2-3 years apart. The reason I bring this up is we had very different body types. I was tall, six foot as a junior in high school at 155 pounds. Long and lean as my dad used to say about me. Varsity basketball was part of my life, I was a standout high jumper on our track team, and my intramural volleyball team kicked everyone's ass. Then we come to my chum: Philip was short, again the baby fat; he was first-chair trumpet in the school band and had a job at his father's "five and dime" store after school. So my mother nicknamed us Mutt and Jeff from the old cartoon strip. Misfits we certainly were. So different, yet I wanted to be with him. I even talked the other teammates into letting him be on our volleyball team. He was absolutely no good as a player, but I had some pull with the team and I wanted him there.

I already had a girlfriend. I would be with Lynda on Friday night and with Philip on Saturday night. The difference was she had to sleep in the spare bedroom, Philip could sleep in my room. Thinking back I wonder if my mother knew more than I did. Boys don't get pregnant; girls do.

It's a long story as to how I got a kick-ass stereo in my bedroom when I was 14 years old and I will fill you in with the details someday. Philip would come over after school and we would go to my room and play music until dinner. Dad didn't get home from work for an hour after we got to the house and my mum would let me play albums loud (maybe that's why I play loud when I deejay). When my next oldest sister moved out I got the "big room"; it was the largest bedroom in the house. It was a perfect footprint of the living room, just one floor above. I had my stereo, recliner, queen sized bed, study table and a built-in closet. I was golden. I always slept on the right side of the bed, except when Philip stayed over. I could walk around my bed on three sides but we always sat beside each other and got ready for bed. I would crawl across the bed to be on the left side so at night I could put my right arm around him.

That summer Philip and I planned a weekend trip to camp. His parents were very protective and I think the only reason they agreed was they wanted a reason not to let him go for a week with me during my week-long vacation from the saw mill. I worked for my dad in the sawmill and Philip worked for his dad at the five and dime type store. We both had to work Friday but the plan was to food shop Thursday with my mum and leave Friday as soon as my dad and I got the boat

ready. At that time my father had two work trucks, same make and model, just one was a year newer.

For the first time I was going to drive to camp. No more lectures on home shore about safety and boat mechanics. Dad said, "You might as well take the truck just in case you boys need it." We were only going to be gone from Friday afternoon until Sunday afternoon. It's funny – once we launched the boat we never saw the truck until Sunday, but knowing it was there meant something to me.

When we got to home shore I knew we were in for a mess. The wind was blowing straight in and very strong. Three-foot white caps breaking at the boat landing is not good for putting in a 14-foot boat. I'm not sure if it was excitement or fear in Philip's eyes (I had the same in mine) but we got the boat in the water and were on our way.

I had launched a boat many times with my dad in bad weather with the wind blowing straight in. We would get it backed into the lake, off the trailer, and turned bow to the wind at the dock. I had done this a hundred times (just never without my dad). As a seventeen year old, and really all my life, I wasn't cocky, I was confident. I pulled the pickup truck and trailer into the landing and started backing the boat into the water. Before we hit the edge of the lake I stopped the truck and had a talk with Philip. I explained that we were backing the flat stern of a 14-foot boat into three-foot whitecaps. There was a chance we could sink the ship before we got started. I could tell he was a little scared but so was I. We got out and unstrapped the boat from the trailer and just had the final wench release to go before we were committed. I gave Philip the bowline and told him: "As soon as the boat is afloat, I will jump out of the pickup and release the wench. When I do, you run to the end of the dock and get the bow of the boat into the wind." As I got into the truck I told myself, "You have to do this right." I loved Philip so much the thought of something bad happening to him hurt me.

The launch went off without a hitch, Philip did a great job with the bowline and I was able to cut the bottom off a plastic soda bottle with my pocket knife to bail out the one or two gallons of water that splashed over the stern. We loaded the boat by putting our duffel bags up under the bow because I knew we were going to have spray over the bow it was that windy. We loaded the food and coolers in the center of the boat for balance just as I had been taught to do. The last step to getting headed to camp was the actual boat leaving the dock. I

had launched a boat many times in inclement weather with my folks. I was in charge of the bowline so we would get my mother and my sister Honey seated, dad would get in and start the motor, and as he put it in gear to drive off, I would jump in. Philip and I used the same maneuver, he pulled the boat as far out into the wind as he could and I got the motor going and he bailed in. We were on our way.

As we pulled away from the dock I knew it was going to be a hard first two miles. The lake was only three miles long but it was a very windy day and it was rough going. No matter how slow or fast I had the boat going there was a lot of water splashing around. I slowed the boat down as much as I could and moved Philip up under the bow and had him lay on our bags. If nothing else I could keep him dry and safe. I got fucking wet. Every third wave would send what seemed like a shower of water over me. As we rounded the last island headed for camp, we had reached the two-mile mark. The lake settled down, and the waves were much much smaller. I told Philip he could come back to the center seat and we could go faster. When he came out from under the bow he started laughing like a school girl. I was soaked, from my head to the bottom of my Converse All Stars. I looked liked a wet rat (at least according to my best friend). The only two good things about that lake crossing was we survived and I had to get naked to get out of my wet clothes. Philip wasn't as wet as I was but he got naked too and we went skinny dipping.

Philip and I never kissed each other on the lips but one time. One day after school Philip and I were riding around in my car just killing time together. We got into a quarrel about something. As we were going down the country road being verbal dinks to each other, Philip took my sunglasses off the dash of the car and threw them into the backseat. My hand came off the steering wheel and I backhanded him across the mouth. The big problem was I had just days before broken up with my girlfriend and I had my class ring on my finger. I had had only one physical confrontation in my life before that. In fourth grade a fifth-grade bully at school picked on me. I split his lip open and he never bothered me again. Unfortunately I slit Philip's lip open. We pulled to the side of the road and for a minute we both cried. As a true Maine boy I had toilet paper in the glove box and we got the bleeding to stop. Then it turned into panic as to what we would tell his parents. I don't recall the story we told them but at the time I knew they didn't believe it. As strict Catholics they didn't like

me, but they knew Philip did. After it healed up is the first and only time I kissed him on the lips. I think we both felt I had an excuse to do it. I was kissing a boo-boo.

I had two older brothers and three older sisters, all of whom were married or living with someone at the age of eighteen. From seventeen and a half until eighteen and a half years of age I couldn't understand why Philip and I couldn't do the same. I had a job at my dad's lumber business and I knew I could support us. I watched my brothers and sisters make a life for themselves at a young age. Why couldn't Philip and I? The time, the place, and Catholicism would not allow it. I loved Philip with all my heart.

Chapter 10 – I Am What I Am

by P.A.

In this section P.A. describes how he is attracted to both men and boys, but is able to find an emotionally satisfying relationship only with boys.

જી

At 12 I knew I was attracted to my male friends. As I got older, I found myself attracted to their little brothers. I said in the past that I'm just a gay man who loves males of all ages, but that's not really correct. I see adult men as sexual partners, but I could never be "in love" with a man. I love the sex I can have with a man, something that may not be possible with a boy, but a loving, long-term relationship is impossible. I love boys beyond the sexual aspects. I prefer their company, I relate to them, we enjoy being in each other's company. I've always thought my ideal lover would be an eleven or twelve year-old boy with a large strap on dildo.

Strangely enough, growing up I was never pressured by my family or friends to find a girlfriend. I was never accused of being gay either. I never experimented with any of my friends sexually. As much as I wanted to, I was afraid of what might happen if my advances were denied, maybe with disgust. At the age of 14, I did masturbate in front of a seven-year-old neighbor boy on several occasions, and he allowed me to put my mouth on his penis, but this ended after a few months when his parents told him to stop coming down and "pestering the neighbors."

I had two adult relationships in my life. Both of them were at

least 20 years older than I. The first was when I was around 21. It was the first time I had sex. After about a year I ended it. All I can say is that it just didn't feel right. Not the sex. That was fine. It was everything else – the social part of the relationship. About five years later, I met Norman.

In those five years between adult relationships, I had five relationships with boys. When I say "relationships" I mean ongoing affairs – not one-time "you show me yours and I'll show you mine" occasions (of which there were a couple).

Karl was my longest relationship, man or boy. I first met him in 1990 when I would watch him as his mother and my brother went bar hopping on Saturdays. We stayed friends and lovers until my arrest in 1996.

Oliver and Henry were friends of Karl. My lovers always started as friends, and even if they no longer wanted to have sex, we still stayed friends. We enjoyed riding bikes, building models, playing Nintendo, watching movies. They were eleven at the time, but I was just in my 20s myself, so we still had a lot in common. On the sexual side, sometimes they would initiate it, and sometimes I would. If they didn't want to do anything, we wouldn't.

With Karl I would give him oral sex and he would masturbate me. Sometimes he would penetrate me anally. He was nicely endowed at an early age and could manage the action successfully. Henry was the first boy I had a oral sex with, and the first to give me oral sex. I didn't have sex with Oliver until three years later.

Then one day Henry's mother told them not to see me anymore. Did the boys' parents know something was going on? I think they may have thought so but couldn't get the boys to admit it. Otherwise, I would have had legal problems earlier. I fell into depression and began drinking more – always at home, not in a bar. I was working the graveyard shift at a truck stop and taking no-doze to stay awake at night, then washing down sleeping pills with rum and coke to get to sleep in the morning when I got home. I was lonely as hell. Besides my co-workers I didn't have any friends. For some reason, as an adult I didn't seek out adult friends. Perhaps I'm a bit of a loner. Perhaps I was friendless because I wasn't allowed by society to have the type of friends I wanted. On a few occasions, the boys snuck into my building and we would spend the afternoon together but they had to be careful because my neighbor was friends with Karl's mother.

I met Norman at the truck stop where we both cooked. Partnering with Norman was my attempt to have a "normal" gay relationship with an adult. He was 20 years older than me and gave me the sense of settling down which I thought I needed at the time. I later learned he was also attracted to boys, and had actually done time for it. After a while, we quit the truck stop and moved into a house the next county over, leaving my boys behind.

As Norman's partner, his friends became mine and I tried to live the "normal" gay man's life – going to parties and gay bars, being seen as a couple. It was all a sham, though. I missed my boys. My attempt to deal with these emotions of loss and disappointment led me to keeping a journal, something that later, during my sentencing, would be used against me. Norman read my journal and discovered that I still yearned for boys and had doubts about my relationship with him. Since he had also had affairs with boys in the past, he was understanding and at one point even tried to find a boy that would join us from time to time, but was unsuccessful.

We decided to open our own small business and settled on a video store which we thought would be easy to operate and profitable. It was easy to manage, but not very profitable. Norman went back to work to help pay the bills and I managed the store full-time. The video store was back in the town where I met Norman, and was closer to the boys I loved. We eventually got an apartment nearby. I hoped to see the boys again but they were teenagers now. I thought they would not have forgotten about me, but they would have moved on with their lives and maybe made new love interests.

Then one afternoon, out of the blue, Karl and Oliver showed up at the store on their bikes. They were 14 and 13 now. I introduced Norman to them. Karl had heard my sister mention to his mother that I had opened the store across from Target and they came down to see. Regrettably, I couldn't spend a lot of time with them since I had to watch the store and Norman had to work at the truck stop, so sometimes we would close the store early on very slow days and the four of us would have sex there at the store.

Norman and I had a flawed relationship. I'm sure he loved me. I was about 27 when we met, and he was an older man, as I mentioned. Because of my attraction to boys, I couldn't honestly love him back and he knew that. Life, at the end was stressful. The store wasn't successful, I couldn't give him the love he desired, and we were both

drinking too much.

One day when I was at the store alone, I caught a boy looking at the binder we kept the adult movies in. He was masturbating. Before, we had an entire room with a door to keep the porn videos in, we flattened the cases and put them in a binder with the corresponding numbers of the tapes. When I caught him, he denied it, but I put him at his ease, saying it was no big deal. We talked for a bit. He said his name was Josh and he was 15. He was small for his age but I believed him. It had been a very slow day and no one was in the store so I took a chance and told him to pick an adult movie and we would watch it on the TV behind the counter. He chose a movie (a straight one) and we set about watching it. While he watched the movie, I watched him grope himself through his sweatpants and occasionally look back at me and smile. "I wish we could do that," he suddenly said.

"What, have sex?" I asked.

"Yeah," he said, looking at me. Long story short, he let me give him a blow job and then allowed me to fuck him. He became a regular at the store. He never let me have anal sex with him again but he did let Norman and me have oral sex with him many times.

Then Josh became jealous of the time we were spending with Karl and Oliver and he went to the police saying we had sexually assaulted him. They got a search warrant for our store and apartment and we were arrested. During the searches they found my journals, where I had written about my affairs with boys. I had stupidly written their names. Josh had already fingered Karl and Oliver as other victims but thanks to my meticulous notebooks, the police were on the hunt for more boys. Of all the boys I wrote about, though, Henry was the only one that talked. The others couldn't be found or, if they were discovered, they denied anything sexual happened or flat-out refused to talk to the cops.

After I was sentenced, I was moved from the county jail to the state prison. During the evaluation the nurse asked if I felt suicidal. I had just got sentenced to sixty-five years. I was a shy, timid man looking at life in the "big house." I made the mistake of saying yes. I was immediately ushered off to the maximum-security prison where I was stripped naked and put in a cell containing a mattress and a security camera. That's it. At one time there had been a table fixed to the wall. But it had been removed with a blowtorch leaving a jagged piece of steel behind, so if I really had been suicidal, I could easily

have tried to do myself in.

How do I think the boys felt about our relationship? Well I assume they enjoyed our time together. I never bribed or coerced them. I have to think that they kept coming back to me because they wanted to be with me. Karl often said he loved me. Does an eleven-year-old know what "love" is? Maybe not in the sense that an adult uses the word, but I think they understand its strong emotional attachment. Why then, you may ask, did the boys confess to our sexual affairs? Well I think we both know how intimidating the police can be. Imagine if you're 14-year-old boy.

My family and friends did not explain to me why they abandoned me. They just stopped visiting and stopped writing. The only real "friends" I had were Norman's. Perhaps our mutual friends blamed me for what happened to him. He was also indicted for sexual abuse, but I didn't twist his arm to do anything he didn't want to. Actually, since he had been in prison before for sex with a minor, he should have known better.

I had written in my journal about masturbating in front of my brother's son when I was around 19 or 20. That came out in court so perhaps that's why my brother stopped writing. My mother writes infrequently, but my dad has really had my back during all this. He paid for the lawyer who handled my appeal. It wasn't successful but he's on retainer if something happens in the sentencing policy that would lower my sentence. My dad is 81 now and still healthy; he visits me when he can, but I can't help but wonder who will be in my corner after he's gone (God forbid).

In 1990 I became a member of NAMBLA (something else that came out at trial which I'm sure didn't help me). When I was arrested I wrote to them and told them to discontinue my subscription to their newsletter, *The Bulletin*. At one point they informed me that they sent a special newsletter to prisoners so I started receiving that. Something else they used to do was have volunteers send Christmas cards to prisoners and that's how I met my first pen-pal. After that I put listings on a couple of pen-pal publications: "GWM prisoner seeks gay man for correspondence," etc. I tell them up front what my "crime" was and I usually don't hear from them again. I'm always honest with pen-pals that being a "minor attracted adult," or an "MAP," as it is now called, is a big part of who I am. I currently have four pen-pals but only one is an MAP. (I don't know if I can get used

to this politically correct "MAP" term.)

From the horror stories I read about other prisons around the country, especially in the South, I'm grateful that my prison is not one of the worst. That said, prison is prison. I don't mean to stereotype "MAPs" but for the most part they are easy to pick out in a lineup of murderers and druggies. Personally I'm small in stature and pretty meek. I got no tattoos on my muscles; heck, I got no muscles. The first few years were hard, but after a while, a new crop comes in and they set you aside in favor of the "fresh meat."

I'm a very easy-going and likable person so that helps. I don't make waves, I keep my distance from the predators and troublemakers. I keep to myself a lot. I don't even seek out the company of other "MAPs." I don't like to draw attention to myself. That said, in the 18+ years I've been inside I've accumulated a list of 20 or 30 guys I can be sociable with because they don't know what my "crime" is, or don't care. I'm lucky enough to have someone who is now my cell-mate who is willing to stick up for me if any threats are made. He is serving a life sentence for murder. He used to live in my hometown and is a loner like me.

I've worked in the prison workshop for nine years. We build the stuff they sell in the prison showroom. I can put my artistic talents to use and make enough money to live so I am not begging my parents for money.

My stupid journals played a large part in my excessive sentence. They were used by the prosecution to claim that I had committed many more criminal acts than I was charged with. It's called "uncharged criminal conduct." The prosecution didn't have to prove I did any of the things I wrote about. However, a few years ago the Supreme Court ruled that this practice is unfair and unconstitutional, and could no longer be used to make a sentence more severe without proof that these acts actually happened. The problem is the new rule isn't retroactive, meaning it doesn't apply to old cases like mine – just to new ones. Until the U.S. Supreme Court makes the ruling retroactive, it's of no use to me. I also think the judge just wanted to make an example of me. It looks good on his resume if he's tough on "child molesters." Coincidentally he got bumped up to the Maine Supreme Court shortly after my case closed.

I'm not much of a "navel gazer." I am what I am. I'm not ashamed of what I am or anything I've done. A caseworker once asked me what

is it that I find attractive in boys? I wanted to ask her, what is it that you find attractive in men? Chances are they're the same things. After almost a decade in prison, I still don't see myself as the problem. Society is the one with the problem.

Chapter 11 – Visions of a Drug Dealer

by T.J.

T.J. was a homeless drug-dealer much of his life. Living from hand to mouth was not always great, but he chose to live that way. In many ways he found that kind of life was intense and satisfying. He is a reflective and intelligent thinker. As he lived outside the mainstream of society, he also thought outside the mainstream.

ଔ

Near death

Raleigh, North Carolina – late 1980s …

I was living with Jamilla, a roommate-with-benefits, so to speak. More correctly, she was kind enough to let me use her couch and her bed, as long as I wasn't the jealous type. I wasn't.

What I was, was a young, drug-dealing, out-of-control youth with no direction, to speak of – adrift in life, and letting the winds of change blow me where they would. "Jami," as everyone called her, was a step above me, if you will. She, at least, had a steady job and was paying her bills on time. I, on the other hand, had drug-addict friends and customers, and was one step from being homeless – again.

At this particular time I was working as a temporary clerk for a temporary warehouse. It wasn't my best career move, but it was a job. I was still constantly looking for a building job, though. I was, by then, a carpenter by trade, and wood has always been my first love for money-making.

On my way to the warehouse one morning, I saw that what appeared to be a construction company had begun work in a field on the same street as the warehouse. Within a few weeks, it was obvious that a building of some size was going to soon be standing there, and I knew I wanted to be a part of it, rather than penciling in storage space for lawn chairs. On my way home from one particularly tiring day, I stopped in the construction site to see if I could locate a supervisor, and maybe procure a job as a carpenter.

I found him readily enough, and found that I'd have to relocate (officially) to Texas to be hired. However, in the meantime, as I was local, did I happen to know where I could find some "party supplies"?

Now, to those who don't know, there are a LOT of construction workers out there who are clean, sober, Christian, law-abiding folk. There seem to be considerably more who are NOT. Being asked by a supervisor for clandestine drug deals didn't surprise me in the least. Besides, I SOLD drugs for extra money. He asked the right guy. Mushrooms? SURE! No problem.

What were the chances? The Grateful Dead were coming to town. For those who don't know, they have a hardcore group of followers called "Deadheads" who make ticket money by selling t-shirts, home-made jewelry, their bodies, LSD, mushrooms, and anything else necessary to procure tickets for the shows. They were already filtering into town, and the main body of "Deadheads" would be here in two or three days. Perfect. More importantly, Jami had a friend who was one of these hardcore "Deadheads." She traveled extensively and had multiple contacts for things, including mushrooms.

Jami made a call, her friend made a deal, and I bought some very inexpensive mushrooms from said friend when she arrived in town. As Jami had invited her to stay with us for the duration of concert time, when she arrived we made to "sample" the goods. (Oh yes, the guys were going to be VERY happy with their purchases, and I was going to make a bundle!!)

I was to meet the construction guys on Friday afternoon, after everyone had gotten paid. Jami's friend arrived on Wednesday afternoon. After one day of my own recovery, and assuring the construction guys I most definitely had what they were looking for, Friday morning rolled around.

As an experienced drug user I was pretty certain that I could eat just one little mushroom and continue to function at work. At six AM

that morning I ate one small "cap" on the way to work, and by eight o'clock, I was TOTALLY unable to be useful at my job – or WALK, for that matter! I knew I had to leave.

I begged off sick. The boss very much liked my work and wanted to keep me healthy. He paid me and sent me home with the admonition, "Go home. Get better. Take Monday if you need it. Just come back." Moaning and groaning, out the door I went. In my car in the parking lot, now that I wasn't in view and having to fake anything, I realized "I'm off work Friday MORNING, and PAID! I can go do ANYTHING I want to! Even eat another cap!" So that is exactly what I did.

I popped down another cap, then went to see if my friend Gary was home. Gary lived out in the country with his girlfriend. He worked nights, she, days. By the time I arrived I was feeling QUITE unattached to the earth. I knocked on the door, and a very sleepy looking Gary answered, invited me inside, and turned to address me. He looked into my eyes and face and, making a "Gimme" motion with his hand, said, "I don't know what you got, but c'mon with it. Don't even try and deny it."

We both ate a couple (in my case, MORE) caps and stems. In very short order Gary knew he wasn't going to go back to sleep, and I knew I wasn't driving anywhere. I explained to Gary that I had a deal to do that afternoon, but I was off until then. Either I was staying there with him, or he was driving us wherever we were going. My new chauffeur was ecstatic.

For the rest of the day we drove around, smoking pot, meeting friends, eating mushrooms, drinking. Oh, it was a wonderful, long party! Eventually I had to go meet my buyers at their motel rooms. I found them, and as promised on both sides, the deals were made and the product happily changed hands. Said buyers were so happy that I had a witness to the quality of the product with me, that they (ALL FOUR different buyers!) offered me some of my own product back – which, as etiquette dictates in the drug world, I should partake of immediately to A) receive the goodwill of those customers thanking me for a job well done; and B) make them more comfortable with the idea that I was NOT, in fact, a law-enforcement officer trying to "set them up." I happily welcomed their thanks.

However, by the end of all the dealing and goodwill, I think I had consumed close to a quarter ounce of high potency mushrooms – all

by myself. It was time to go home – immediately.

When we arrived at the residence, Jami's friend was in the throes of musical ecstasy at the concert. Gary and Jami had never met, but they hit it off immediately when Gary and I got there and I introduced them. Probably a really good thing, as that was about the last social act I could coherently handle. I lay down on the couch, fully ready to surrender to the forces of euphoria. Jami and Gary said something to me about going shopping to get foodstuffs for a very late dinner. IF I replied at all, I don't remember. They were gone and I was out, Out, OUT.

Nearly everyone has heard of NDEs (Near-Death Experiences). I'm no exception. But I certainly had never dwelt on the phenomenon, as I personally had never known anyone who had experienced one, nor experienced one myself. Experienced or not, almost everyone has heard of the "white light" or the "tunnel" (or some combination of those) associated with NDEs. We've all got our own ideas about what this may look like, or have a picture in our minds of what it is from reading about someone else's experience. I had MY idea as well.

What I witnessed did NOT match my vision of what the "tunnel" or "white light" was, even though it WAS exactly that – and more.

I'm tempted to tell the reader why I believe this to be a "spiritual" experience at this juncture of the story, but it might take away from the absolute AWE I felt as I was experiencing it, so I will wait until the story is told. Some reader's will undoubtedly call me either hallucinogenic (certainly understandable, considering all the drugs I had ingested that day), or a liar (well ... I guess those people will just have to get to know me personally), or just plain crazy. I can understand this as well, but please keep in mind that I am a die-hard skeptic as much or more so than many of those people reading this. I probably wouldn't believe it either if it had been the ONLY piece of the "other-world puzzle" that I have experienced. If you will keep reading past the first part, I think you'll see what I mean.

In the meantime.

I was out, Out, OUT.

But I WASN'T.

I don't know how long I lay there, oblivious to all, but suddenly –

There I was, fetal position on my right side, curled up at the feet of the Virgin Mary. My spirit was calm ... Calm ... CALM, while my mind went "WHAT THE ??!!??" Understand, reader, that I have nev-

er been Catholic, nor would I ever bring myself to pray to ANY human – and I don't give a DAMN if she IS the mother of God or not. She's still HUMAN. To me, that makes her a TOOL, at best, of the Gods. NOT "Holy" herself.

And for that matter (I can hear you asking already), how did I know it was the Virgin Mary anyhow? Couldn't it have been "just" a female angel? Answer: I suppose it could have been. But somehow I KNEW it was the Virgin spoken of in biblical terms. Quite possibly the "Gods" knew I wouldn't accept anything less, considering them as ghosts or some such, and the answer to their query would never happen, or I would believe I was just hallucinating.

"Query," you ask?

We'll get to the "conversation" in a bit. Let me describe the setting first.

There I was, fetal, on my right side, fully dressed at the feet of who I believed to be the Virgin Mary. Coming down from above us was the "tunnel," and we were inside of it. It really appeared to be more of a very thin cone shape, with the point at the farthest point away from us, but I think that was an optical effect of distancing. If I WAS, in fact, laying there, then the light cast a circle around us, radius about 5 feet or so from center, with us in the middle.

It looked like a concert laser effect. It wasn't steady at all. Thin circular bands traveled up and down constantly during the whole episode, crossing and recrossing each other, always in a level, horizontal posture. Outside of the tunnel was dark. Nothing to be seen at all. It was just myself and this – personage, spirit, angel, Holy Woman.

The entire "tunnel" was steady in an up/down posture, but the bands of light moved, some quickly, some slowly, never deviating from the horizontal.

I was positioned, my right shoulder lined up exactly with the bottom of her feet, had there been a floor ... but there wasn't. The light stopped at this plane, leaving the entire underneath us dark.

The light at the very "top" that I could see was the classic "brighter-than-bright" kind. I'd never seen a light so ... white ... and PURE ... and BRIGHT ... but it didn't hurt my eyes. It was beautifully crystal clear – and that doesn't really describe its clarity or loveliness.

The woman ....

She was in a seated position, except there was no kind of seating apparatus. IF there had been a chair with armrests, that's what

she would have been sitting in, with her arms on the rests. She was dressed in the classical all white robes ... and SHE GLOWED. From INSIDE her. I wish I could describe this phenomenon, but "glowing from inside" is as close as I've ever been able to come to an accurate description. EVERYTHING glowed. Her skin, her robe ....

I couldn't make out the details of her face. Strangely enough, I never felt like I HAD to. I ALREADY KNEW WHO SHE WAS. Why would anyone question The Virgin? I never even looked at her feet.

It was at this point, I think, when I basically told myself that this was SOOOOOME trip! And it was immediately communicated to me: "Choose." In a gentle command. (I say "communicated." No verbal words ever were spoken during the entire episode. All communication to me from her AND FROM ME TO HER were ... thoughts?)

"Choose what?"

"Whether to live or die."

I remember thinking, very clearly, "Man! This is REALLY ... Wait a minute. If I'm just [drug] trippin', then it shouldn't matter what my answer is, right? So if I say I want to die, then ...."

... And the light started to slowly close underneath us in a bowl shape, equilateral from all sides. I felt my (soul? spirit? life force?) being "pulled" out of my body. I could FEEL it! (Which raises the question: Was my BODY actually there, or is there in fact ANOTHER plane of existence ... the "ghost-plane" maybe, that we go through BEFORE we actually lose a soul or spirit or life force permanently from our physical selves?) In any case, feeling the pull of my soul/spirit out of my body scared the crap out of me!

"Wait! WAIT! Just WAIT A MINUTE! Let me think about this for a second." And the light returned to it's original level as my soul/spirit settled back into my body. So much for hallucinations.

Note my thought process at this point: "Okay. You're trippin' HARD, dude, but THIS does NOT feel like a trip .... So ... Okay. I'll just treat it like it ISN'T a trip. Just like it's really happening and I have to choose to ..."

– WHOOOOSSSHHHHHH –

ALL emotion left me right then. It was the calmest, most peaceful feeling I'd ever experienced (even since then!). If any readers have ever experienced shooting up heroin ... Imagine the peace of that ... now multiply it by a factor of 100. There's nothing to describe it, really.

In my mind was PURE logic. "Did I want to live, or die?" This weird computer thing was going in my head, albeit peacefully. "Okay. If I die, what happens? Well, Mom is all upset. I become another police statistic drug overdose. I haven't gotten married or had any kids yet ... and I'd like to do that. If I die I won't have anyone to leave anything to. Jami will be upset because it's in her house, and I'm sure she's got reason NOT to have police in here. It'll mess up her visit with her friend. Gary doesn't want any police questioning him ...."

I went through a whole list of "What-if-I-die?" questions. All quite logically. No emotion at all. Pure science.

Then I did the "What-if-I-live?" routine. "Well, Mom won't be upset; I won't be a police statistic. Maybe one day I'll get married and have kids and grandkids to rock on the porch when I get old ....

I don't think I'm ready to die yet."

– WHOOOOSSSHHHHHHH –

And that fast, it was all gone. The Virgin, the light, the choice ... everything ... and I woke up.

I sat upright, and realized I was dripping sweat. So much so that I felt like I'd just stepped into a shower fully dressed, turned on the water standing underneath the nozzle, and as soon as I was soaked, went and lay down on the couch still fully dressed in the wet clothes ... and while I was laying there, someone came along and poured a bucket of hot water over me.

I was uncontrollably shaking all over. I couldn't stand up. I couldn't speak. I could barely turn my head. I felt like I was sitting in a puddle. I felt the couch under me. Soaked. I felt upwards where I had been laying. Soaked. (Well, at least I hadn't urinated all over myself and Jami's couch ... I don't think.) It was a VERY traumatic return to reality.

And on the verge of crying, like I'd just made a HORRIBLE decision. (Do you know how embarrassing it is to be embarrassed for YOURSELF over something you've done, even though you KNOW that no one has seen or knows? That is EXACTLY how I felt.)

I don't know how long I sat there like that, recovering. Not long, I think. Very soon I saw the lights of Jami's car pulling in. Jami came in first and headed straight for the kitchen, carrying bags. Gary, right behind her, saw me sitting up ... and PROBABLY saw me shaking ....

"Dude! You okay?"

I tried, but couldn't answer. I shook my head in the negative, try-

ing to force the words out. THAT got Jami's attention. "Hey! What's up? Are you ... ??" I waved off her question and tried harder to answer. This time I at least got a squeak out.

"Hold ... Hold on," holding my hand up in the universal "wait-a-minute" sign.

They waited only a moment. Jami came and appeared as if she was going to sit down next to me ... on the wet side. I again waved her off to stop her. Again Gary spoke up: "Hey man, for real, what's up?"

"Jus ... jus gimme ... just gimme a minute," I gasped. "You aren't gonna believe this anyway."

In a couple of minutes I was able to stand, get a glass of water and return to my wet seat. Then I relayed to them my experience.

Of course, their reaction was just what you would expect. It's EXACTLY what I would have done in their places. They both burst out laughing hysterically! "Wow! Dude! That was some GOOOOOD 'shrooms, huh?" Tee hee har-dee-har-har. Yeah. They were just lovely.

Well, what did I expect? I already KNEW that they were going to react like that ... and so would anyone else I told. I decided on the spot that there would be damn few people who ever heard of this.

And so now you ask: "WHY, for pity sake, would you POSSIBLY think this was REAL?!!?"

Let's regress a bit. Remember I said everyone had heard of the light and the tunnel, and that we all had a vision of what that looked like? Ask yourself ... Don't YOU? So did I.

Except it didn't look like what I'd always imagined. Seems like if I'd imagined the same thing for so long, that my sub-conscious would have used THAT picture to convince me of the reality of it. WHY CHANGE IT?

Next ... Remember that I said to myself, "Well, if this is just a trip, it shouldn't matter my answer ..."? I KNEW I was tripping, AND I TESTED IT – even then! More importantly, it caused a physical reaction (or what felt like one) that actually scared me. I've NEVER had a "bad trip." EVER. And this wasn't really a "bad" trip anyway. It was a message, delivered, and a CHOICE. Nothing more. Would my sub-conscious purposely scare me into staying alive? Especially when it was obviously SO PEACEFUL there?? Possibly. But WHY? In the end I chose to live. I didn't HAVE to scare myself.

AND ... why would my sub-conscious send a messenger whom I

considered to be ... human ... and nothing more? Why not send an angel, or a ghostly-type presence? The Virgin Mary? Whom I am loathe to call "holy"? WHY?

And the two things that I will NEVER be able to explain. The PURE LOGIC of my reasoning, combined with the absolute absence of emotion during my decision-making. I've always imagined that this must be what Vulcans felt during all those Star Trek episodes.

And the PEACE. The utter peacefulness of it all. No way to explain. Ever.

Now the REAL kicker ...

Ever since this event I have felt protected. I have no reason to believe I am, but I constantly feel a (roughly) 10-foot circle of safety around me.

Also, whenever I am just THOROUGHLY stressed, if I listen closely, I hear music. In my head. Nothing I could ever duplicate, nor even try to. Sort of "classical," but not really. Very soothing. It usually doesn't last long, but always long enough to calm me. More about this later.

Third, I feel that at some point in my life, I am going to be witness to, or involved in a life-and-death situation for someone else ... and it will be for me to put hands on this person and say, "Oh Great ???, I need your help to save this person ..." or some such. Just one time only ... and it shall be so. Faith healing? I dunno. Again, more about this later.

Washed in the sphere

Yea, let it be known that I was now a believer!

A believer in ... what? I believed that a higher power than myself existed, and that for whatever strange reason, I was given a CHOICE to live or die. I felt doubly honored. I think it's actually very rare when humans are visited by spiritual beings in any visible form. To the best of my knowledge (although SURELY there MUST be others!!), I am the only one I know of or have heard of that was given a choice. Why do you suppose they would do that? Hmmm ....

In any case, I now KNEW, and knew that I was protected from any "evil" spiritual forces. Again, let me state, I have absolutely no rational basis for this protected feeling ... but I've not been seriously hurt, physically or emotionally, since. And I knew that all those religious texts were just "starter manuals," so-to-speak. Koran, Bible, Talmud, Dead Sea Scrolls ... ALL of them trying to teach us that there

was more, and we would have to pay close attention to "get it." And it didn't matter which text you chose. All that "Do eat this, or don't eat that," that's PHYSICAL nonsense, written by men, regardless of who it was inspired by. Keep this rite, or you'd better do this ritual, or fast on this day, feast on that ... Malarkey! MAN-made ideas. Probably by men who HAD been in contact with the spiritual – or alien – worlds. A little confusion here, a little "unable to explain it" there, and you have a genuine goodwill attempt to share good knowledge, but it just didn't come out exactly right.

I understood a LOT, without ever having been TOLD anything! And the music was a beautiful gift which I've heard on maybe 6 or 8 occasions since. I dread the day of the "laying-on of the hands." (That's probably going to be a REAL bad day for someone – or maybe a GOOD one, if what I think and believe will happen, happens.)

But for the moment, if nothing else, I had made a "God"-given choice, and now I WAS PROTECTED. I wouldn't have been given a choice, only to have it taken away immediately, right?

I was protected from "evil" spiritual influence, true enough, but we still have free will. Spiritual gifts given freely, are not really free, and should be used wisely. "Evil" in the spiritual world is NOT the same as what most living humans consider "evil." Mostly, we make up our own rules to appease the sensibilities of the morals of the people at the time they live in.

Two examples:

Until very recently it was considered, not just okay, but PROPER for a middle aged man to marry and start a family with a 12-year-old girl ... without horrible, dastardly, dire lasting ill effect on said young lady. Now to do so is considered TERRIBLY EVIL and will land that same man in prison for many years. And the poor girl ... *sigh* ... Just think of all the therapy she's going to have to endure to make herself feel "normal" again .... Alas, and woe-is-me.

And...consider the native populace of America from the late 1800s and earlier (Many, MANY years earlier!). They had been killing each other, and stealing from each other for THOUSANDS of years. It wasn't considered "wrong." As a matter of fact, in many of those populations, a young man couldn't be considered a "warrior" or take a wife UNTIL he proved he could be a good thief and killer.

I say again, many of the things we consider "evil" are simply societal constraints. Evil in the spiritual world ... well, fortunately, I

didn't experience any. But if the "evil" THERE is as horrible as the "good" was wonderful ... YIKES! I shudder at the thought!! In any case, I was protected from it, thankfully. But I was NOT protected from Earthly law.

Precisely BECAUSE I felt protected I was not using my gifts wisely. KNOWING that the likelihood of injury is infinitesimal, and the likelihood of immediate death almost nonexistent, makes for a very dangerous person. A person who doesn't care if he lives or dies can pretty much make anyone else do whatever he wants them to, by any force needed. It's very easy to convince someone that they'd better give up their wallet/dope/jewelry if you convince them that if they don't, then even if they fight, something possibly lethal WILL happen...especially if you mean it! (Because, it really isn't "bad" anymore in your mind. I KNEW that "The Place Beyond" was a wonderfully peaceful place. To GET there might be traumatic, but once there, SURELY I would be forgiven?! Right? Rationality isn't always rational. I repeat ... I wasn't using my gifts wisely.)

As with all lawbreakers, spiritual protection or not, I ended up in prison for breaking human laws. I hadn't cared about anything or anybody in quite some time. Why should I? Most people were ignorant of what was beyond, and even more refused to see the logic of what was the greatest gift the Higher Powers have tried to give us repeatedly over the millenniums. Why shouldn't I take advantage of them if they are going to refuse to see? I SAW. And that was enough.

What I couldn't articulate, and what they didn't know, I can now speak freely of. Most people think the one binding we all have is Love. That's a nice thought, but it isn't correct.

The ONE connection that we all have, is that WE ARE CONNECTED. Through love OR hatred, good times and bad, human, alien, animal, mineral or vegetable ... WE ARE ALL CONNECTED. EVERYTHING we do affects everything in God's created world, somehow. "Karma" is the only real law. "As you sow, so shall you reap." There is no hiding from this. Oh, it may not "get" you in THIS world, or time ... but it WILL come back. The GIFTS are love and free will.

❃

In the interim, I had dues to pay in modern America for my infractions. In 1996 I went to prison, and for the first two years I was

the movie version of a convict. Drugs in prison, infractions, resisting guards, underworld business ... all of the clichés a person sees in the movies.

I eventually grew up a bit, though, calmed down some, quit the drugs, and began my own rehabilitation back into society. I wasn't perfect, by any means, but I was trying. Sometimes I tried harder than other times. I may have quit the drugs, but I still didn't care too much about people. I was somewhat mean and very intolerant of those people not in my realm ... whatever THAT was at the time.

I had been in "the hole" ("jail," while you're in prison, for naughty boys) more than once, and certainly wasn't afraid to go again. In Arkansas at that time, when a person goes to "the hole," you are put in a one or two man cell for segregation from the population, the guards would take your mattress out of your cell every morning at around 5 A.M. and bring it back in the evening around 5 P.M. The whole day you spend on concrete or a slab of plywood with only a single thin blanket for padding. The only things allowed in the cell were your clothes, one religious text (in my case, a Bible), 2 envelopes per week, 4 pieces of lined paper, a pencil, and whatever food tray was available. (Obviously, it being prison, inmates often had books or other foodstuffs, cigarettes, radios, etc., etc. ... whatever you could afford to pay for, depending on whether a guard brings it to you, or another inmate doing custodial duties.)

When it all comes down to it, if you could get past the daytime concrete rule, it really wasn't bad. I had never had anyone send me money in prison, and Arkansas doesn't pay prisoners like most prisons do – but even I had books and the occasional cigarette. Even better, "the hole" is a WONDERFUL place to go for some ALONE time. (One of the most precious commodities in prison is time to yourself. Inmates are almost NEVER alone. Time apart from others is golden!)

I don't remember what I'd done to get there, but eventually I ended up in "the hole" – again. And this time I was going to be in for awhile. I'd been in long enough that I'd gotten tired of them waking me up at 5 A.M. just to get my mattress. I finally refused to take it back one evening, and just slept all day AND night on the plywood bench. (Living outdoors CAN be helpful, at times! I was already used to hard sleeping places with very little for covers. :)

And there I was, alone. It was early afternoon, and I had been sitting up on my plywood bench, watching the little "tweety birds"

hunting grass seeds outside my window. I don't remember what the last conscious thought I had was. One minute I was watching birds, the next I was standing in this sphere of light!

It had to have been at least 50 feet across. The "floor" (that wasn't there) was about a third of the way up from the bottom of the sphere. I could see below me to the bottom of the sphere, even though I was standing on a plane that wasn't the bottom. Outside of the sphere was absolute blackness, but coming and going ONTO what would be the outside of the sphere were what appeared to be your classical "movie ghosts." Whitish apparitions that drifted in and out of view. When they got to the sphere they followed the contour of the light around where I was standing. As I was looking at the 4 or 5 that were drifting by, to my left, right, over and under me, one actually LOOKED at me for a moment, then continued on its way toward the top of the sphere.

I realized I wasn't alone. I was standing next to a very tall individual. Again, robes and glowing countenance (but not glowing as brightly this time), and this was a male. I'm about 5 foot 9-1/2 tall. This long, white-bearded giant was ... well, as I was standing to his immediate left, when I looked horizontally level to the right, my eyes looked right at the curve of his left shoulder. He glanced at me for just a moment then looked toward his front. I followed with my eyes and realized that WE were not alone.

We were standing only about 15 feet from the wall of the sphere, with our backs to it. In front of us, taking up much of the center of everything else was a "seated panel" of others. I'm wanting to say there were 7 of them, but I honestly don't remember for certain. They were seated like my previously encountered "spiritual being" – that is, no seats in evidence. All males. All long, white beards. All glowing and robes.

I looked again to my right to my "companion" – and realized that he was "speaking" for me! (Again, not verbally.) I had time to wonder why someone was HAVING to speak for me, and then realized that even though I knew he was speaking for me, I couldn't understand – or even HEAR what was being said! *What kind of trial IS this?! ... TRIAL???*

It looked and felt, well, not as a trial would – but certainly maybe a hearing. It felt ENOUGH like a hearing that I was slightly concerned. Probably not as concerned as I maybe SHOULD have been, considering the circumstances ... but there was that peaceful feeling

again. Not nearly as prevalent as last time, but still present. In any case, I DID feel sort of out-of-place, not knowing what was being discussed.

It was as I was looking around, feeling left out, that I decided to look closely at the robe of this man next to me. I was standing no more than about 6 inches off his left shoulder, so I knew I could get a good look at the weave and style. It was quite coarse. Almost like a burlap sack, except the weave was tighter, and of course, the whole of it looked considerably cleaner than any burlap I've ever seen.

I had no more than got the thought in my head about the burlap, when ...

If you've read your Bible, you'll know this story. If not, bear with me a moment. In the Bible there is a story of a harlot (or prostitute, depending on your translation) who, as Jesus walks by, reaches out and touches the hem of his clothing. Jesus, being Holy, knows it immediately and asks, "Who has touched me?" The woman replies (I'm paraphrasing here), "I, Lord." Jesus asks why she would do such? The woman answered that she KNEW if she could only TOUCH his Holiness, then she would be cleansed of her sin and evil. Jesus says "By your faith you are healed. Go and sin no more." ... Or something close to that. (I may not have the wording exactly right, but you get the idea.)

As I was studying this man's clothes, that story popped into my head, and I wondered to myself "Now ... I wonder what would happen if I reached out and touched him?" I remember very clearly thinking these exact words. I reached up with my right hand to his shoulder, and using just my right index finger and thumb, very lightly pinched/plucked his robe, just below his shoulder, and ...

!!! Ka-ZAP !!!

I can't even come close to describing the IMMEDIACY of what hit me. "Instantaneously" doesn't cover it.

Do you remember putting your tongue on a 9-volt battery to see if it was still good – and half hoping it WASN'T, so you wouldn't get a full dose of shock? Okay, now imagine it WAS a full dose ... and then some. Only it started in my fingertips – the two I touched with first, then slowly working it's way into my other fingers, then my hand and wrist, then up my arm ....

But it wasn't electricity – even though it half felt like it. It was ... well, let me finish ... no. I have to tell you what it was first. It felt

electrical, true enough, but it was EMOTION, and ... It was Love, and Faith, and Forgiveness, and Compassion and Caring .... It was EVERY "good" feeling a person could possibly have, toward myself or others!

And I could feel it EVERYWHERE!! As it traveled into my hand and up my arm and through my chest and down my legs, I could feel all that good emotional electricity pulsing IN EVERY CELL of my being! In every vein and artery, every muscle, all my organs, in the cells of my hair and finger and toenails ... !!! (I may not know the names of all these parts, but to this day I can tell what part of me is sick or hurting, down to the smallest part – exactly located.)

By the time it reached my elbow I very clearly remember (at first,) saying, "Oh God." I looked at the seated gentlemen to see their reactions. Only the one on the end even looked at me. (He only glanced at me for a moment, then went back to paying attention to whatever it was that previously held his attention.) Then this emotional "washing" started to pick me up off of my feet and lay me out horizontally in the air at about waist level of the man next to me, like I was a board. Just before I reached "level" I called out again, quite loudly, as I was looking at the man, "OH GOD!" This time he looked at me for just a moment, then he TOO went back to whatever had his attention ... like this was an everyday occurrence (which, I guess for THEM, it may well have been!).

This "washing" was a steady progression to all of my parts, but it wasn't steady. It PULSED. In and out, over and over, never completely leaving me. And every time it "re-entered," it was like getting a shot EVERYWHERE of good and wonderful loving, forgiving emotions. Over and over and over ....

Eventually it began to stand me back upright. I don't know how long it lasted, but it was the most ... I've come to describe it as a huge, emotional "body-orgasm," for lack of better terminology – but really it was MUCH better than that. Finally, back on my feet and looking at "my companion" in utter astonishment – at his LACK of it ....

I'm actually not sure exactly what was going through my head for some time, but once I (sorta) "had it back together" again, I knew that was THE BEST I would ever feel in my life. I then wondered what would happen if I REALLY reached out to touch him, like, grab his arm or something??? I lifted my hand to do just that, but when my hand got close to him I could feel it starting again ... a sort of "re-

sidual" pulsing again beginning in my hand – which was nice, but ...

I thought to myself "Oooh. Don't want to be greedy," and ...

!!POOF!!

Just like snapping a finger, it was all gone, and I was sitting upright in my cell again – soaked. Broad daylight.

This time I was sort of prepared. I quickly got up and wobbled to the window in the door of my cell to see if anyone had seen anything. Of course, there wasn't a guard in sight. I wobbled back to my outside window in the slim hopes that someone had come by cleaning up the outside yard and had looked in like they do on occasion. Of course not.

Right where I'd been sitting was a giant wet area, like I'd been sitting upright the whole time and someone had dumped a bucket of water over me. I peeled out of my wet clothes and hung them up to dry. (Inmates in "the hole" in their underwear isn't an unusual sight at all. There's really not much reason to get dressed all day long.) When the guard finally did come around, I asked him if he'd noticed anything unusual, as they have view of all the cells, even if they can't see into all of them. He replied in the negative, asking, "Why did I ask?"

Ummm ...

How in the HELL am I supposed to answer that?!!? "No reason. The birds were acting funny, is all."

Middle of the day. No drugs. No witnesses.

I've heard of being "washed in the blood" or "washed in the spirit."..but I was washed in the sphere of light. Well...my SPIRIT was washed. I came out a few days later, after having mulled over this experience in my mind repeatedly and coming up with ZIP for answers. When I was released, I realized that ALL OF A SUDDEN I CARED!! About me, about other inmates, about guys I didn't even like! Guards. My step-dad. EVERYONE. I CARED.

I wasn't sure what that meant to me then (although I do now), but it has affected my whole life since. I see everything and everyone differently. It's one of the reasons I don't think I could ever have an exclusive relationship with any one person again. I love EVERYONE too much.

Blue butterflies

You may choose to believe this narrative, or not. It doesn't matter to me. But somewhere out in our big, wide world, if nothing of ill

nature has happened to them, there are four witnesses to the following story. And because strange things happen all the time...

Taylor, Ray, Margo, and Danielle, I hope you cherish this memory. (Should you ever read this – or write your own, I hope you'll remember me fondly.)

About 6 or 7 years ago I was living in Bullhead City, Arizona – across the Colorado River from Laughlin, Nevada, and about 20 miles from Needles, California. Taylor was then 14 years old; Margo, 12; Danielle, 10; and Ray was 9. I was a parole violator, so I was trying to live completely "off-the-grid." I was literally camped out on the river in a no-camping area.

I need to explain this. Bullhead City was then almost TWO towns, known to the locals as "Old Bullhead" and "New Bullhead." New Bullhead had Don Laughlin's money being used to build a retirement town in a beautiful desert setting. Saguaro, cholas, mesquite, paddle and prickly-pear cactus ruled, but palm trees and varying fruit trees were being planted. New commercial enterprises – bars, Wal-Mart, restaurants, and a massive new homes project were all part of this "newness."

All of it had to be built but the local workforce that was not big enough to handle the job. Workers – mostly homeless modern-day cowboys: veterans, construction workers, drug-addicts and alcoholics, illegal aliens – all poured into Old Bullhead, straining the temporary housing available there. There weren't enough motels, hotels, or rooms for rent. Much of the workforce moved into the space between "old" and "new" Bullhead out of convenience.

Between "old" and "new" Bullhead was a section of desert belonging to the Parks and Recreation Department. On the Old Bullhead end was a city park with restrooms, water, and pavilions with tables and cooking areas.

Beyond that park was a "day-fun" desert. It was about 200 yards wide from the river to the main road. From the park to the nearest apartments in New Bullhead was about 500 yards of unstable sandy river bottom and 2 flash-flood wash areas, one reinforced, the other natural.

The higher portions of this area were quite safe, especially in the daytime. The lower areas of the flood wash plain and the river bottom were PERFECT for experienced homeless folks to hide and live in. Sand everywhere meant the police couldn't get down to arrest anyone

for illegal camping unless they either came on foot or by all-terrain vehicles – which meant we could hear them coming from quite some distance away.

The thing about most homeless villages (and this WAS a village: in just that one section, about 30 people lived), there is no such thing as "normal" police. Drugs, alcoholism, theft and prostitution abound. There was SO MUCH methamphetamine use there (it was very literally easier to get meth so we wouldn't have to eat, than to get food) that someone was ALWAYS awake. If you know anything about methamphetamine, then you know that one of the effects of its use is sleeplessness.

No law enforcement officer EVER – NOT ONCE – slipped up on us, unaware. They got tourists, but never the homeless population.

While there are campsites everywhere in the bottoms (I suspect people have been camping there since the Native Americans ruled that area), most of the current sites were full of trash, cast-off furniture, and cars. It was an old, unregulated dump, full of stolen and abandoned shopping carts...and self-arranged toilet areas. The trail system, while being heavily "guarded" by the deep and heavy brush, was also well-known to everyone, including the police. I decided to make my own camp rather than use one of the "established" camps.

After I made my camp, I found a garden rake and a shovel. In my (considerable) free time I went camp-to-camp cleaning up, leaving trash bags "up top" (on the highest sides of the riverbank where the Parks and Recs sandy roads were), so the Parks and Recs guys could get them easily to be hauled off to a dump somewhere.

One afternoon they and the police were on a "sweep" to remove the homeless, illegal campers. This happened about once per month, the Parks guys leading the way, scouting out camps for the bulldozer behind them. The police would bring up the rear to make sure no one came back to dig out personal items. (In their defense, these camps REALLY were a terrible fire hazard! More than one had resulted in use of town emergency vehicles.)

Anyway, they found me bagging trash down away from my own camp, and asked if I was the one who had been cleaning up all the camps. I replied in the affirmative. They asked the location of my own camp, THANKED me, warned me the police were coming, and SKIPPED my camp with the bulldozer, directing the police away from my "home."

Later that day I saw their dump-truck driver on the road with many of my neighbors' beds, furniture, kitchens, etc., being hauled to the dump. He recognized me, gave a little salute and smiled. Later that evening when I went back to see if anything was left of my camp, I found it totally untouched.

My camp:

Most of that section between "old" and "new" Bullhead was short scrub desert plants or brushy, thorny river-bottom greenery. Almost exactly center between the apartments and the park were the two equally spaced flash-flood washes, dividing the whole section into thirds. Almost exactly center between the two washes were four "salt" cedar trees, very large ones on the edge of the riverbank, near the top of a 30-foot tall, 45 degree slope. One end of this particular slope had been cleared by fishermen for a traveling path from bottom-to-top (and vise versa). On the other end was HEAVY brush, loose sand, wasp nests, and beaver holes. (Yes, BEAVER.)

It was also MUCH, MUCH cleaner, quieter, and well-hidden. It just needed some excavation work and I'd have a nice SHADY, hidden camp unknown to ANYone. I got to work.

Four days later I had the most enviable camp in the bottoms. Before the week was out I had much of the village coming by just to "shade" and relax. My camp wasn't wide. From 2 feet to about 10 feet, at most, but was 30 to 40 feet long ... "Bedroom," with cot and sleeping bag (it's COLD in the desert at night!), kitchen/social area, hidden trail entrance, tool storage on the other side of the down slope access trail, and beyond that a hidden camp toilet that could be used repeatedly and carried out or buried (NO defecated tissues blowing around MY camp!!). I even built a brush arbor out into the river big enough so that even in the daytime I could stand totally nude and bathe and wash clothes without (much) fear of discovery. It usually served as a pretty good refrigerator as well. It was comfortable, to say the least. I had wasps for security (gotta know which branches NOT to grab!), quail and skunks as occasional visitors, and a pet chipmunk with babies (she LOVED frozen waffles!).

One of the transient family units I met consisted of Big Dan, his wife (I forget her name – she was an older, heavy-set, "housewife" type who didn't work), and the four kids, Taylor, Ray, Margo, and Danielle. As it was summer and Mom COULDN'T keep up with them, they pretty much ran wild, wherever, mostly in the park area ... but

not always.

These were good kids. Mom and Dad were wanted somewhere in California for meth sales, I think, so the kids knew all about the drug world and all it entailed. Two of them had already had sex, three had smoked pot, three had smoked cigarettes ... all of this the parents knew.

Things were pretty hard on Dad. As the only worker in the family, he would leave the clan in their old bread delivery truck (that served as home to them) in the park during the daylight hours while he went to work – the idea being that Mom could watch the kids, as such. No such luck.

Very shortly the girls knew how to dress provocatively and scam the boys on the baseball fields for money, hot dogs and sodas. The oldest boy sold newspapers he got from vending machines to sympathetic business people, and the youngest boy learned how to turn on the charm and beg. As a little blond-haired, blue-eyed, rapscallion pixie, he was incredibly successful in his endeavors.

These kids weren't always right with the law, but they were SPIRITUALLY "mint." I never saw any of them be mean or bullyish to anyone, nor steal from any individual. In very short order I was in love with these kids. Gawd, how I wished they were MINE. They were fun, and caring. They always shared everything they had with anyone who was nearby. They were curious about EVERYTHING, they helped work and clean, and they were respectful of their mom and dad, even when I thought they shouldn't have been! FABULOUS kids!!

They were allowed in my camp at any time, day or night, whether I was there or not. I'm pretty certain they liked me pretty well also. They visited a LOT, with Mom and Dad's blessings.

...As they were to do on the day of the blue butterflies.

Having lived in California, I knew of monarchs and others, but I'd never seen live, solid blue butterflies before. And here in the desert, I hadn't seen ANY butterflies at all.

Another (then) homeless friend of mine, Leanna Brooks, gave me my "Arizona name" of "Maverick Dundee" by accident. She thought I was some kind of naturist guru because I happened to live well outdoors. The kids loved her. (She had the thought process of an approximate 12 year old, due to cerebral palsy.) She made sure the kids knew my camp was the safe place to be, because I was "the real deal" outdoor guy.

Not really, but I've learned over the years to be comfortable and SAFE outdoors. Leanna, being newly homeless, mistook my experience for natural mysticism.

Early one afternoon I heard the kids coming up the trail, heading toward camp. (It was easy to tell it was all of them, and maybe a friend or two: boisterous Danielle, rambunctious Ray, and calm Taylor keeping them in check. They never would've been in that configuration without quiet Margo ....) I loved these kids and was quite liberal about what I allowed them to do around me, but some things still had to be cleaned up and put away. I didn't leave meth needles and porn out for 9-year-olds to see. So I started cleaning up, getting out the extra camp chairs for them, listening to their progress as they got closer.

Very soon they were at the top of the trail, "helloing" down to me (a camp courtesy, akin to knocking on the door). I hollered for them to come on in, and looked up to see them starting down the access trail. As I looked up to them I saw movement above my head. I looked straight up... into this BEAUTIFUL BLUE CEILING OF BUTTER-FLIES over my head, spread out over my sleeping and "social" areas! It was so ... SURREAL!!! I lifted my arms to reach up into the "cloud" right as the kids reached the turn into my camp. I saw Taylor stop suddenly and put out an arm to stop the rest of them at the entrance as he saw what I did. They all stopped and stared open-mouthed.

At the exact moment they all stopped, all these beautiful blue butterflies began to land on my arms and head, beginning at my upraised hands, moving down to my elbows, then head and shoulders – until almost the whole cloud had settled on me! There must have been hundreds! I was covered, from hands held high to my waist!!

I didn't know what to do! I didn't want to hurt them. Here's the REALLY cool part. I REALIZED THAT I HAD A SPELL-BOUND AU-DIENCE. So...

Out loud I said, "O.K. you guys. I have company. You'll have to come back later."

And very gently, starting at my right shoulder, I blew down (up?) my right arm to my fingertips, sending butterflies back above my head to flutter around at ceiling height again.

(Smiling hugely to myself!) I said, "You, too," and repeated the blowing on my left arm. After they were all cleared, I gently shook my head and said, "ALL of you!"

The whole "cloud" had gathered above me again as a fluttering blue ceiling. I raised my hands, moving a little faster (lest they try to land again), and using an upward "air patting" motion, I said, "Really. I'll talk to you guys later. Go on, now. The kids are here. LATER, I promise."

And OH. MY. GAWD!! The whole ceiling lifted and dissipated through the tree branches (!!!) like I'd ordered them to leave and come back later!!

Keep in mind, I AM ABSOLUTELY FLABBERGASTED at this moment, but I'm STILL aware of four TOTALLY SPELLBOUND kids who haven't so much as twitched!

When the butterflies had all left, I dropped my arms and looked directly at my human visitors. Quiet Margo, bless her heart, took two or three tentative steps toward me and asked breathlessly, "HOW DID YOU DO THAT?!!?!!"

I've since tried to picture this from their viewpoint. I always see the "Walt Disney princess" moment. You know, the princess or Cinderella or Snow White sings a song with all the forest birds and deer and critters..."Whistle while you woooork! Ta – da da – ta – la- dee – da – dum..."

... Only now instead of a princess, they saw an honest-to-goodness nature wizard TALK TO BUTTERFLIES ... a LOT of them!! ... AND THEY LISTENED!!!

How amazing that must have appeared! I am forever thankful to the powers-that-be that I was allowed the presence of mind to "speak magic" into the moment ... into the moment when I MYSELF was being blessed by a vision from Mother Nature.

My answer to Margo was: "Hon, when you live with nature long enough, you become part of it. Those guys are my friends just like YOU are. (Like this was a normal, everyday happening for me.) Are you guys going to come in and sit down?"

They did, of course, constantly watching the trees to see if the butterflies would return.

I loved those kids with all my heart and soul, and I am eternally grateful that I got to share that moment with them.

Are we our brother's keepers?

Without a doubt in my mind, I believe that, yes, we are.

The only time I ever saw my little crazy friend Phoebe disappoint-

ed in me was when we had been sharing a sunny afternoon, walking together in some deep sand and heavy brush lining the Colorado River, heading for my camp on payday to partake of freshly acquired party supplies...and we got ambushed. Three guys with clubs surrounded me while a VERY largish woman grabbed Phoebe from behind. Yes, I probably could have run and gotten away, but the Amazon wench had a firm hold of Phoebe, and all little Phoebe's kicking like a mule and squalling like a rabid cat were doing her no good whatsoever. Yes, I could have fought, but the odds were less-than-comforting, and there was no telling what they would do to Phoebe if I lost.

It was only money and dope they wanted. The leader demanded half of each, of whatever I had. Somewhere in my mind the echoes of Bible reading came to bear on my soul: "Don't allow your brother to become a thief." Well, I had personally believed and preached for years that we are all connected, thereby making these my brothers – even if I wasn't happy with them at the moment. In the end I gave them the $60 I had, along with the quarter-gram of methamphetamine, mostly to make them leave Phoebe alone, but it certainly would benefit me as well.

I told the leader of the group outright "Here. If you need this stuff that bad, then here," holding it out to him, "I want you to have all of it."

"No, I only want half," he replied. Called it a "camper's tax for newbies here."

"No sir. I'm giving this to you," I said. "Take it. Let Phoebe go, then do whatever you want to. That's yours, my present to you."

When they were gone Phoebe blew up on me. "WHY DIDN'T YOU FIGHT THEM!?!?!"

"Phoebe, I wasn't going to let you get hurt because they wanted to rob me of sixty dollars."

Phoebe stormed off vowing evil torture and death on them all. Rob HER friend, would they?!? She was tiny and she was crazy, but she certainly was a loyal friend. I was glad for my actions and glad that she had escaped unharmed to BE mad at me.

For the next two weeks every time I saw the leader of that group, I tossed out a cheery "Hey Billy!" to him. "... You alright?" He never verbally replied, but I always got one of those "this crazy dude" looks. The confrontation day came one Saturday. I was in the shade of a large tree out in the desert alone above the river, enjoying the morn-

ing, about to put fire to my happy-stick... when here appears Billy on the trail, also alone, no club in his hands nor friends nearby to help him now – and he knew his predicament immediately.

Credit to his bravery. He offered to "settle the whole matter right now, no cops, no witnesses, no help for either party."

I never even stood up. I just asked him, "Settle ... what?"

The confused look on his face and his answer dying on his lips told me that he really didn't know what to say to me. "The ... huh?"

I told him "Billy, you were so busy being the big bad boy leader that you missed what really happened. YOU think you robbed me, BUT YOU DIDN'T. Think back. I told you SPECIFICALLY, "Here, I give this to you as my present." If I had let you rob me then, you and I both know that one of us would likely end up dead over 60 bucks. I GAVE that to you so I COULDN'T be resentful of you. We have nothing to fight about. Sit down," I said, gesturing to the large fallen tree beside me. "You wanna smoke this with me?" It took some convincing to prove to him I wasn't trying to lull him into a false sense of security just to jump on him. We shared smoke and talk, and at the parting of our ways that morning he was apologizing profusely and promising repayment.

About two weeks after that meeting, very late one evening, Billy "hello'ed" me in my camp, this being the polite method of knocking on the door in most outdoor living arrangements. After receiving my permission to enter, he came into my camp, bag in hand, looking quite worn out and bedraggled. I offered peanut butter and jelly sandwiches and a cold drink of water which he hungrily accepted. Apparently the Amazon wench had kicked him out of the house and he'd been wandering all last night. Today, not sure what to do, he was confused, homeless, and at a loss as to what his next move should be.

We ARE our brother's keepers to my way of thinking. This was a human being in need, and I wouldn't refuse him the help we all should be able to find. I offered sleeping arrangements and breakfast. Billy actually ended up staying in my camp for most of a month, and he made sure that NO ONE ever molested me, my camp, or my friends again while I was in that area, becoming MY keeper.

Funny, after he left, the Amazon that had kicked him out eventually made it to my camp as well with her new boyfriend – also hungry. Yes, I fed them too. Sixty dollars for peace-of-mind? I'll pay that anytime.

Social garbage

There I was, homeless and not caring about anything, hanging out outside of the local video arcade, selling illegal products to immoral youngsters. I didn't know most of them, but the few I did helped me by acting as go-betweens, so teens and preteens could spend their allowances on things not approved of by most parents.

As I stated, I didn't care...about ages, nor where the money came from, nor even what bodies these products might be entering. I just needed money for my own habits.

I should enter a note here – however little good it will do me. I never sold anything to anyone under age 20 that might kill them, even accidentally. Products to an "underage" buyer might include no more than a pint of any liquid, a small bag of marijuana, or (up to) 3 "hits" of LSD (never more than that per customer), cigarettes, information on where to go to hide, or varying forms of pornography, etc., etc.

Hey! I already said I was social garbage.

Anyway ...

Of the ones I DID get to know, most of them were street kids. They either were as homeless and uncaring as I was, or they HAD homes where the parents didn't care themselves (this usually involved large quantities of drugs or alcohol in the home), they weren't home enough to know what their kids were doing (LOTS of this going on!), or the parents were in denial of what was happening.

Occasionally there was the rare case of a kid that was SMARTER than the parents. Oh, the parents cared, all right. ...Would've beat that little 13 or 14 year old butt – IF they had known. But let's face it... Some kids ARE smart enough to cultivate good cover stories that hold up pretty well under scrutiny.

They didn't have to hold up well with guys like me around.

"Mom, I'm going to the arcade for awhile. Can I get some money?"

"Okay. Get $10.00 out of my purse. Be back by dark."

" 'K."

... And he SWEARS later on that he only saw the $20 bill (so that's what she MUST HAVE meant). And he was INSIDE. How could he know it was dark so soon? In the meantime he's met with me, spent $5.00 on weed, found his girlfriend, charged three other friends $5 each to smoke a joint with him and his girl – and he's now "up" $10 from what he started with AND hooked up his girl and his friends,

making him look like a junior high kingpin, and now he has ... more ... to do whatever with – and I'm still close by, eager to help.

Of course, things don't always go well for them, any more than they do for adults or full-time "streeters." For the good hustlers, street kids or not, like the adults, I'll provide credit. (Believe it or not, only ONE credit debt ever went unpaid to me by anyone under age 17... this one.)

– No real names, please. for obvious reasons –

Oliver was 14. He was the best hustler of the 10 to 16 year old set in that area. He would sell weed, porno mags, rob a house or turn a trick. (Oh yes. Your kids ARE out there selling themselves without pimps or protection, at ages as young as 10 and 12. It's not nearly as uncommon as you might think. And yes, boys sell themselves to men, as well as girls sell themselves to women. Happens every day.) He was, I assumed, "street," and he was good at it. I saw him almost everyday at the arcade, plying his trades. His credit was good.

On this occasion he was having a run of sour luck and asked for a 3-hit LSD "loan." Sure, why not? But two weeks later he hadn't repaid me. Three weeks and he had started avoiding me. A month later I saw him on his bicycle and called out to him... and he saw me and pedaled off in a hurry.

Wait. WHA?! A FOURTEEN YEAR OLD thinks he's going to beat ME out of a credit debt? REALLY?? (I'm thinkin' maybe not. I carry a loaded pistol all the time. Would I shoot a kid over $18.00? Of course not. But I WOULD scare the ever-lovin' B'Jeezus out of him!) I put out the word that he had two weeks to "get right, or ..." A week passed. No sign of him. Week #2 came and went. Then I put out the word that I was now actively hunting him with plans to make his nose and ears change places on his head – permanently. The arcade was now "off-limits" to him. (I KNEW that would hurt. It was where he did most of his money-making.)

On week #4, after continually making it known that I was indeed mad, but indeed waiting to be paid so that I wouldn't have to be mad anymore ....

Another Saturday, early evening. Business outside the arcade has been good. I'll be able to leave soon to go do "big-boy" things in the night. The arcade has a very wide concrete walkway on two sides of it, one of which has a low brick wall running along it, much like a beach side boardwalk. This is where I'm sitting, watching the world

go by, listening to the bells and buzzers and jingles and music coming from the open wall of the arcade. ...Just a few more customers and I can go...

... Ahhh. Here comes one now. I recognize her. Valerie something-or-other? A slightly pudgy (but certainly not fat, nor even chunky) 12 year old, smokes weed sometimes. Not always out with the street kids, but enough to know what's going on. I've never actually spoken to her, but I've seen her around enough to make inquiries. She's actually one of the "better" kids out and about. I'm sure she knows, if not ME, then certainly who I am and what I do.

You know, growing up, I've learned to love or hate certain mannerisms done to me by different people. I loved the way Grandma would come up behind me and hug me. To this day I love being hugged from behind. Evil step-dad had a "mad" habit of poking a finger in my chest repeatedly to drive home a point. "YOU are the oldest! you should've known..." Poke. "You could've done..." Poke. Poke. "WHY DIDN'T YOU THINK?!?!" Poke,Poke,Poke. GRRRRR!!

To this day, if you wish to start a fight with me, don't hit me. Poke me in the chest with one finger. GAME ON.

So here comes cute lil' pudgy Valerie-something in her cute little shorts with her cute little top and her...VERY determined looking walk and mad-as-hell face? Huh?? ...STOMPING my way.

This incredibly brave, incredibly foolish, incredibly INCREDIBLE young lady, stomps up to me on a semi-crowded public walkway, up to a KNOWN drug dealer that she's never spoken to before and...

Oh. My. Gawd!!

Stretches her face up to mine in absolute defiance and anger, and starts POKING ME IN THE CHEST with one finger!!!

(W.T.F?!!?!)

"I want to talk to you!"

"Not while you're poking me, you don't. (Menacingly leaning down into her face and grabbing her hand). Don't do that."

Smart girl. She "got it" immediately. She "stood down," but didn't physically back up at all. Still within arms reach, left arm akimbo on her hip, pointing at my face, emphasizing...

"I want you to stop selling drugs to Oliver."

"Whoa. Whoa! WHOA!! First of all, lower your voice. Second, get your finger out of my face. Third, I HAVE stopped selling to him. He owes me money and as long as he does, he can't get s**t from me.

Fourth, you obviously know who I am, so who the f**k are YOU to come tell me ANYTHING about who I do business with?!!

"Well, he's got a family who cares about him. He doesn't have to be out here. He goes home every night."

"Yeah. They care SOOO much they know he's out here on Saturday afternoons giving blow jobs to strangers and robbing houses at 3 A.M. Don't give me that s**t, girl. Why should I give a damn about his home life or you making his habits your business?"

(Raised voice, again with that finger, poking me ONCE) "BE-CAUSE I CARE!!" (as I catch her hand again.)

Three simple words spoken in exasperation and anger (and love) caused the year-long silence between us.

I noticed the people walking by, staring. I look back into this young girl's face and see that she's on the verge of tears. (Oh no. Oh NO. No, no, no. Not crying. NO! Ahh, DAMN IT!!) I release her hand and "stand down" myself, deflated.

This girl...this TWELVE YEAR OLD girl...cared enough as a friend to approach a known, gun carrying drug dealer at least double her own age, that she had never spoken to previously, and ORDERED him to stop doing business with her friend – because SHE CARED.

Honor is a funny thing sometimes, isn't it?

This girl had just done a more honorable thing in 2 minutes than I had done in the last 5 years, AND shown a hell of a lot of REAL courage in the process. There she stood in front of me, still defiant, shaking slightly and on the very edge of bawling – but not backing down a bit – for her friend – waiting for me to speak.

Now you tell me... HOW IN THE HELL am I going to be less honorable than a 12 year old, and still collect my money? Answer: Ain't happening.

(Considerably calmer and quieter) "Valerie, right?"

"Yeah."

"I wish I had a friend like you. (pause) You tell Oliver he doesn't owe me anything. I'm not coming looking for him. He can come back here safely, with no problems from me. O.K.?"

"Okay."

"You also tell him that from now on I don't exist to him if he wants ANYTHING. EVER. I'll see him, say 'Hey,' but he's not allowed to ask me for anything else, ever again. Got it?"

"You mean it? Really? You won't sell him ... ?"

"Shhh! Yes, I mean it. Nobody has ever come to me to ASK me to stop selling to someone else, much less DEMANDED it because they care, like you did. I think he's got a really good friend in you – and he probably doesn't even know it. Let me say this again: I wish I had a friend like you"

(Throwing herself at me in a giant hug, THEN I felt the tears on my neck.) "OH THANK YOU! THANK YOU!"

"Yeah, yeah. (People watching again. One quick hug back for a brave young lady, and) Stop crying. Whatcha cryin' for? Quit. (Sniffles) Go on. Get out of here. (Wipes her eyes and turns to leave) Hey, Val?"

"Yeah?"

"If you ever need anything, you know, not THAT stuff, but, like, help or anything, you give me a holler. You know where to find me."

"'K."

"I mean it."

"Okay. I will."

"Promise?"

"Promise."

She turns to leave "Oh yeah. Hey, Val?"

"Yeah?"

"You got a cute butt!"

Snort, rolled eyes, big grin, and a back-handed wave, and she's headed back into the arcade.

Oliver found me later that week. Rode straight up to me on his bicycle, obviously a little nervous, but ...

"Hey, Cheyenne. I got your money. Can I get a couple more hits?"

"Nope."

"Huh?"

"Don't want your money. Did you talk to Valerie?"

"Yeah. She told me what you said, but it's O.K. I got your money, plus some more."

"Dude. Listen to me. You don't owe ME anything, but don't you EVER ask me for anything ever again. You got it?"

"Yeah, but I got your money."

(Now I'm leaned into HIS face, poking my finger into HIS chest!) "Let me tell you something ... That girl, Valerie? She loves you, you dumb-ass. I know she's a little chunky, but dude, you better grab a hold of her, make her your girlfriend, grow up and marry her, and

stay with her FOREVER. If you don't, you're even dumber than I thought. It's HER you owe."

"Aww, c'mon man. You aren't gonna stick to THAT, are you? She's just some ...."

Leaning into his face in a VERY menacing manner. "Oliver, Get. Away. From. Me. Don't you ever come near me again. I mean it. And if I find out you've been mean to Valerie for ANY reason, I'll smash your legs. I'm not kidding. You understand me? Now go find her and tell her your sorry for making her come see me. And tell her I said, 'Hey Girl.'"

Can I call myself "honorable" for honoring the request of a young girl to cease illegal activities that I probably shouldn't have been doing anyway?

I don't think I should, but it sure FEELS like it.

By all the "powers-that-be," I hope that brave little 12 year old became the Grand Old Queen Swan.

She certainly had a damn good start.

Just for a moment

Have you ever heard the saying "Living in a moment you would die for"?

... Florida, mid-to-late 80's, and I'm a piece of trash... and I know it. Street trash. My days are spent working day-labor jobs or casing houses to rob for dope money so I can sell illegal substances to the tourists and party kids on the weekends. No one would miss me if I disappeared. No one would even know to look for me.

"Trash"... on any given day and time but Sunday mornings. These are special times for me, and I won't give them up easily. This is the beach where... well, it's the beach. ALL beaches have one thing in common. They remind you of another beach back in time somewhere. The smell, the color of the sand, the traffic or nightlife, the FEEL of a place. My hard-living doesn't exclude me from this.

One Sunday morning I was strolling farther up the beach than was normal for me after an "all-nighter," just enjoying the solitude and the morning, feeling like I felt when I was a young, healthy, idealistic U.S. Marine walking the beaches of Hawaii, where I'd been stationed. As I continued down the beach I found a beachside café open and decided to stop in for coffee. As soon as I walked in it was like being transported back in time instantly. The café smelled EXACTLY

like Keones, another tiny café in Waikiki. The wooden seating, the table arrangement, the atmosphere, all like Hawaii. I WAS YOUNG AND A MARINE AGAIN!!!

The older woman working as the cook/waitress I later learned was the "Mom" in the "Mom-and-Pop" operation. She was there early to get ready for the lunch crowd, but opened in case any stray beach-combers came by ... which was rare where we were located. Mostly the tourists were farther south, and the locals didn't do much early morning walking here. It wasn't really safe until later.

That was fine by me. Just she and I, and I didn't want any company. I just wanted to bask in the atmosphere and be alone for awhile. Our entire time of being acquainted, we probably never spoke a total of 200 words to each other. I explained how her place made me feel and why I liked to just sit there watching the waves. I didn't tell her what I REALLY was at this moment in my life. For some reason I felt ashamed to THINK this "Mom" might find out ...

I never did tell her. It would've ruined the whole situation some-how, but for some reason I couldn't to this day explain, I felt she understood. She wasn't MY mom, but she was A "mom" – and that was enough. No one wants their mother ashamed of them. That began a weekly tradition of me spending my Sunday mornings at that café, where no one knew who nor what I really was, where I could be who I was meant to be in my mind.

As I said, I'm a piece of trash ... except on Sunday mornings. Then I become that young Marine again, and make my way to the café and spend a glorious two hours or so "hiding" from the rest of my life and the people who know me, resting and enjoying the beauty of Mother Nature.

Unbeknownst to me, this is my last weekend there. I'm early. I've watched the sun creep up and "the Marine" is very near the surface, ready to take over at any moment. I'm walking slowly because I'm not sure what time the café opens. It's within sight, but just barely. I can also see on the beach, up near the sedge grass, a ...

... a what..?

... a CHILD?!?

Surely not. NO local would allow a child on this beach alone this early. This is a fairly dangerous place to be for the night-movers who are experienced, much less for someone who doesn't know what can happen ....

Certainly no place for a child to be building sandcastles, or whatever she's ...

MUST be some tourist's kid, visiting, or ...

Hmmm ...

Maybe she's not as young as I first suspected – but she DOES look like she's building a castle or ...

I don't know. She's quite a ways up yet. Not quite to the café, but closer to that than to me. Really not even sure it's a "she."

... Yes, I am. It's a "she" in my mind. And she's young. Too young to be out here like this.

"The Marine" takes over. He'll stand guard until she leaves, and make sure she gets somewhere safely, or better, go tell her she needs to be gone until later, and escort her "home," wherever that is. She's WAAAAAY too early .... The sun is just coming up good. Stupid tourists. This is how kids get stolen. GRRRRRRR!!! It's OK for her now, though. "The Marine" won't let anything happen to her.

As I get closer I realize she isn't just a little child. She's got to be at least 12 or 13. She's just waifish. Tiny.

Closer yet and I realize she's even older. Maybe 18? 19? What the hell is she doing out here building sandcastles at this time of the morning? ... Or for that matter, AT ALL? She's sort of oldish for that.

Ahhh ....

I recognize her! I don't know her, but I "know" her. She's one of the nightlife denizens that inhabit the beach the same way I do. Sometimes she sells dope, sometimes turns a trick, sometimes robs someone, I'm sure. Eats when and where she can, does drugs when she can't eat because it's easier than finding food. No wonder she's small. Probably had a late night herself and couldn't find a place to crash for the night. No blanket. Clothes stained and ragged around the edges. No telling what ...

Oooohhhhh ....

(As I get closer I recognize the signs ...)

She's stoned "out-of-her-mind." Yup. Even from here I can tell.

I've actually gotten pretty close now. Then I realize it isn't a child, so I can comfortably approach her. The café is now close enough that I can see it's open, and "Mom" is standing outside, shading her eyes, looking in our direction.

I don't know what I'm going to say, but it seems rude to just pass the girl by without acknowledging her presence. Maybe ask if she's all

right? Don't know yet. She finally realizes that someone is approaching her, but the sun is in her eyes. Gawd! She really DOES look like a cute 10 year old, just being a kid, unless you look closely. She's not building a castle after all.

Shells ...

She's got a collection of shells in front of her, all lined up in perfect (?) rows of sizes and colors .... And she's SMILING BIG!!! I recognize that smile, the glassy eyes ... yeah. Mushrooms or acid ... But hey, she's happy, and not hurting anyone, so it's none of MY business. I've done my share, and I can tell she recognizes me.

Just as I'm about to speak, she holds up a hand, palm up, offering me what she's got. More shells. She gives her hand a little shake in a "take them" gesture.

So I do.

She's handed me 8 or 10. Nothing particularly special about ANY of them ... but that SMILE ... I can see that she thinks they are treasures beyond words at the moment ...

... And she has just offered to share with me something beyond the streets, beyond the prostitution, beyond the drugs and schemes and scams and misery ...

She just offered ME a moment of her beauty. She knows I'm like her. She's seen me around too. She KNOWS!!! Yet she offered me her treasures. These shells aren't special. They're small, cracked and chipped, kind of dull and faded. I'm pretty sure that her sight is being affected by her drug trip. She would never look at these shells twice in a sober state of being. But it doesn't matter. Right now they are the world's most beautiful shells, and she just offered them to ... ME.

All of this realization in an instant. How could I NOT find them wondrous?

"They're beautiful!" I tell her. (Ahh, that smile!!)

I crouch down and take my time looking at each of them, giving them each an examination worthy of the world's most beautiful seashells. Plenty of "oohs," "aahs," "wows," and "oh my's."

I try to hand them back to her, but she won't take them. (Keep in mind she has not spoken one word to me during this whole encounter!) I try again to return them to her. I can't keep her treasures! Again she refuses. I kneel down holding them out flat in my hand, presenting them to her as regally as I can, the same way she presented them to me, and said "The most beautiful seashells in the world

MUST ONLY belong to the most beautiful mermaid. Won't you please take them back?"

Can you imagine a smile EXPLODING into a morning? Most women have prettier smiles than they realize ... wedding days, graduations, newborns ... The times you get those HUGE smiles ... were DWARFED by hers!! It simply challenged the sun for the morning! In that instant, I fell in love with a girl I didn't know, on drugs, and had never spoken to before today. In that instant, I would have died for her, and died a happy and honorable man. I wanted to reach out and caress her face, but no ....

I told her I had to go, and with shining eyes, she waved me a child-like goodbye with her hand. Almost to the café I looked back. She was crouched down, picking up her treasures to leave. She stood up and looked my way, gave a quick wave, and walked off the beach and out of my life.

When I arrived at the café, "Mom" asked me if I knew her? "No. Do you?"

She said that she had seen her around a time or two, but that was all. Maybe once a week. I ordered breakfast, had coffee, and watched the beach where she'd been, hoping to see her again, hoping she would find a blessing somewhere.

When I paid my bill, I gave "Mom" an extra $10 (which was almost all the money I had at the time), beyond her normal tip. "The next time you see her around," I asked her, "strolling around looking lost or hungry, would you please feed her good once or twice? Will you do that for me?" She said she absolutely would.

"You really like her, don't you?"

"I don't even know her name ... but for just a moment, I loved her."

I'm pretty sure "Mom" didn't know what I was referring to, but somehow I felt like she understood. She gave me an impromptu hug and went back to work.

I never saw either of them again, but I hope that "street" girl got a good meal, or two – and I would bet she did.

And I hope and pray that someday I'll see that smile again, somewhere, sometime ... just for a moment.

Excerpts from the letters

It has been my experience that most people do not understand

pedophilia – that it is not a matter of morals. They are so quick to pass judgment that they will not even discuss the issue, but behind closed doors they are either doing or at least thinking about the same thing. I've met many people in prison that were in for murder, or burglary, or something other than a sex offense against a child. Once they found out what I was in for, they would secretly confide in me things that they have done but had never been caught for.

ജ

I have what you might call a global empathy deficit. I don't really care what happens to people I don't know. For instance, the earthquake in Haiti. I don't feel sorry for them. Life is what it is. There are good things and bad things for everyone. When I was growing up we were dirt poor. No electricity. No water. Very little food. But I was still happy. I played with sticks instead of toys but I had just as much fun in life as any other child does. .... I made the most of what I had. It did not take much to brighten my day. If I couldn't find the toy to play with I found a stick and pretended.

ജ

One thing no one can take away from me is my mind. No one can stop me from thinking any thought I want to think. I think about things that make me happy and I don't hurt anyone. Sometimes I think about things I've done in the past during the happier times of my life. Sometimes I just daydream about things that never happened but are just nice to think about. Sometimes I see a movie or even a commercial or even a picture in a magazine and I think what it would be like to be in that moment of time having some fun. These are the highlights of my day and what gets me through from one day to the next year after year.

ജ

I can't change the fact I'm in prison. I can't change the fact that I'm around a bunch of ignorant and violent people. I can't change the fact that I am a pedophile. I can't change the fact that this is the most miserable place I have ever been in, but I can change my thoughts. When I want to I can use my imagination to go to any place I want

to be. I can look like anyone I want to look like. I can make others do and say anything I want hear. They can do whatever I want them to do anyway I want to do it. I can go fishing with my brother on a beautiful lake. I can hear my mom say I love you for mowing the grass. I can have any sexual partner I want who is willing to do everything I want to do. This is how I cope with prison. Yes, once my dream ends I'm still in prison and everything is still miserable, but at least I had a little respite. I did what I wanted to do and it felt good. That's not much. You may even think it is pathetic, but it's all I've got, and if I ever get out of this place for even for a few minutes, then it is worth it.

☙

Over the years I have been in federal custody and have experienced a lot of hostility by staff because of my offense. Once I was put into a two-man cell with four other people. One was a gang member who had a knife. He told us that if they ever put a child molester in his cell he would kill him. I was there for three days before I finally faked a medical emergency and refused to go back into the cell.

☙

Being a good listener has helped me learn a great deal about other people. I learn from their experiences so I don't have to make the same mistakes they've made. Of course I find out about a lot of personal things too. People do have a tendency to want to unload their guilt as a way of purging themselves. Many of the people who have confided their most intimate secrets with me did so because they felt guilty and were ashamed about them. But when I explain to them that there was nothing to feel guilty or ashamed about because they were as normal as anyone else, they are relieved. I give them the analogy about how a person who likes vanilla ice cream is no different than a person who prefers strawberry. They are able to understand that. We all have desires; we all have specific things that trigger those desires. Just because my desires are different than somebody else's does not make me a bad person and the other a good person. A person can be mean and violent, and still like strawberry ice cream or a person can be kind and gentle and like strawberry ice cream. Our interest has nothing to do with what kind of person we are.

CS

Most people are taught from a young age what they are supposed to like and what they are supposed to not like. So what does a child do when he or she likes something that is supposed to be bad? They hide it! They tell the world what they think the world wants to hear but in secret they like what everybody else says is bad. The funny thing is, if you think about it, what if everybody really liked strawberry ice cream but only said they didn't because of what they thought everybody else believed. Each person would think they were the only one, and no one would be free to eat their favorite ice cream openly. But when a person finds another person likes strawberry ice cream, that has a healing effect. Not that it changes their taste, but they don't feel alone anymore. They don't feel as much guilt or shame. They stop believing at least a little bit that there is something wrong with them. I believe we're all created the way we are supposed to be. I also believe that people change [from who they really are] because they never express their true selves. They are so wrapped up in what they think others think that they repress their true selves and never reach a level of maturity that maximizes their potential. At the end they realize their lives have not been as full as they could've been. They die with regrets, wishing they had the chance to do it all over again. I will not die with regrets. I will die with memories!

CS

I can imagine that it would be lonely with no one to care about you and with no one for you to care about. I was lonely like that for a long time for the same reason. I wish they would allow us to have pets. Maybe that would help. I don't expect anyone will ever love me again, and if they did, they would just go and tell their mom! (sick joke). I'm not really looking for love. I guess all the years in here alone have made me give up on that aspect of life. Of course I would like to be in love, but there is no one to love me. Very simply, there is no one in my life. No one even knows me. I have no friends, no pen pals, nothing! Who will love me? Well I think I will just leave this alone because I could really get onto a soap box if I started feeling sorry for myself, and that's where this is going.

ೞ

We moved to a small town near _____ Florida where I went to the second grade and started the third. Then we moved a little further away to a town called _____. That was when I was introduced to nudist colonies, swinging groups, and oral sex (giving, not getting). This was the period when I was introduced to a lot of different sexual things. Between the time I was in the third grade and the fifth grade I had done or seen just about everything. Men with boys, boys with boys, men with girls, men with women, women with women, and lots of incest. This was the first time I remember deliberately getting drunk. That was the first time I smoked pot. This was also the first time I saw a dead person up close. A woman committed suicide right in front of me by jumping in front of a dump truck. When I was in the fifth grade, I was separated from my family. I was sent to live with my aunt. I was never really happy after that.

ೞ

Now I have 9 years to go, and life supervision. With being through all this, I still look at the positive side of things. First of all I have my integrity. I have never compromised myself for fear of anything. As a young boy, I allowed men to have sex with me because I enjoyed it. As a young man I had sex with boys and girls because that was something I chose to do. I never hurt anyone. I never forced anyone, and the experiences were awesome. And even though I have spent years and years in prison because of that, at least I know within myself that I did what I wanted to do. I was not afraid of the risk and I did not deny what God created in me. I still look at the positive side of things because I believe that I have lived my life the way God wanted me to.

ೞ

One important thing I did learn through my years of growing up the way I did: I learned that if you limited yourself then you would wind up with limited experiences. As I said I've done and seen a lot. I've also met many people over the years that have liked a variety of things from one extreme to the other. I don't judge people because they are different than I am. We don't all like nuts sprinkled on our

strawberry ice cream. I am no one's judge. I am me and they are who they are. Just because we may like different things doesn't mean that we can't be friends.

An email from prison
a day after being civilly committed

As I sit listening to my modern MP3 player, Native American flutes playing tributes to older Powers that I know very little about, it doesn't escape me that the feelings evoked by the flutes in my Spirit are the same as I feel deep in my soul every day. It wasn't always like this.

At one time in my life these flutes would have been something "Indian" and "mystical." Now I know they are "me," as is the singing of some religions, the chanting of others, and the various musical types of yet more God worshiping exercises. The strange rites of so many different cultures blend into one, coming together, becoming me and everything around me. God, by whatever name a person chooses to use: "Yahweh," "Gitchi Manitou," "Allah," "Jehovah," Sun Goddess, or science ... we all strive to understand the unknowable. I suspect in my heart-of-hearts that it will ALWAYS be mystical.

My story began in middle-class Christian America, in a chapel in school one morning at the tender age of six. I made the long walk down the aisle alone to accept the love and teachings of Jesus Christ. Of the 365 days of my life that year, why is that one the only day I remember? Mystical, to be sure. The love of that acceptance was neither here-nor-there in my young mind. "Love" was what I got from Momma, and it was enough.

... And the teachings? All those funny words in the Bible certainly didn't mean much to me, and the ones I fully understood, well, it was either much like another school classroom, or a Harry Potter story. To me, seas didn't part like Charlton Heston portrayed. Angels didn't really speak to people, and who would be so mean as to make a baby be born in a barn? ... But Momma and Gramma believed it, so I guess I would too ... at least, in my mind I would.

That part of my story is easy to tell and believe because many people identify with religion the same way. The following may be more difficult, and I would understand if most would think I'm a crazy person. I believe it, and that's enough for me.

Eighteen years after my six year old self accepted Jesus as correct,

during a near-death experience, I was blessed with a vision of "The White Light" and "The Tunnel," and was visited by an "other-world" being that I believe was Spiritual ... and I was given a choice to live or die. In the end I chose to live and was therefore granted a Spiritual "protection" that I had not previously known.

That didn't change my mind about anything concerning how I lived in the physical every-day world. I was still the footloose, oat-sowing, wild young drug user I had been. The difference was that now I knew in my heart and soul that greater Powers exist than we humans ... and it was HUGE! Bigger even than the Bible. Bigger than the Talmud. Bigger than the Quran. I knew that all of these books were just "starter manuals," so-to-speak. The reality of a loving God (and, I suspect, a vengeful one as well) had exploded my world into an eternity of possibilities – and I knew I had protection. A gift. Why would the Spirits protect me, if not for me to go live and enjoy life?

... And enjoy I did, for many years. Fortunately, I hadn't physically hurt anybody seriously in that time, but I suspect the Powers-That-Be don't care to see their gifts being used for theft or drug dealing or other manner of not-so-nice activities. "Protected from evil" doesn't mean escaping dues-to-be-paid for breaking Earthly laws.

My scandalous actions eventually landed me in prison, quite likely saving a life. While incarcerated I had my second visit from the other world. Again, believe or don't, your choice. MY choice changed my life completely.

I'm not sure what other religious texts call it, but the Bible refers to being "washed in the blood" or "washed in the spirit." My second visit happened while I was in a period of solitary confinement for disciplinary reasons, in the middle of the day. I chose to reach out and actually touch the being I was being visited by ... and that's when the Spiritual "cleansing" occurred. Not because I had asked for it, no. Simply because I was curious. The reason didn't matter. I'm certain the end result would have been exactly the same.

I no longer just believed in "higher powers." Now I knew that all those things I'd been taught as a child by way of the Bible were real: Love, faith, forgiveness, charity, "Love thy neighbor," "Do unto others ...," "Suffer not the children ...," and "A child shall lead them ..." – ALL real, and I understood it. I FELT it in every part of me. I CARED!! ... About you, about me, even those people I had called "enemy." Now what? I was a prisoner in a den of evil.

"Now what?" turned out to be "Have faith" that I would be led in the right direction, growing into a whole new frame of mind. During and after my incarcerations I've written multiple stories of my new self and how my faith in the Spiritual has always led me in the proper directions.

I couldn't tell you all of them, and indeed, you may not even want to hear them – especially as you might already believe me to be a "crackpot-religious-freak." That's okay. But one story I've repeated often to friend and foe alike is a story I called "Are We Our Brother's Keeper?" It's a story of how, while living homeless and wild, a young man was set to rob me. Rather than allow that event to happen, to avoid a confrontation that may have resulted in an innocent person being injured, I freely gave the would-be robber all I had at the moment. In so doing I would be morally unable to bear a grudge against him and would guarantee the safety for the friend that was with me.

That young "robber" eventually came to me, hungry and in need after a meeting between us during which I refused to fight him. I explained my lack of ill-will toward him and invited him to join me in rest and relaxation ... which he did. Now later, hungry and alone with no help at his call, he had come to me ... not to his family or so-called friends.

I know the native flutes blowing their haunting, beautiful tributes are "me" ... as are the chants and dances and rites ... because I was honored with Spiritual visitors, not once, but twice. The evidence is by that young would-be thief that came to me for help when he couldn't go anywhere else. We were from wildly different backgrounds, but Billy became my friend and protector out in Arizona.

Does it matter if we call God "Yahweh" or "Allah"? Does it matter if, to reach and understand that power, to be thankful for the gifts provided, we use flutes or chant or dance or sing? Personally, I think not. Billy, was "me." YOU, are "me." Maybe someone in Japan or Turkey or Australia is praying for me ... and Billy ... right now, as I pray for people I don't really know ... but in reality I DO know, because they ALL are "me."

... And then I'll go have a meal.

I happen to like the wooden flutes. They remind me that we are all connected in of the circle of life.

Chapter 12 – **Spanky**

by M.D.

M.D. tells about what it was like to be "different." It led to conflicts within himself, with others, and eventually with society. As is so often the case with sex offenders, his sentence was grossly out of proportion to any harm he may have done to others.

ଔ

I've known I was "different" for as long as I can remember. One of my earliest memories was getting caught wearing Mom's panties (I liked the feel of the silk). I never was into girls, and was always trying to talk my friends into taking their pants off. In fact, the first time I can remember getting seriously beat by my stepfather was when I talked a friend into running naked down the driveway.

That friend's name was Andrew; my name was Andrew too. He always had an unruly cowlick, and I was the chubby kid who was always getting into trouble. His nickname became "Alfalfa," and mine became "Spanky."

As I got older, I learned to hide my gay tendencies (even though I didn't think of myself as "gay"). Anytime I even acted a little "effeminate," I would get clobbered by my stepfather who wanted (as he'd say) "to beat the pansy" out of me.

My first real gay experience was when I was 16. I become tired of frequent beatings, and ran away with a friend of mine who was a year younger. We ended up staying at a place called "Bibleland." The owner was a sand sculptor who sculpted various Bible scenes and had a flat big-bed trailer with a mattress on it that we were allowed

to use. Neither one of us called our "fooling around" gay – but some of it definitely was.

As a young adult, I went to Bible college, and I became extremely religious. Secretly, though, I would buy books that had pictures of boys, or stories of underage sex. Every time, I would feel condemned and end up throwing them away after I had "used them."

It was many years before I ever did anything sexual with a boy. Then, in a church I was active in, I met a boy I fell head over heels for. He was 14, and very affectionate. The first time he met me, he gave me a big hug that I didn't want to end. I later found he liked more than just hugs. It wasn't long, though, before I felt so condemned that I abruptly left town – without even telling anyone goodbye.

For quite a while after, I was on and off "the wagon." I didn't actually have sex with most of the boys I interacted with, but I'd find excuses to get them undressed (like going swimming, etc.). Every time I began to get close to a boy, I'd get scared – actually, felt "condemned" – and take off. I believe the greatest harm I ever did was abandoning them without an explanation.

Eventually I married a female friend of mine in the hopes that I could put my "sinful ways" behind me. Then, I went a whole different direction. Another friend talked me into writing a bunch of bad checks. Just before I was sentenced to three years in prison, I found out my wife was pregnant. My son was born six months after I'd gone to prison. Because the state I was in had both "good time" and "half-time," I only had to do nine months before being released to a halfway house, so I was able to spend time with my wife and new son, Julian. I was fortunate that I was able to, because Julian had been born with a three chambered heart. Five days after his second birthday, he died.

After that, I "lost it." I left my wife and sort of "wandered" for a while. Finally, I pulled myself together – sort of. I launched a number of different businesses: a secondhand store, baseball card sales, flyer delivery business, ice cream vendor. In every case, I'd have two or three boys to work for me. I still resisted having actual sex with any of them, but mutual fondling began to happen more and more. Every time, true to my nature, I'd feel I was "sinning," and abruptly break off all ties – usually closing down whatever business it was – sometimes even moving to a different state.

Finally, I did give in, and had oral sex with a 14-year-old. I tried to shut out the part of my brain that was telling me I was evil. I suc-

ceeded for a few months, and then one evening the boy told me his mother knew about what we were doing. He assured me she didn't care, because she felt I'd been very good for him (his grades were going from Ds to Bs with my help). Someone else knowing triggered the old "flight" impulse. I told him I had received a job offer out-of-state and had to leave immediately. He began crying (which made me cry), and begged me to stay. I promised I'd write and come to see him whenever I could. (I never did). I left town that night – crying the whole time.

I vowed after that to stay away from boys, altogether. I was a NAMBLA member by then, and bought all their books and magazines, as well as books from a Dutch company that was called "Acolyte Press" that had stories of boy love. That, for a long time, kept me from actually seeking boys out.

Then I met a beautiful Chinese trans-gender who, although she was older than I, looked like she was in her early teens – actually like a teenage boy. We got married not long after we met. She was too much of a "girl" for me, though, and I didn't really have a lot of sexual attraction to her. We were married friends who occasionally fooled around. I began to bury myself in my new business – as a professional photographer.

There were two parts of my business: 1) I made photo CDs of different subjects, and 2) I printed out pictures of boys I saw at the beach, workplace, etc. I even got a few boys to model for me. No nudes, but frequently in underwear. I sold the pictures on-line and was making a lot of money. I also had a side business, selling books and videos (mostly those of interest to boy lovers). My wife put up with this because we were making good money.

Then "9-11" happened. For a while, people stopped sending money. Between rapidly depleting funds and finding out my parents in Idaho were about to lose their home, my wife and I decided to move to Idaho. The rent there was 10% of what it was where we lived (near San Francisco), and I could help my folks with a little extra money.

To be honest, one of the reasons I wanted to move to Idaho was to be near my two nephews – seven and nine-year-old boys who absolutely adored their "Uncle Andrew." I opened a little store in Idaho that sold books. My main business was still the photography. I found a lot of eager models swimming in a nearby river. But my most exuberant models were my two nephews, the older one especially. I hired

him to work in my store. He was constantly telling me, "Take my picture!" One day, he came to my back office and saw a picture I was printing out of a boy who had been swimming in his underwear briefs. He asked me if people actually paid for pictures like that. When I told him "yes," he offered to pose in his underwear – or even naked – if he got some of the money. I was too afraid of taking pictures of him totally naked. I figured, if someone recognized him on the Internet, it would get back to his mom (my sister). I never actually thought I was breaking the law. In fact, I'd been very careful in that area.

Before long, though, I began to do stupid things. The first was masturbating while he took my picture. A week later, just after my nephew's 10th birthday, the two boys and their nine-year-old cousin were dropped off at my store by my sister. I was to babysit, and then drop the nephew off at his home later in the day. I gave the boys a job sorting books while I worked on the Internet. Then I checked my email. A man had offered me $100 for a picture of boys kissing. I had the perfect opportunity. The boys kissed each other goodbye all the time. I gathered the three together and told him what I needed. They were happy to oblige – making a game out of it. I actually had to rein them in, because I didn't want to get caught with any pictures that were that were actual porn. At one point, the two oldest actually mooned me. But the only pictures I took had them only with their shirts off, kissing and hugging.

A lady in the office next door had heard the commotion and started listening through a door that separated our offices. She called the cops and told them, "A man is taking pictures of little boys."

The cop investigated. A couple days later I was arrested. After almost a year, I was tried and convicted of sexual abuse – because I had "caused them to make physical contact," saying that my intent was "sexual gratification."

I kept insisting the pictures were legal, and I hadn't taken them in order to "get off" – but to sell, as a professional photographer. The jury didn't buy it. And because my past activities came out in my pre-sentence investigation, I was deemed a "threat to society." I received 15 years fixed, for the masturbation episode, but that was later dismissed on appeal, as it only amounted to "indecent exposure." But I still got a total of 25 years fixed, and 20 years indeterminate... 45 years in a row. Worse than most rapists received.

My job now is to try to educate people. The worst harm done was

convincing those boys that hugging and kissing was "wrong."

I've had very few adult friendships – mainly because I was afraid they would find out what a "monster" I was. I've made more friends since being in prison than in the 40 years prior.

As far as I know, every boy I've ever interacted with loved me, on some level. At the very least, as a friend. I didn't engage in a lot of sexual activity, although in many cases I would've been able to. Many tried to encourage me to do more. Only my own self-condemnation prevented me. I hurt more boys by abandoning them than by any other way.

Almost my entire family has abandoned me. My mother says I "tore the family apart." Nobody will tell me anything about my nephews.

I don't really have any pen pals. People don't like to write to "sex offenders."

I stay busy in prison. I do a lot of writing. I lead a pagan prison chapel group. I take younger vulnerable inmates under my wing and show them how to stay safe. I'm a "companion," which is someone who stays with suicidal inmates while they work things through. And I watch a lot of TV.

My sentence is incredibly harsh: Three 15-year sentences, running, concurrent. I've been in prison since 2002, and am not eligible for parole until 2027. I've actually watched people here with rape and deadly assault come in – and get out – since my being here.

I most enjoy reading fact and fiction about ancient Greece – when boy lovers were expected. I also read sci-fi, fantasy, and horror. I must be honest: if a book doesn't have a boy as a main character, I usually lose interest.

Chapter 13 – I Praise God for Those FBI Guys

by K.T.

The narrative by KT is rather unusual for people in his situation in that he felt that getting apprehended by the authorities was a good thing.

ଔ

It's been 12 years since the FBI came and got me at my door in Beaver Dam, Wisconsin. The paper said that the agents came to town to arrest us. They woke me up early in the morning pounding on all the doors and windows in the house. I thought it was an earthquake. When I opened the door. Half a dozen men with FBI on their vests pointed machine guns at me. I knew right away what they wanted, but I didn't say. All I did was ask if I could smoke a cigarette. I figured it was going to be my last one.

I was maybe three or four when I first noticed there was something odd about me. My little brother is 18 months younger, so this would have been 1966 or so. I remember wishing I could wear diapers like him. Maybe that was normal thinking for little kids, but I remember thinking it was strange to think that way. I have three older brothers. We were all about 18 months apart. I'm the fourth.

My dad and mom were always fighting. We could hear them in the other room yelling at each other a lot. There would be a loud slamming sound. Then it would get quiet, as my mother cried off her beating, I guess.

My mom said I was my dad's favorite. I remember always being on his lap and speaking with him all the time. Now I think it kind of strange that just one of us boys was always on dad's lap. Why didn't my brothers sit on his lap? I'm not saying he molested me or anything like that. I don't remember anything like that happening.

My dad was a Navy vet and was off to the VA hospital a lot. He was gone for a few months through Christmas when I was five. He came home in March. My birthday is January 7th, so by this time I was six. It was late at night when my dad woke us up. He had a deer rifle. He put it in his mouth and pulled the trigger. I remember the blood going all over the wall. The thing I remember most is the smell. Like raw hamburger. I didn't cry at the funeral. My little brother didn't either. We wanted to, but couldn't. I remember yelling to him we should pretend we were crying because everyone else was.

We moved to Minneapolis. Soon after, we stayed at relatives' houses for a while. Then we moved to the white slums there. I remember a few different houses and apartments. My mom always moved around a lot. Every six months or so. She still would if she wasn't so old.

The apartments we lived in were about five stories tall. They had outside stairways where everyone hung out their wet laundry. The apartment buildings were U-shaped. There were burn barrels in the middle for trash. I can still remember the smell of bread burning in those barrels. This was 1968. I guess there were a lot of race problems. The black people didn't live in the same slums as the white people there, and we (the whites) were always fighting with the blacks. I remember one time when a mob of black people was coming to attack our apartment. All of us little kids were headed up to the top floor. I don't remember how all that turned out. Okay I guess. No one died.

There was this girl a year younger than me who lived way up on one of the top apartments. I remember her sleeping and I wanted her to wet the bed. For some reason I peed on her. Yeah, weird as hell, I know. I was a weird kid. I don't think the girl even noticed me peeing on her.

When I was in the second grade, me and a second-grade friend hitchhiked to the St. Paul mall. There was a new Target store where we heard we could get free stuff or steal stuff. I don't remember which. A nice lady picked us up. Another nice couple brought us home.

One time, my little brother and me were playing out back when a

man asked us if we wanted a hamburger. We went with him and ate hamburgers at some restaurant. Then we went to his house. He first taught me about sex. He said he would give me 50 cents if I went back to his house the next day. I said sure. We were gone all day.

There were police at the house when we got home. My mother took us to the station. They took naked pictures of me. When we got home my little brother and me took a bath together and asked what was the big deal. I couldn't figure out why everyone was so upset. I don't remember, but my mom said I went to the court and sat on the judge's lap and told him what happened. I don't remember what happened. Not really now.

My mom met a country music singer there in the apartment. She married him and we all moved to Pine River out on a farm. He (my step-dad) said that his dad planned a kidnapping. My step dad and his father kidnapped some kid for a ransom. It was $40,000, I believe. They split the money. Our family got caught in Illinois by the police who were following us through two states.

My little brother was six and I was eight. He kicked the cops and told them to leave us alone. We ended up staying with my aunt for a while. Then we went off to a foster home. Good and bad things happened at the first foster home that I don't really want to talk about.

My three older brothers went somewhere else. I guess my mom had a hard time getting us out of the first foster home while she was in prison. We did finally move to the same town where my older brothers were in a different foster family, but they were good people. All of us went to the same small town school. I loved it there. I wish I would have stayed there. My life would be so much better than this.

After a few years my mom got out of prison. We all moved back with her to Pine River, Wisconsin. I was eleven. We didn't have a father. They were starting a new thing called Big Brothers/Little Brothers program. It was brand-new. A bunch of us kids signed up for it and went camping with a bunch of big brothers. I guess to match us up. I got Adam. He's dead now so I won't bother with his last name. He was super nice. He drove a bus. His dad was rich. He was a Vietnam vet with a bunch of medals. He was wounded and got a silver star. That sort of thing.

He was great. I loved him to death. He was just for me. My best friend. All I ever had to do was ask and I would get it.

I don't remember when the sex started. I think it was at his

house. I took a bath, and then watched TV with only a towel on. There was this couple kissing for a world record and I asked him if two guys could do that, and we did. After that our times together were making-out sessions. My brothers were telling me I was gay because Adam was. Stuff like that. I never told anyone about Adam.

We moved to Texas when I was 13 – to a trailer park. I found girls. I never thought much more about gay stuff with men or boys.

I joined the Army at 18. When I got out I became a security guard at special events in Santa Barbara, California. I was working at a horse show at the fairground, when these two boys started talking to me. One was 15, the other 12. They hung out with me all day. Then the 12-year-old asked if he could sleep at my house. His friend snickered and said that he was a horrible fuck. "He just lays there." All those old feelings came back to me at once, and I told him yes.

We did stuff for about six months until I met a girl and moved to Virginia. I ended up moving to Illinois and went to college for a year. Then I went to Texas for the summer and met a girl who had three sons: ages nine, eight and five. We fought all the time but her boys were perfect. So I knew that no matter what kind of problems I had with her, I would have to give up the boys if I left her. We got married. We moved back to Illinois. I went back to college.

9/11 happened. I went back in the Army.

I wanted to molest the boys but not knowingly. I mean I wasn't making plans or consciously thinking about it, but always wanted one of them sitting on my lap. I never molested them.

One night I was home on leave. The youngest was eight now. He fell asleep on my lap and I started to play with him. The next day we were watching TV and he climbed on my lap and put my hand on his crotch. A few minutes later my wife came downstairs and saw us. She freaked out and I left the house with plans to kill myself. She called the police and told them everything. I went to jail. My life turned upside down.

Three years later my wife and I were still together. I started doing fairs, selling stuff at them. I made a lot of money and bought a restaurant. I got a computer. It was 1997. The first thing I did was type "boy" in the search engine. I didn't leave my office for three days.

When I learned what a boy lover was, it possessed me. That was all I wanted to be. I chatted with them all over the world, and looked at pictures all the time. Up until then, I just thought I was some weird

kid liking boys. I didn't ever think there were so many people like me.

We had two other kids by now. They were four and two. The older boys were 17 and 13. I took my wife and kids home to Texas. On the way back I stopped in Arkansas and went with some friends and hooked up with a 12-year-old and then went back to Illinois. I sold everything and went on the road doing fairs. I took the 12-year-old and his 17-year-old brother with me. I was on the road all that summer.

Later I went to live in the woods with a bunch of hippies. This family lived in a bus and had five kids. Three of them were boys: nine, seven and three. The older ones were always with me.

My BL friend, Bill, called from Illinois. He was having problems at home. I told him to come to Florida with me. He did. He was into electronics, so we went into selling electronics at flea markets. We made lots of money and met lots of boys. Two years later we went on the road. I wanted to go to Wisconsin. We were selling cell phones at the fairs and doing quite well. I looked up Adam and found out he was dead. People who ran the Moose Lake fair asked us to come set up there. So we did.

I met a lady there who had a kid. Like I said, we sold electronics. We had lots of computers and cameras. Bill made lots of movies. The electronic business started to get too hard. So I moved to Wisconsin to become a psychic at psychic fairs. I stayed with the lady who was a psychic too.

Then Bill came. We met lots of boys and made lots of movies and made a living selling them on the Internet until that morning I thought there was an earthquake.

I never could figure out why I was the way I was. It doesn't make much sense. Not really. Maybe people like me exist to keep an eye on any lost boys in trouble. A cute boy would never drown around one of us, because we would always be watching him. Maybe back in the old times, when there were a lot of orphaned boys running around, we were like Fagan in Oliver Twist – there to keep the boys alive. I don't know. I do know that we are absolutely not needed anymore. There is no place in this country or even the world for people like me anymore.

I don't know when I became like this. Maybe some demon snuck into my soul back when I was a little kid, just to corrupt me and all the boys I met as I got older.

Back in 2005, I decided I had a choice between two things: either

become really bad or turn to Jesus to fight my sins. I turned to Jesus. As the years go by, I become closer and closer to Jesus. It's become easier and easier not thinking about boys. Since I am locked up away from them, it's better. I have two life sentences in federal prison, with no hope of parole. So it's not like I will ever hurt another boy. I don't have to worry about that, but nowadays I'm at a point where I don't even want to think about it.

To be honest, I never hurt a boy – never made a boy do something he didn't want to do. They were always happy, always having fun.

The Bible says we should have sex only with our wife, no one else, so that leaves boys out, anyway, even before all the messed up psychological stuff it does to them.

I'm doing okay these days. No sex with anyone. I love Jesus. I'm looking forward to going home to meet him. I thank God every day that those FBI guys pounded on my house.

Chapter 14 – **I Led A Double Life**

by H.G.

I've no idea why I've been blessed with the continued love, support and letters from devoted friends and family members. I'm eternally grateful that they, unlike so many others, haven't abandoned me. It may be the religious tenets that we grew up with, or our unique views regarding intergenerational and inter-familial love. It's most likely an amalgamation of various views, beliefs, and behaviors.

S.O.'s in prison simply have to know which battles to fight and which to avoid. Harassment is inevitable, but I have to rely on my wit, wisdom, grit and social skills to carve a niche for myself, even in a place where I do not belong and I am not accepted. Most S.O.'s must give up the idea of being "accepted." The best they can hope for is being tolerated. I have no idea how those without wit, charisma, charm and social graces manage to survive in hostile environments (aside from staying in the S.H.U.). I barely eked out an existence in some prisons. Thankfully not all prisons are alike-whew! I'm charming, clever and sexually experienced. That's how I've survived in prison, for better or worse.

I've been attracted to other males for as long as I remember. I simply didn't know what "being gay" was or meant. Why did everyone laugh at me when I asked for a Barbie at Christmas or when I wore heels, dresses and mascara and ran like a girl? Why did the other, usually older, boys do sexual things with me in private but would then spit, threaten and yell at me in public? All while I kept their secrets. I simply knew that being gay meant I'd "go to Hell." I had extremely low self-esteem, hated my body, was socially insulated. I escaped into the world of reading and let others use my body. I wasn't

emotionally close with anyone.

My intergenerational attractions where a well-kept secret. I led a double life. I would indulge/binge for a short time and then purge and starve for a period of time. It was very cyclical. I'd move from self-hatred and disgust to apathy to defiance to acceptance. I felt dirty but wondered if I was indeed dirty or if society was simply throwing mud at me. I believe it's a bit of both but more-so the latter.

I did really well socially but no one knew the real me, no one knew my secret. In fact, I gave myself up to the cops once they openly started sniffing around. Had I not done so, I truly would have avoided prison for a short while longer. At the least, leading a double life is extremely difficult and draining. I was tired of playing the game and was relieved in a way not to have to pretend anymore even though it meant going to prison.

S.O's receive long sentences and harsh punishments because it's easy to draw and quarter a social pariah. Most people can understand wanting to kill someone or to do drugs or to steal things, etc. But few people want to admit to or understand intergenerational attractions and/or sex. Plus, same-sex desire is punished more severely than opposite sex desire. I'm not sure why. Yet I believe that society punishes those who are willing to do what they wish they could do themselves. Or, more pointedly, punish those who get caught doing what they wish they could do, i.e., "How dare you turn a spotlight on us/this activity?" Yes punish them to further separate "them" from "us" even though we're all closer than we'd like to believe. After all how did Justin Bieber become a sex symbol at such a young age? The over-18 fans far outnumber the under-18 crowd. Yet it's not an intergenerational attraction – correct? I disagree.

Chapter 15 – Degradation

by E.J.

The following two sections contain journal entries. The first describes what happened the night in the receiving unit when the other prisoners learned what his "crime" was. The second concerns his struggle with a desire to end his life after his release from prison.

℃

The back of the bus

That night I jotted down some of the things that various people screamed [at me] out of their doors, so that I would not forget:

"We're going to strap you to the toilet and fuck you in the ass."

"Push the fucking buzzer you piece of shit."

"Ripper."

"Kill yourself you fucking piece of shit."

"Die, ripper, die."

"I'm going to stick it in your hairy ass."

"Burn skinner, burn."

"Check in, Martin."

"Why'd you do it?"

"Little boy fucker!"

It went on for about 45 minutes.

Then I was able to settle down and try to sleep.

I woke at about 3 AM and could remember several dreams. One seemed especially nice:

I am sitting with a young boy of maybe six or so. He knows that I can tell stories and he asks me for one. I sit on a couch. He curls up in

my lap and snuggles in close to me. It feels wonderful.

Then I am with a small black boy at a bus stop. We run to catch the bus. A woman sees us. She likes us. The boy goes to the back door. I call him to the front and we get on. I worry whether I have enough money for the fare. I pull out a billfold. I have money. I give the driver a five-dollar bill. I worry that he may have a wreck while he makes change and drives the bus at the same time, but he does OK.

One of my thoughts about the dream is that I want to take my feelings about boys off the back of the bus, and bring them up to the front – where they are freely acknowledged – and become first class. My association is to the beginning act of the civil rights movement in Montgomery, Alabama, when Rosa Parks refused to accept a seat on the back of the bus. Whether I have enough money for the fare might refer to whether I have the resources to endure the degradation that is heaped on me. The price might be too great.

A pinch of incense

About five year ago I purchased some thick rubber bands, an allergy mask, and a plastic bag. These were most of the things that would be needed to commit suicide fairly painlessly, as described in a book put out by the Hemlock Society. I was 63 years old, happily married, and in reasonably good health at that time. The occasion that prompted my serious contemplation of suicide had to do with my release from being incarcerated for 3 1/2 years in prison, as a sex offender.

After talking recently to an individual who was in a similar situation, I decided to pull up some entries from the journal that I was writing at that time. I felt this might be of interest, and perhaps even of some help, to the person with whom I had conversed. My initial intent was simply to locate a copy of the Journal entries and send them on to my friend. As I looked at the entries it occurred to me that this material might be of some interest to a variety of other people as well.

It was however clear that some general explanation of various circumstances would be necessary for a person to follow what I was talking about. My intent has been to keep this explanatory material to a minimum so that it would be possible to hear the voice of the person who was very much in the middle of these circumstances when the entries were written.

Before I was incarcerated I asked my lawyer to negotiate with

the prosecutors an agreement that I would not be required to attend the usual sex offender treatment programs after being released from prison. As a psychotherapist I had heard several descriptions of such groups. Based on these descriptions I had come to consider such groups as degrading forms of brainwashing with which I wanted nothing to do. Without going into any detail about the so-called "cognitive/behavioral" approach to the treatment of sex offenders, suffice it to say that such groups are based on forcing the participants in the group to agree that the therapist's pre-formulated – one size fits all – narrative of the sexual offense is the true one, and that the "offender's" own experience of the event consisted only of rationalizations and denials. In short, treatment was a matter of forcing a set of beliefs and self-defining narratives upon the participants. I felt that Russia under Stalin and China under Mao had developed such techniques adequately, and that we did not need to be experimenting with them in a society that purports to believe in freedom of thought.

I had agreed to arrange for treatment on my own and with a Jungian analyst, and was presently seeing one.

Shortly after my release from prison a friend of mine talked me into joining a writers' group. I was interested in sharing some of my writing with them. Specifically, I wanted to get some feedback as to how a random selection of people might respond to descriptions of my prison experience. I had not been in the group very long when one of the group members reported me to the Department of Probation for "advocating pedophilia."

I was confronted by my probation officer who said that a decision had been made. It was no longer acceptable that I should evade the standard group sex offenders treatment program. I reminded him that my not being required to attend the usual sex offender treatment was a part of my plea bargain. I suggested that we take it back to court and let the judge decide whether the Department of Probation would be required to respect this aspect of the plea bargain. I was told that, should I pursue the matter through legal channels, the Department of Probation would take it back to court with the recommendation that I be required to serve the entire outstanding 11 years that were still hanging over my head. In effect, I would be punished by 11 years imprisonment for attempting to seek a legal opinion as to the enforceability of the plea bargain.

It was this situation that led to the crisis that is the background

of the journal entries that follow. I have added a couple of the headings that are under the dates, and had to do a small amount of reconstruction in a few sections because my documents were slightly damaged by my computer program. But the words here are as I wrote them then. Any other additions are just for giving enough relevant background to enable a reader who is unfamiliar with my situation to make sense of the journal. These additions are in brackets. Also, the names have been changed. But this is not fiction.

10/15/03 – Degradation

Yesterday I was told by John Shannon [my probation officer] that I would be required to attend a sex offenders treatment group after all. By the time I got home my stomach was hurting a lot. I guess I must secrete a huge amount of acid in such situations. I took several antacids, and after a bit that seemed to help.

Some time last week a woman in my writing group turned me in to the state for "advocating pedophilia." My "Preface" to the writing I was planning to do on my prison experience was delivered to the hands of my probation officer. Actually in that preface I was neither advocating for, nor condemning, pedophilia. I was asking to be seen as a human being. But I guess in her mind this was too fine a distinction. This report that I was "advocating pedophilia" was what caused my probation officer to do that-180 degree turn around about therapy. So much for my experiment with re-entering the world in something resembling a normal manner.

I struggled the whole day with the issue of suicide and whether that was the sensible thing to do at this point, or at least at the point where it becomes apparent that there is no way out. If the degradation is going to go on and on it hardly seems worth living. I reviewed the method I would use, [The thought had occurred to me before, and I had gathered information on how I might do it.] and talked some with B [Boo, my wife] about it in the evening. To actually do such a thing to myself seems almost unthinkable when I consider it concretely. At the same time to spend the next ten years in prison also seems unthinkable. I am certain I would rather be dead if it appeared that this was where the whole process would end up.

I woke at about 2 AM thinking about it. I realized that the whole question of "treatment" for me centers around the issue of degradation. So I asked myself, "What does it mean to be degraded?" What

came to me almost immediately is that there are two forms of degradation – internal and external. I made the following lists to distinguish between the two.

External degradation — This is what is done to you. The elements of external degradation are as follows:
- Being exposed to ridicule, derisive comments, and name calling
- Having a negative identity imposed on oneself from the outside
- Being prohibited from telling one's own story
- Being coerced into living a life that is not in keeping with one's essence
- Being forcibly subjected to the micromanagement of one's activities
- Being treated with complete disregard for who one is

Internal degradation — To be inwardly degraded pertains to what a person does to him or herself, or to others. We are inwardly degraded in the following circumstances:
- When we willingly participate in the external degradation
- When we internalize the views of those who are degrading us
- When we tell our own story in a way that is devoid of compassion and understanding
- When we abandon our own principles
- When we fail to protest, as fully as is reasonably possible, the external degradation
- When we actively degrade others

To be inwardly degraded is a matter of fact. To be externally degraded is a matter of appearance. To determine who is inwardly degraded and who is only externally degraded one must look at who is active in the ritual of degradation. The one actively doing the degrading, whether to one's self or to another person, is the one who is inwardly degraded. The one doing the name-calling, for example, degrades himself. Also the one who internalizes the names he or she is called, and incorporates them in his or her self-concept is inwardly degraded.

The archetypal story about this is the crucifixion of Jesus. What is happening here is a degradation ritual. In terms of the above categories, it shows that one can be degraded externally in an extreme way,

yet not be internally degraded. Jesus was even forced to participate in his own degradation. That's the meaning of his having to carry his cross. And his main strategy for not allowing this external degradation to become an internal one? He kept silent!! Ah, I must learn his discipline in this matter. My task is to talk. Yet there are times when I must not speak. Or when I must speak in modulated tones.

The people in the world do not want my truth. In fact they will kill me once again if I persist in telling it – not quickly, which would be a tolerable sort of thing, I think, but slowly over a period of years. So, okay. Finally I saw it. I really do have only three choices:

• I can allow myself to be sent back to prison.
• I can go out into the woods and put a bag over my head.
• I can cease being a teller of the truth and go underground.

[In case it is not clear, the third option listed above was what I felt would be necessary if I was to join a sex-offenders group.]

It is not easy to be confronted with such bleak alternatives at 62 years of age. They all seem almost equally unacceptable. But I know that going back to prison is the worst of them.

Yesterday I thought a lot about suicide. I have been, off and on, for some time now, but I gave it perhaps, more careful consideration than ever before. The main method I contemplated was taking sleeping pills and putting a plastic bag over my head. This is described in the book *Final Exit* [a publication of The Hemlock Society]. The book, of course, is aimed at people whose lives are intolerable because their physical bodies have deteriorated past either repair or usability. In my case it is my social body that seems to have deteriorated almost to that point. I had already bought some thick rubber bands that would be adequate for the job of holding the bag in place. Yesterday I looked in a drug store for sleeping pills. I couldn't locate any, and then decided I might not need them anyhow, and put off buying them.

I am not aware of being much afraid of death at this point. I would welcome a nice cancer. Doing it to oneself, however, introduces new convolutions to this matter of dying. To make such a choice would be an awesome thing. One has the feeling that it is forbidden. Is it in reality a sin against creation?

I don't know. In some situations I think it is not. Still, the weight of that moral imperative – thou shalt not kill – is hard to shake off, even if the life one is thinking about is one's own.

Of course I would not know really, until I came to the point of

doing it, but I do not think the process itself would be that unpleasant. The method described in the book *Final Exit* would be painless, physically. I am inclined to think that at this point I would feel more relief than dread or fear. One holds the bag open a bit until the sleeping pills take effect. Then one simply goes to sleep and dies of oxygen deprivation. It sounds very peaceful. I would not even experience myself suffocating.

One of the things that causes me to turn away from this option is that it is so ugly from the outside. Whatever I might be experiencing from the inside, the image of my face turning blue inside a plastic bag , secured in place with a thick rubber band around the neck, is not a pretty one. It is grotesque. Suppose someone would find me in that condition by accident. I would notify the authorities by mail where to find me. Even for them, prepared as they would be for what they would find, it would be a shocking sight. Why that matters much to me, I'm not exactly sure. But somehow it does.

How would I go about separating from Boo? And what would this do to her? I cannot overlook the possibility that she might feel some relief. Not that I think she wants me dead. But this whole situation is difficult for her too. I could not just tell her, say goodbye, give her a hug and drive off into the woods. I would have to just leave sometime without making a point of it. I think this would be very difficult for her. Phoebe [our daughter] would also be shocked, though I think she would manage with it now that she has Matthew and a life that is separate from me. A few others would shake their heads. Some might actually feel genuinely sad. I don't think it would be devastating to them, though. The two boys who gave the information that sent me to prison might feel guilty, but they would be re-assured by therapists. But it would be very difficult to do this to Boo.

It is also unfair to Boo to leave her hanging up in the air, not knowing from one minute to the next whether I am going to go out and do that ugly and unthinkable thing. So I need to make a choice.

Going underground

Yesterday I decided to withdraw from the world as a teller of truth and to re-enter it as a teller of lies. [In other words, I had rejected the suicide option, mainly because of it's probable effect on B.] If I had my choice, I would not re-enter it at all. Lies constitute the warp and woof of our social life. Others seem either to accept this or not

to notice. Underneath it, are they wishing to tell the truth? Are they lonely? It's hard to know. I suppose it varies from person to person. I know that I have little interest in adding my thread to this huge fabric of dissimulation. But it seems to be necessary. I must become a teller of lies. I must go underground.

I believe that without truth we are meaningless phantoms. We barely exist at all. Perhaps a little bit of reality seeps around the layer upon layer of persona that we place between ourselves and others, but only enough to let us know that the other person is not the one we are seeing. Can one be a phantom in the world, and still exist as a substantial being in solitude? Or is living a lie and thereby becoming a phantom the ultimate betrayal of our reality – a betrayal that leads to the loss of that reality? I am not sure.

It does not come naturally or easily for me to become a teller of lies. But I will have to give it the very best effort I can.

At the same time I have decided to become a teller of lies, I have decided to begin a new journal – so that I will have someplace to tell the truth about this part of my life.

Possibly some still unforeseeable event will throw me back into prison no matter what I do. Perhaps my rage at not being able to be a real person in the world will get the best of me at some point and I will undermine myself.

It was difficult saying goodbye to Sanford. [The Jungian analyst I secured in order to be in compliance with the plea bargain.] He is a good and gentle person and has been quite supportive to me. A part of his idea is to provide a warm and safe place for people to sort out their problems. This is the old and genuine concept of psychotherapy. He should be able to practice this if he doesn't run into too many people like me. Herbal teas, hot water, and earthy attractive mugs were always available in the waiting room. It was a quiet and safe environment, as he intended it to be. The waiting room and consultation office were in the basement of his house, snuggled back in some trees on a peninsula. One could not see the ocean there, but you knew it was not far away. When I drove in yesterday, I discovered that my usual parking place was inaccessible due to a branch that had fallen there. The previous day a storm with high winds had pushed through the area. I got out of my car and pulled this branch out of my parking place. I could have parked elsewhere, but the place where the branch was, was mine. I had always parked there. Paul's wife noticed me

moving the branch. She waved at me from the window upstairs, and thanked me.

I told Sanford about what happened with my probation officer. He told me that the probation officer had called him and told him that I had been reported by an anonymous person from my writing group. That's how I discovered that fact.

When I discussed the fact that I wouldn't be seeing him again, I started crying. And when I actually said goodbye and left the office, I began once again. I cry so much these days.

I am beginning a new section of my journal in order to still be a teller of the truth. I wonder whether it is it important to tell the truth if there is no one to hear. So I ask the question all beginning writers are instructed to ask: who is my audience? It's not easy to answer this. Before, when I wrote my journal, it was to Sanford or to Boo. I won't be writing to Sanford anymore, and I tell Boo what I think as we go along. So to whom am I writing? To a hypothetical grandson, possibly – one that may never exist, and if he does, with whom I may never have a relationship? To a lover of boys in some future, possibly freer time? To the Buddha? I don't know really. To whomever it might concern. That's the best I can do for the moment. It seems likely, of course, that it will be to no one.

The final question as I embark on this new journey has to do with the issue of degradation. Am I degrading myself by accepting this option? It feels degrading, of course, to agree to go to one of their sex offender treatment programs. Even the kinder programs that are not deliberately set up to be degrading are attacks on the dignity of the participants. But is that just a matter of external degradation? If I really have only alternatives that are more degrading and more harmful to others, it would not seem to be inwardly degrading.

10/18/03 – A pinch of incense

The question is whether one should throw a pinch of incense on the fire at the altar of Caesar. Some years ago I read "The Martyrdom of Perpetua and Felicita." I had to be impressed by the courage of these people, if not by their theology. Even during some of the most severe persecutions, all that was required to avoid martyrdom and continue with whatever passed for normal life in those days was to drop a pinch of incense into the hot coals at the altar of Caesar. I'm not sure I remember, or ever knew, the exact set-up at these altars. In

my mind I see a statue of the current Emperor of Rome, and beneath it a brazier full of hot coals upon which the incense was to be dropped. However accurate the details of this picture may be, that was the gist of it. A simple pinch of incense, and you got away scot-free. Shameful. All Sunday-School-trained children have heard at some point of the early church martyrs, and they know what judgments to pass on those who gave their pinch of incense: shameful.

Of course these good children know that they have dropped their pinch of incense into the braziers provided by Caesar. Well, let's be honest. They have thrown fists full of incense into the braziers provided by their peer groups, by their parents, by their teachers, and by all the representatives of society in their lives. If they hadn't noticed, then some preacher or Sunday school teacher would have pointed it out at some time or other. "When have we thrown our incense on the brazier? Michael?" He hangs his head, pauses, and then confesses. He used bad words in order to impress his peers. A hook of guilt, from which he may never escape, has been set in his flesh. It is no accident that it is the peer group that is generally cited for tempting the child to give his pinch of incense. No church wants to encourage the children to question adult authority. Caesar and the church are getting along very well these days, and we don't want to raise boat-rockers.

Such is our training.

Even though they may sometimes be used in repressive ways, there is a pinch of truth in the pinch of incense stories. We all do betray our essence in our interactions with others. We act as though we are not who we are, do not believe what we believe, do not want what we want, and do not feel what we feel. We do this in order to get along with others. We do it with our bosses, with our parents, with our teachers, with police officers, and with all the authority figures we encounter. We also do it with our friends and our spouses. We give not just pinches but whole fistfuls of incense at the various altars of social expectation. We do not behave like Perpetua and Felicita. We do not allow ourselves to be thrown to the lions and hanged upside down on crosses. We are guilty.

Perhaps now is the time to ask that most fundamental of all questions asked in Sunday school. What would Jesus have done? By consulting a concordance I find we are in luck. There is a biblical passage that speaks directly to this point. The Pharisees are questioning Jesus.

"Tell us therefore, 'What thinkest thou? Is it lawful to give tribute

to Caesar, or not?' But Jesus perceived their wickedness, and said, 'Why tempt me, ye hypocrites? Show me the tribute money.' And they brought him a penny. And he sayeth to them, 'Whose name is this image and superscription?' They said unto him, 'Caesar's.' Then saith he unto them, 'Render unto Caesar the things which are Caesar's and unto God the things that are God's.'"

That's mighty close to recommending that we put that pinch of incense on the altar. And in fact, Jesus is actually doing something of that sort in this little scene. Wily as a serpent, he was. And he recommends this quality to us.

With this little encounter in mind we return to our question: what judgments should we pass on those who throw a pinch of incense on the altar to Caesar? Shameful? Well, not necessarily. It all depends. Yes, that is the answer to this question. It depends. But upon what?

It depends on what our task is. We need a starting point here. A task. Suppose our task is to bring light and warmth into this dark and cold place that is human society. And suppose we believe that we do this by feeding the hungry, clothing the naked, ministering to those in prison, providing help to the sick, and listening to those who have stories they need to tell. I'm not pushing this agenda. A person can pick whatever life task he or she wants. But suppose a person picked a life task similar to the one I have just described. What then? Does refusing to put a pinch of incense in the brazier further this agenda? Well, again, it depends. It depends on the probable consequences of one's actions in a specific situation. If refusing to throw the pinch of incense in the fire will in fact increase the light and warmth in this world, then one should refuse to do so. If throwing it, on the other hand, does the trick, then it should be thrown.

The ideal that I would uphold is the Bodhisattva as a political activist. The Bodhisattva would point out that there are many powerful images of political action, such as Arjuna the warrior, arrayed in his armor, standing in his chariot, facing the enemy and preparing for mortal combat. Jesus parrying with the Pharisees. The Maccabees resisting oppression with guerrilla warfare. The sage who acts like water that never directly confronts or struggles with anything in its way, as described by Lao Tzu. These models suggest very different kinds of action or non-action. Which is correct? Once again, it depends. Different situations require different responses. If one follows the example of Perpetua and Felicita as to when it would be best to give

onto Caesar, one may fail to effect an increase of light and warmth in the world.

Perhaps it is our identifications that get in our way of seeing what is required. I am this or that kind of person, so I will do this. We are identified with a particular way of being in the world. Wouldn't we be more effective Bodhisattvas if we did not feel so compelled to be this or that sort of person? This is essentially what Krishna tells Arjuna on the eve of battle.

There are situations that require of us that we behave like Perpetua. There are others in which we need to be like water, flowing around and through and under the obstacles – refusing to struggle with them. It's a question of strategies. What will change things?

It seems to me that we need to approach the world with a strong bias against the use of violence. Only rarely does the sort of battle that Arjuna is preparing to fight lead to the increase of light and warmth in the world. There is a more subtle kind of violence in Perpetua's action as well. Perhaps it was called for. I don't know. But to act in a manner that will predictably bring down the violence of Caesar on one's head does increase the amount of violence in the world. In this case it was at least on one level successful. The sort of fearless self-sacrifice evidenced by the martyrs undoubtedly played a role in the eventual victory of Christianity in the Roman Empire, and following this, the ascendancy of the church throughout the middle ages. But the church then became Caesar. It's not altogether clear that this was a good thing. So at best, Perpetua's sacrifice led to mixed results.

What is clear is that, if I follow the path of Perpetua in my present situation, I will be martyred. I will end up either out in the woods with a bag over my head or back in prison. It is hard to see how either of these outcomes will increase the light or warmth in the world. Therefore I must throw my pinch of incense on the altar. Handfuls of it if necessary. I will go to the treatment group. I must give up my identification of myself as the one who is always out there, speaking his mind and letting the pieces fall out where they will. For the most part I feel that this was not a bad way to be. But a new challenge has come into my life. I must learn to be water.

10/19/03 – Rubber bands
[I told Boo about my decision not to commit suicide and to become – to use her term for it – a "gopher" – which is to say one who

lives underground.]

Two nights ago while Boo and I were out doing our evening stroll around 9 PM, she began talking continuously. This was unusual for her. She recalled a variety of key points in her personal history that pertained to her choice to live as a "gopher," as someone who lives in hiding from the social world, and she talked about how she would handle the situation I am in, especially with the group. Her comments seemed to have two underlying messages: 1) living as a gopher isn't all that bad, and 2) here's how you do it. She was the welcome wagon, welcoming me to Gopherville.

She seemed to be trying to resolve something in her mind, or perhaps in our relationship. I was puzzled. Finally after we got back to the house and were sitting on my couch, I observed that it seemed almost like she was wanting to do the treatment group task for me. Yes, she said. She wished she could do that. Also back when I was in prison she had fantasies that she could come and take my place some of the time so that we could share the difficulty.

Whatever was driving her seemed resolved.

But last night she started in again, and again there was a drivenness about her talk. She recalled that she first started living as a gopher as a way of escaping from her mother's insistence that she be somebody other than who she was. Then she recalled events, such as her hospitalization in Boston from liver failure, and K Street [a private mental hospital she was in briefly for an acute psychotic break many years ago], when she had to make special efforts to maintain her gopher manner of being in the world. I felt she was trying to teach me how one would do it. I explained that it wasn't too hard to see how one would go about doing this. For me that was not the problem. The problem was overcoming my intense emotional resistance to doing it. It felt like a betrayal of who I was. But I went on to say that I had pretty well resolved this in my mind. That's what the last two journal entries, which I had shared with her, were all about. She nodded and confessed that she had not had the time to read the second one. I encouraged her to do so. They were my efforts to resolve this issue in my mind – to persuade myself that it was all right to choose this path for myself, at least with regard to the "treatment" group. I felt I was pretty successful. I did in fact feel okay about it. When the Gestapo is at the door, it's okay to lie. "No. we don't have any Jews here. Can't stand them." Reading those papers, I felt, would further reassure her

that I really was in a different place.

I felt that my explanation might have helped her resolve this issue in her mind, but when we got back to the house and were sitting on the couch, she continued with her gopher stories. The issue was somehow not yet sorted out for her.

"You are afraid that I just won't be able to pull it off in the group, aren't you?" I asked. "That I won't be able to lie. That's why you want to do it for me."

"It's what I've always done," she said. "I'm like a duck in water in that kind of situation. It doesn't feel degrading to me."

"And if I can't pull it off, you think I'll end up killing myself."

She nodded. "That's what you said you would do if they made you go to the group."

"And I gave it a lot of consideration," I said.

"I know that," she said.

"But I am in a different place now. That's what those journal entries are about."

"I couldn't read them," she confessed. "I couldn't get past the point where you bought the rubber bands."

"I see," I said. "I can understand that."

She wanted to know where the rubber bands were. I told her.

"Let me have them," she said.

I took the package of thick rubber bands out of the plastic container where I keep the miscellaneous odds and ends connected with my writing. "Here they are," I said, handing them to her.

She commented on how useful they looked but said that she really just wanted to get rid of them.

გა

This morning, about an hour ago, Boo came to my room. She said she couldn't sleep. I asked if I had made too much noise.

"No," she said. "It was very quiet in your room." Her implication was that it was too quiet. "And your light was off," she added.

I explained that almost every morning I turn the light off, and try to get quiet. When it's dark, I use a candle.

She nodded and came over to hug me.

"Didn't you read the papers [journal entries]?" I asked.

Yes, she had read them. But I could see that they had not per-

suaded her that I really was in a different place now.

"I really won't do that to myself," I said. "You won't come in here some morning and find something grotesque."

I think she was re-assured. She went back to bed.

10/20/03 – Hunger strike

Yesterday evening while we were out walking we talked some about Phoebe [our grown daughter who was now living with her significant other in St. Paul]. We have both experienced Phoebe withdrawing from us. With Boo this withdrawal began to occur after Phoebe got involved with Matthew. This is understandable and is undoubtedly to the good. That's her new primary person. But her withdrawal from Boo became more complete after I came back home. I don't think this is an accident. Her withdrawal from me occurred after I got into the trouble that sent me to prison. It didn't happen right off, actually. But after I went to prison, I began to be aware that she did not really want to visit, and the letters became more infrequent and more distant in their content. It seemed to me that this was connected with the Columbus [where I once lived and where my mother still resided] scene. I think that essentially she was drawn into a slightly modified version of my mother's view of the scene – which was that I had committed an unforgivable act. At least it was unforgivable if I failed to show more remorse for it than I did. Phoebe is inside the circle of acceptable humanity. I am on the outside. We talk across that wall.

Boo got to talking about her own isolation from the larger community. She had been to church this morning and talked about her discomfort there. She goes because Mary [the choir director] wants her to, and she feels some loyalty toward her despite their fundamental differences. But then she talked about her father visiting her while she was in the hospital. [This was a few years before. Boo had an eating problem that caused some health problems. I had tried to avoid the label "anorexia nervosa" both to avoid the *Reader's Digest* kind of stereotyping that goes with that label, and because her situation did not, in fact, fit the label in a number of ways. Also, because we both feel that labels are handles for society to get a hold of you and control you.] Langly [her doctor] told her father the diagnosis – "anorexia nervosa" – and he was livid. He came into her room and said "I thought you were really sick, but you just have this anorexia thing."

I said something about the fact that her "illness" was a consequence of her differences with her family. It was part of a struggle that was essentially political in nature. In that sense her father was right about one thing – it was not an illness in the usual sense of the term. It was political. It was connected with her effort to emancipate herself from him, from Georgia, and from her membership in the upper class. In a sense she was on a hunger strike.

She couldn't see the connection. I'm not sure I do either – at least I am still unclear as to the exact meaning. It was not as straightforward as "I will not eat until you make some concessions," which is the usual concern in hunger strikes. Or perhaps it was. The concession she was looking for was that she should be allowed to be in the world who she was in her soul. In her soul she was a socialist, a mystic, and a universalist. Was it likely that such a weed would be allowed to grow in Georgia soil? [Her family were very well-to-do Republicans.] Certainly not in the gardens of the wealthy. She longed to escape and join the blacks or the white trash. Maybe she would be allowed to grow in one of their backyards. In the world she was born into, she could only hide.

Shame prevents her from seeing the dignity of her struggle.

As I see it, the issue she struggled with back then was essentially the issue that has come to a head for me much more recently. We cannot manifest in the world who we are in our souls. We cannot bring who we are in the implicate order into the explicate order. With me it was my love of boys that catapulted me out of the world of social respectability. Once we experience the overwhelming power and hostility of the world, we retreat back in our souls and try to protect what we are there as best we can. Once we do this, to be seen becomes the dangerous thing. So now we both live underground. With her it is a familiar place.

me to pleasure him. Instead he chose the video of a boy masturbating a man. "I can do that," he said. He did that thing that kids do so well where they arch their backs and slide down to the ground.

"Are you sure?"

By the time he gave his answer, "I can do it," he'd already unzipped my pants, stuck his hand in, and was stumbling about in search of the hole in my boxers. He pulled my penis out and with both hands grasping it tightly he began masturbating me, almost expertly, slowly at first but gradually going a little faster until, without meaning to, I climaxed and ejaculated. He looked at me with wide-eyed wonderment, one hand still holding my penis, and the other raised out palm up, as if he were asking silently, "What's this and why didn't you warn me?"

It was very cute. I sent him to clean his hands, and cleaned myself up with another wipe. From there we hung out and, if memory serves, I introduced him to Power Ranger, which we watched until his mother called him so they could go home. He cried and begged to spend the night with me. It wasn't convenient for his mother, so the answer was no. Before he left, I pulled him aside for a private moment. I knelt in front of him, cupped his face in my hands, kissed him gently on the lips, and said, "Your uncle loves you very much." I also told him when he comes back we'll hang out again and do whatever he wants. Then I hugged him tight and he calmed a bit and went home peacefully.

From that day every time I saw him privately I dropped to my knees, cupped his face, kissed him softly on his lips and told him how very much I love him, because I do love him and because I felt that it was important for him to know that someone loves him. I couldn't think of a more important contribution I could make to his life.

When I explained to him why I didn't want him looking for porn on my computer, about a year and change after that incident, he begged me to teach him how to search safely. I told him that it's not easy to learn to recognize malicious sites (I called them "bad sites" for his benefit), that it takes experience and trial and error, and in the mean time one of his errors could blow up my computer. "What could I get from it?" I asked him rhetorically. I was pulling his leg a bit. I didn't actually want anything from him.

Apparently he'd already thought it through and knew exactly what he was willing to pay. He answered "I'll rub your dick again." (I

hadn't taught him that word. He was learning a lot from the Internet on his own.) His answer caught me by surprise. I didn't think he even remembered doing that with me-to me. But he did. And more than that, he knew what the act was. He understood it. And he still wanted to do it. So we made an agreement.

Our agreement was simple and we both gained from it. Every time he wanted to look for porn, he masturbated me first. Then he got unrestricted but supervised access to my computer, plus my lessons on safe computer searches and answers to his questions about sex and sexual acts, most of which I answered before he asked to save his pride. He was grateful for that and after a while his questions, likes and dislikes flowed freely from him. We were both happy with our little arrangement, which held for two years until my arrest.

Banana bread

I've got a lot of mixed feelings about the memory of making banana bread with Tobias the day before my arrest. I'd known him for two years at that point. It was just getting to the point where I could really nurture him and teach him. His father (who was my friend and only had custody of him on odd weekends) loved him, but taught him a lot of macho "boys-don't-cry" crap which is damaging to any kid. He was also often impatient and short-tempered with the poor kid. I was working to undo some of that damage. I showed him patience, love and affection which he didn't receive anywhere else, and which I feel he and every kid needs. It's the little moments that mean the most to both children and adults. He loved to sit on my lap while we worked on a video game together. (He had sharp eyes and often saw things I missed.) I live right across the street from Flushing Meadows Park, home of the 1964 World Fair and the semi-famous Unisphere. I took him to the park a few times to see the Unisphere, kick a ball around or learn to fly a kite.

The day we made banana bread was a very good day. He spent the previous night with me and slept with me in my bed. He was always a ball of energy, up at the crack of dawn. (I'm more of a noon riser.) He woke me up to fire up a video game for him. We played games for a few hours (he repeatedly refused breakfast – he never ate much). Then we hit a couple of yard sales we saw postings for within a couple of blocks of my house. I bought him a vintage lava lamp he saw and fell in love with, for five dollars. It still worked and polished

up real nice. I often wonder if he still has it, and if so, does he still think fondly of me when he looks at it?

When we got back to my place I showered while he played another game. When I finished my shower we made the awesome banana bread. I taught him – or at least I tried to teach him – to throw darts while it baked. I don't think he hit the board once. There were plenty of little holes in the wall. We had lots of fun though. After we enjoyed the fruits of our labor with some ice cold milk, it was time to take him home. On the way home he refined his theory that I'm actually an elaborate robot in disguise, That was the last time I saw him.

The FBI raided my home a few hours later.

I guess that brings us to the mixed feelings. I'm very sentimental and very nostalgic. Because of that sentimentality and nostalgia I can to look back on days like the one I just described often, and when I do the feelings are intense. I can't say if said feelings are more or less intense than they would be in the average person. I have no standard measurement for the intensity of others' feelings, so it's difficult to gauge. I know the feelings of love and loss are profound and often overwhelming. And I don't just feel what I've lost. I feel what Tobias has lost as well; all the things I would have taught him and all that the system and the therapists and even his parents have taken from him since my arrest. That's the part that hurts most.

It's interesting that you referred to Tobias as my friend in your letter. While I was locked up in M.D.C. Brooklyn going through the pretrial motions, my lawyer managed to convince my judge to bring in a couple of top-notch shrinks to give me "therapy" (attempted indoctrination) while I waited for sentencing. They drilled it into me that anyone who hasn't reached that magical moment of sudden clarity and enlightenment that hits like a Mack truck at exactly midnight on one's 18th birthday does not have capacity to be anyone's friend or lover; that they can only ever be dependent. I disagree. Tobias, for example, thought of me as a friend, and I thought the same of him. I don't see how having to hold his hand while crossing the street or fight him to get his teeth brushed before bed has anything to do with the bond we had. We shared more than a few intimate moments together and we always made each other laugh. Right to the end he conspired and begged to stay at my place for the weekend and I was always happy to receive him.

Chapter 17 – **No Parole For Love**

by S.R.

One of the nice things about this selection is the author's sense of humor. He describes many different aspects of his life, from his experiences growing up, to some of the things that happened after he was incarcerated.

৪৩

Baby pigeons

I'm one of the few people alive who has ever seen a baby pigeon. During the seven months I was in a cell in the county jail, I watched two pigeons build a nest on the ledge outside my six-inch window. Pablo and Lefty is what I called them. She (Lefty) had no right leg, but that did not slow her down at all. She laid two eggs. The nest was less than a foot from where my head was. A combination of light, shadow, and glare, and years of grime prevented me from being seen. The eggs hatched. Lefty was an attentive mother, while Pablo flew security. One day a blue plastic bag from Walmart was blown up to the ledge by an updraft. It was an impressive sight to see Pablo defend the nest. Actually, I think he was trying to mate with it. Pablo would mount Lefty often, but be pecked off. After a while the little ones would leave the nest and walk along the windowsill. The window ran the length of the cell but was only six inches tall. Outside, the opening was larger with plenty of room for them to stand. The babies were reluctant to fly. Lefty would try and try to force them off the ledge but they were determined. Pablo would try to climb on their backs, only to be fought off by Lefty. I guess he and I share a common attraction to youth. Finally, they flew off. I was blessed to get to see the whole thing.

Wrestling

When my son was 10 through 12, I helped out at his wrestling practices. The team was run through the "Boys and Girls Club" – mostly lower income, single-parent kids. They craved attention more than anything else, and I loved to give it out freely. One day I met a boy named Eric. He was a tiny little kid. At 12, he wrestled at 61 pounds while my son was 118. Still, they were good friends. Eric lived with his grandma. His dad came and went, and he never knew his mom. Because I was a coach, father and schoolteacher, his grandma trusted me. I even tutored him in math. I was taking my son to an out-of-state tournament, and Eric really wanted to go. The club would pay his entry fee. I had room in my car and in the hotel room I was renting. He only needed money for food. After my explaining this to the grandma, she gave me $40 and asked me if it was enough. I assured her it was. If not, I'd pay for his food, but I didn't tell her that.

So I pulled them out of school on Friday at noon to make the 6 to 7 PM weigh-ins. It was a 6-hour drive, but all highway. I stopped at Arby's to get a stack of beef-n-cheddar – 5 for $5.55. I got 10 of them, four for me, and three for each of them. Also a large-mouth Pepsi for each of us. We were off.

An hour later Eric said "Hey Greg, I need to pee."

"Already?" I asked.

"I drank that Pepsi."

"So use the bottle."

"What?"

"That's why my dad gets large-mouth bottles," my son added.

"No way. I'll wait."

Driving a little Hyundai, I got good gas mileage. An hour later, I still had half a tank, but my bladder was full. I took my bottle, and doing 75 miles an hour, I refilled it.

"Oh, gross!" Eric said.

"That's one of the pleasures of being a man."

"So we really aren't going to stop?"

"Dad never stops at above a quarter tank."

"Fine, don't look."

"Nothing there to see."

"Well, just don't look.."

Finally Eric relieved himself.

We got there at 6:30 PM, went to weigh-ins, and checked into

Boxers not briefs

My son had a friend who was raised with really good manners. When I would take a group of boys out for a 99-cent, 1/3 slab of ribs and fries after midnight, Rick would actually use a knife and fork while the other boys ate like savages. Despite his oddities, my son liked him, and so did I, so he was always invited on outings, though he often could not attend. His family was into " TOGETHERNESS." One night he actually got his mother's permission to attend the group sleepover. My son had invited a couple dozen friends over to spend the weekend. Rick was allowed to come from Friday after school until noon on Saturday.

On Friday night, the boys mostly played Mario Super Smash Brothers Melee on the Game-Cube. With a 2CD projector, I turned the wall into a 114 inch screen and they set up a 32-man tournament (using a few computer players to fill in the empty slots). Since it was summer in Las Vegas, most of the boys wore what they planned to sleep in, or in other words, just a pair of boxer shorts. They did not give it a second thought, much to my pleasure. The only exception was Rick, who was fully dressed and looking rather withdrawn.

I got him by himself to ride with me to get more soda pop (which we did not need) and I had this conversation with him.

"Rick, are you okay?"

"Yeah."

"You seem like something is on your mind."

"No"

"Are you uncomfortable because everyone is in boxers?"

"No."

"I ask because you're fully dressed."

"I can't wear them"

"Boxers? Why not?"

"Mama buys briefs."

"Oh, would you like to borrow some from my son?"

"Eeew."

"What if I got him a new three pack and gave you one."

"Really?"

"Sure."

So we bought a pack. Rick picked out one, and as soon as we got back, he dashed into the bathroom and came out wearing the boxers. He was as happy as he could be.

On Saturday night Rick's mom called to thank me for hosting her son, but she added, "it's the strangest thing. Rick came home wearing someone else's underwear." I told her the whole story. She was amazed that boys that age would actually wear boxers. She thanked me for being so kind to Rick.

I cannot but wonder if she thought about this event when news of my arrest became public. She could have imagined all kinds of reasons her son needed new underpants, but the truth was as simple as he was embarrassed to wear briefs in front of his friends.

Cub Scouts

I was always a socially awkward child, basically friendless. I simply never learned the social skills that most boys have. When I was 8 years old, the family had moved to a new town, and my mom did what she could to improve the situation. She signed me up to be a Cub Scout. It didn't work. On the first meeting at my new den, it was a warm day in November. It was the den mother's child's birthday. The meeting was basically a party for him. I was not even introduced to the other boys. One of the gifts he got was a set of toy guns. There were six guns in the set, and I was the seventh boy in the den. When they decided to play "army" they split into two teams of three. I got to be a dead body on the battlefield.

The next week's meeting, the den mother's older son was home from college. He had been a high school quarterback, so instead of scouting activities they played three on three football. The older brother was permanent quarterback. What to do with point number seven? I would hike the ball, then wait for the next play to hike it again. The next two meetings were spent making a holiday craft. We glued pasta on styrofoam cones and painted them gold as gifts to give our mother at the big pack-meeting Christmas party. After a month in Cub Scouts, I never learned the oath, salute, handshake, law of the pack or anything.

My parents could not attend the Christmas party. They had other plans, but I was dropped off on their way out. I sat there, watching all the boys get badges, beads, arrows, etc. I still had not earned my "Gregcat" which requires all of 10 minutes and three signatures. There was a special visitor: Santa Claus came. In his bag was a gift wrapped "Cub Scout pocketknife" for each boy. They were called up one by one. I wasn't called. The den mother forgot to notify the pack

leader of my existence. One would think they would have had one or two extras ("Oops, the name tag must have fallen off of this one") but nope. Then we were all brought on-stage with our styrofoam and noodle thing to give to our moms. My mom was not there. I'll never forget the pain of that walk home – overlooked by Santa, and not one award earned. I threw the craft into the trash and cried. Thirty-three years later I still feel raw from it. I quit Cub Scouts, but when my ninth birthday came up, my mom allowed me to have a big party. I invited each and every kid in my third grade class, all 18 of them. On the day of the party not one kid came. My mom told my sisters to invite a couple of her friends over for cake and ice cream, as if that would help.

My 16th birthday

I had found a place to fit in high school. Like any other heavyset kid, I joined the football team. I hated practice, and even the games, but the hero worship from the "Pop Warner kids" somehow made it all worth it. Well, one of my fellow offensive linemen had a birthday the same weekend as mine. We decided to have a huge party: pig roasting on a spit, kegs of beer – a typical high school bash. Joe, the other kid, was popular in school. He said he would invite everyone, and he did too. He just did not tell people that it was a dual birthday. No one knew it was my party also.

I was never a drinker but I pretended to do so, just to fit in. I nursed one red Solo cup of beer all night, but would act drunker and drunker as the night wore on. The plan was that after the people left, I would spend the night at Joe's house to help him clean up the next day before his mom got home. We were on his mother's bed, playing grab-ass, and one thing leading to another, I ended up giving him a blow job. I was not out of the closet, but we were drunk, so it didn't count, according to the "guy code." When I finished, Joe said "I'm such a shit. Why are you so good to me, and I treat you like crap. I don't know why I didn't tell people it was your birthday too. How can I make it up to you? I know. Tell me who you like. I'll hook you up with her."

I told him I wasn't interested in a hook-up.

"Come on Greg, anyone at all. Just say the name." I took a chance and jokingly said I liked his brother Dylan. Dylan was five years younger, a Pop Warner football player, and really cute. "Really?

Why? Are you into guys? It's cool that you are. I just never knew. Well Dylan's in our room. Go ahead and have fun."

Joe and Dylan shared a room. Joe had the top bunk and Dylan the bottom. I wasn't sure if Joe was serious or not but I went into the room. Dylan was sound asleep, wearing briefs and a t-shirt. He was curled up in a fetal position. I knelt next to the bed, and rubbed his leg. This was enough to get him to roll over onto his back. He had a noticeable erection which I began to play with. He seemed cool with it, and I lowered my face and took it into my mouth, right over the briefs. His hands pushed down his own briefs, which I took as an invitation. I was kneeling and bent over, not in a good position, so I picked him up and put him on the top bunk. I removed his shorts from his ankles, stood up between his knees, and took him into my mouth. I began to masturbate while I sucked him and too soon I had an orgasm, ejaculating on Dylan's pillow. Being a typical 16-year-old, I was done. Dylan got dressed and went to sleep. I slept in Joe's bed.

We never ever spoke of that night. I don't know if Joe was too drunk to remember, upset that I knew, shocked that I would mess around with the kids, or jealous that I shared his brother. We sort of grew apart. Dylan would ask me at practice why I did not visit Joe anymore. I actually think he missed me.

I like lesbians

One of my son's friends was a boy named Aaron. At the age of 12, he was all of 59 pounds. The law requires kids who are under 60 pounds to be in a safety seat, but every time I took him anywhere, he refused to use one. Aaron was really a funny kid. He could make me laugh. Being a strawberry blond with freckles, combined with his tiny size, he was as cute as could be.

My son, Sam, and most of his friends, would wear boxer shorts as pajamas. Aaron preferred to wear gray briefs, but he made no distinction. He wore them as if they were baggy boxers, with no shame. I really loved the way he filled them out. Like everything else about Aaron, his frontal bulge was tiny. For me, size truly did not matter. Many a night, he would curl up against me to sleep, allowing back rubs, as well as other things. Oddly we never discussed our sex life. I would fondle and suck his dick, and he allowed me to, smiling while I did. Then he came back for more. But there was an unspoken agreement that we both pretended it never happened.

idea what sex was at that age, but while all the boys in my class would hope to see a girl's panties up her skirt, I lived for the chance to get a glimpse of white cotton briefs. Nothing got me more excited, but oddly I lived in fear of mine ever being seen. Having to dress out for physical education in junior high was a really difficult time.

As I grew older, most boys discovered girls, and I never understood the attraction. But as boys tried to look their best to impress them, I enjoyed those efforts myself. At least I did at first. In high school, as zits, facial hair and muscles appeared, I realized I was not "gay," as men held no interest for me, but I always felt some attraction for the smooth face and slender hips of a boy. Naturally I could never admit to my feelings, so I pushed them deep inside of me and lived a lie. To hide from the truth, I got married at 18, had a child at 19, and filed bankruptcy at 23. Life was difficult, to say the very least.

As my son grew older he started having friends over, and life was wonderful. I was "one of the gang" among his friends, and grew to love some of them very deeply. I wanted to share my feelings, and to do so physically seemed natural. Hugs and cuddles became back scratches and massages. This led to the fondling of their penises and eventually oral sex. In Nevada, that carries a life sentence, so here I am.

Since I will never get out of prison, I see no reason to try to change. In some ways, being in here allows me the freedom to be myself. I do not know how much harm is caused from sexual contact with boys, but I am sure no harm can come from my having the fantasy. I can now look at the beauty of boys without worry or fear.

Please do not think my only attraction to boys is what is between their legs. That is simply not the case. My only sexual attraction is toward boys, but I would prefer a good conversation. My happiest memory is floating in "the lazy river" at a water park, sharing an inner tube with a sixth-grade boy as he told me all about his favorite book, *Where the Red Fern Grows*. It took the entire afternoon, and I was in heaven. I grew to love him deeper than I had ever felt love before. When I was arrested in 2003, this boy, who was then 12, never told anyone about us. Sadly I was selfish, and began to groom other boys, and one of them told.

Now, in 2011, the one I first loved came forward. As I understand it, he came home from his Latter Day's Saints mission and had an interview with his bishop. He admitted to his bishop that he thought

he was gay. Being homosexual and a Mormon is not allowed. When asked why he thought he was gay, he said it was because of how much he had enjoyed what he and I shared. That naturally lead to questions and then new charges. So I'm back in the court system once again. It will not affect my parole date, as I will never get out as it is, but my heart breaks. This boy was told he was the victim of rape, as opposed to the love I really felt for him. I no more raped him than Marcus raped Franklin. [*This allusion is to the book* Marcus and Me, *by Jay Edson.*] Reading that book, I could feel the benefit Franklin felt with regard to this relationship. I'm not saying that every boy should have sex with men, but some should. Some boys are seeking the attention.

Being arrested

On the day I was arrested, July 16, 2002, two detectives came to my door, saying they were investigating allegations of sexual misconduct, and they were going to take my two sons, then ages 12 and 8, "downtown" for questioning; otherwise the boys would be placed into foster care. I was invited to drive myself down. Obviously, my wife and I went to the station, where I was questioned if I had ever molested a boy named A.J. I, at first, did what is natural, and denied it, but then I was confronted with the facts as well as lies: "Look Mr. Henderson, A.J. told us what happened, and a child of that age could only know of such things if they really happened. We know what happened, but we do not know why. We do not think you are an evil person; you are a man who made a mistake. We don't want to send you to jail, we want to get you help, but to help you, we need to know your side." The only knowledge of criminal law I had came from "Law & Order" on T.V., and since no one had read me my rights, I assumed my comments could not harm me. I confessed, and the police said "OK, Mr. Henderson, we now need to place you into custody, and read you your Miranda rights ,..." After hearing my rights, I requested a lawyer when they asked me to repeat my statement for the record, at that point I was transported to jail.

Upon arriving at booking, they asked me to remove all my jewelry. I wore only a plain gold wedding ring, which had not been removed in 15 years and I was nearly 100 pounds lighter then. That ring was stuck. The officer did not care, and tried to pry it off. I was in real pain, begging him to simply cut it off. He said, "Shut the fuck up, pervert, you're not dealing with helpless kids now, I'm in charge." Finally

the ring removed skin from my finger and came off with blood. The ring was never seen again.

Then they asked several questions, one of which was, "Are you considering suicide?" I answered honestly by saying, "There is nothing left to consider, I made up my mind," which was a wrong answer. Off to the suicide, 4-minute watch. First I was stripped, and checked for contraband. "Turn around, show us the bottom of your feet, wiggle your toes, squat, spread your cheeks and cough, face us, run your hands through your mouth, lift your tongue, behind your ears, lift your balls, now lift your ... well ... I guess you call that little thing a dick." Come on, I may only have an average white guy issue, but when cold, shrinkage is real, and when afraid, it is like an ostrich; the damn thing tried to hide. Still, at that point in my life, did the cop really need to go there?

Now I was buck-naked in an empty cell, no mat, no blanket, but a really bright light and every 4 minutes a knock on the glass, where I had to move to prove I was alive. Despite all that, I developed a plan to kill myself. If I did a headstand in the steel toilet, when I fell over, my skull should catch on the rim and break my neck. The only thing that saved me was a camera in the corner of the cell. I envisioned my fat, naked body getting into position, flapping around on the ground like a fish, and the video tape being played at the Metro Christmas Party. No way!

Two days later, I saw my lawyer. I assumed it was a public defender, but he said that my mother had hired him. I was surprised she knew, but he told me she saw it on the news. My bail was set at $50,000, which my mom posted at 10% through a bondsman. I would have been out the next day, except the grand jury indictment was unsealed, and the judge raised my bail to 1 million dollars. I never saw the streets, and my mom never got back her 5 thousand in cash.

In court, the media was there, taking pictures of all the inmates in the gallery. They were wondering why, as they did not see anyone of interest. Then the bailiff explained it. He said, "You're the child-molesting teacher, right?" and pointed me out to the photographer. They were able to get lovely pictures and video of it all.

That night, I was transferred from the suicide ward, and sent to a housing module. There were no cells open, I was assigned a cot in the tier area. At 6 PM the tier opened. A hundred inmates came out of the cells, and turned on the TV. There was my face with the caption

"Teacher in court for sex abuse of boys, details at 11." I went to the guard and asked if I was in danger. He asked why and I pointed to the TV. His response was "OH SHIT! LOCKDOWN! Emergency Lockdown!" I was escorted to protective custody – a unit of sex offenders, pimps and transvestites. Even in there I was recognized. I had hit a trifecta of high profile. I was a Mormon, I was a school teacher, and I molested a Cub Scout. Even sex offenders gave me a hard time, thinking my crime must be far worse than theirs, as they were not on the news. I think they were glad to have me, as I drew all the heat from them.

During the 17 months it took to convict me (Nevada courts are not only harsh, but painfully slow) I developed a nasty toothache. Since a county jail is considered to be "short-term housing" the only dental services offered are extractions. A simple drill and fill could save the tooth, so my family paid for transportation to a private dentist. On the day of the appointment, I was dressed in a navy blue jumpsuit, with bright orange shoes, ankle chains and waist shackles. Complete with a two-guard escort, we drove to the dentist's office. We went into the full waiting room like any other patient. I was told to find a seat. There was only one empty spot, next to a boy of about 10 and his mom. I sat down, kept my eyes diverted and my mouth shut, but the kid noticed me. He said "Mom ... mom?" She replied with an uninterested grunt, but he continued, "Mom? Will I have to be chained up to see the dentist also?"

She looked at me with horror and said to her son, "You mind your own business. Don't worry about why that man is in chains."

The guards, hearing this, said to her, "Lady, if you knew why he is in chains I bet you would move your kid."

She thought about it for a moment, and decided she needed a cigarette, and dragged her son outside to the parking lot. The guards smiled and sat in the two empty seats. I'm pretty sure that was their ultimate goal.

The dentist ordered a "dental soft" diet for 24 hours, so that night, I got a special dinner. The menu called for chicken patty, creamed corn and cake. I got chicken patty, peas, and cake. I guess the creamed corn is not on the list of dental soft. Go figure, it looks like "pre-chewed food" to me.

When I finally got to prison, I inquired about programs or counseling for sexual offenders. The answer I received is that I could

sign up for S.T.O.P., which stands for Sexual Treatment Offenders Programs, when I was within two years from release. I asked what I should do until then and the prison psychologist's exact words were, "There are plenty of rocks to kick on the yard." I did join a "treatment" group of inmates, run by inmates with no staff oversight. It was a joke. When they asked me why I committed my crime, I said, "I am now, and have always been, sexually attracted to boys. The abuse occurred when my selfish desires took control of my actions. I did not even consider if I was harming him. I did what I wanted to do." The response I got was that I needed to stop making excuses to justify my crime and be honest with myself. I was also told that if I wanted to be attracted to women I could; sexual preference is a choice. In the group, I was the only person who molested boys. There was a Peeping Tom, two pimps and a rapist of grown women. Somehow these men could offer insight to my thinking.

Reading *Galaxy*

I am re-reading *A Galaxy of No-Stars*, since my first time was an all-night binge. [This is a novel by Jay Edson.] I find much of myself in the pages. Of all the characters, I relate mostly to Kyle. When I was in high school, my best friend was named Thomas. Thomas and I were both social outcasts, and often talked about our feelings. Like most adolescents, sex was of great concern to both of us, as neither of us had ever been with a girl. That changed when Thomas started to date a girl named Corra. I was very much the third wheel, but I tried to cope, and treasured what little time Thomas gave to me. We still talked about being the only virgins left in our class, and I felt oddly good knowing that he and Corra had not yet gone to that level. I did my best to befriend Corra, and accept Thomas' new situation. Then, at some point, Thomas dumped Corra for Kim. Kim did not like me at all, and tension grew. I was still friends with Thomas when Kim was not around, but I also talked a lot with Corra. When she told me how hurt she was to have given up her virginity to learn Thomas was cheating on her, I was crushed. Thomas was still proclaiming to me to be a virgin. I felt his lie to be a betrayal. The worst part was that instead of understanding my pain, he openly flaunted his relationship with Kim, who told him to choose her or me. I lost. To this day, I never spoke to Thomas again, not that I didn't make a total ass of myself trying to.

Reading about Christopher and Melissa [two characters in *A Galaxy of No-Stars*] got me thinking of that painful time in my past, but unlike Christopher, who got that wonderful letter from his mom, I had no one to talk to. To this day I feel alone in many ways. Being who I am makes life very lonely. It is true that every landscape is beautiful, and there are no abnormal mountains, but in today's society, a man like me, who is attracted to boys, is considered abnormal. [The reference to "abnormal mountains" refers to the section in *A Galaxy...* in which Christopher's mother compares our complex sexual orientations, no two of which are the same, as "mountains."]

The Hole

[*In this section the writer is responding to a question about what it is like in the "hole." The question emphasized the value of very concrete descriptions. So this was written in brief sections throughout a 48-hour period.*]

The best way I can describe life in "the hole" is that it is reversal of sleep/wake cycle. Instead of interrupting my day with a nap now and then, my sleep is interrupted with periods of being awake. I am always waking from a nap, sleeping, or getting ready to take a nap.

In the month of November, my cell door was opened up exactly two times. One was to be locked in the shower stall while two guards tossed my cell, the other was for a trip to the eye doctor. The cell search sucked! Every letter, file folder, envelope, or paper was dumped in a pile on my cell floor and mixed with two active lawsuits, discovery from my criminal cases, and personal writings. It was a mess and a half. The one lawsuit has over 500 pages of pleading by itself, the most recent being the order from the Nevada Supreme Court that I be provided Pro Bono counsel for oral arguments in my appeal. Now to wait and see if a lawyer will accept my case. :) Anyways, it was a real mess to clean up. My trip to the eye doctor resulted in him ordering me bifocals. I am still waiting for them to come in. Then I'll be able to read and write in a more "normal" way. Currently I take off my glasses, close one eye and get the other eye within 6 inches of the word on paper. To write, I need to move the pad as I go. It makes writing really tedious.

The reason I continue to write is to fill my deep need to communicate. I do not yell out of my door to other inmates because it only gets the cat-calls of "CHOMO." Even other people who have sex

crimes will join in, to steer the heat away from them. So I very much keep to myself, and go crazy with loneliness.

I guess the best way to share my life is to account for the time as I go through a 48-hour period. I can't really say a day, as my schedule is "off." I hope it does not get to be too boring. To begin, let me make you aware of my clock setting/geography. Ely is on the east edge of Nevada, which is Pacific time zone, but since all of my T.V. comes from Salt Lake City, I set my clock to Mountain time. It is now 7:20 AM on Friday. My breakfast and lunch just came through the food slot. Scrambled eggs / hashbrown potato / corn casserole, oatmeal, french fries, powdered milk on the tray, and 4 slices white bread, 2 slices bologna, pretzels, orange, 1 mayo & 1 mustard in a sack. The powdered milk upsets my innards, so I do not eat it. I ate the oatmeal (3 spoonfuls), french fries (13), and casserole (8 spoonfuls). I am waiting for the guard to open my food slot to pick-up my tray and bring me my Prozac. I will then brush my teeth and go to sleep.

[*Later.*] I waited until 8:45 for the nurse to finally bring me my meds, she was over an hour late. I watched various "morning shows" as I waited. At 9 I turned off the TV finally and rolled over to sleep. I woke up to a knocking at the door. Part of life in the hole is a monthly mental health check-up with a psychologist, mostly to ensure I'm not suicidal. It makes no sense to me. Only a fool would admit to having such thoughts, as the result is being put on suicide watch – being butt naked with no property for days at a time, as every 15 minutes a guard requires you to acknowledge them to ensure you are alive. I was suicidal when I first got arrested and made the mistake of telling the truth. It was 72 hours of pure hell! So, do I contemplate suicide? Of course I do. I'm in prison for life, but for a few reasons, I never act out the idea. The biggest reason is the hope of one day rebuilding some kind of relationship with my sons. Suicide is too FINAL. The other is never knowing what kind of erotic dream might be enjoyed at my next catnap. :) My dreams are so wonderfully enjoyable. Also, I have to acknowledge that at 7 AM and 4 PM, a meal will come, and there might be cookies. I do like cookies!

[*Later.*] Well, I'm awake, but there is snow falling, and it must be building up on the prison satellite dish. As there is no TV reception, I'm missing out on a rerun of Frasier on Lifetime. My 48-hour time-log is now current, so I'll read until I fall asleep.

[*Later.*] It's Friday at 5 PM. Dinner just came and woke me out of

a sound sleep. It was late today. Usually dinner is at 4, so at 4:30 I can watch "Fetch with Ruff Ruffman" on PBS after dinner. Dinner was 2 hotdogs with buns, and chili (9 spoonfuls and way too spicy). For a vegetable we got a mix of pickle-relish and onion, and dessert was chocolate pudding. I was lucky. My pudding must have come early into a pan, as it was nice and thick, but the bottom of the pan it is overworked and soupy. Since my next feeding is 14 hours away, I save my sack lunch for a late-night snack. Now I'll read until sleep comes again. My TV alarm will turn itself on at 7 PM for prime time viewing.

[*Later.*] It's 10:30 PM now. I never did fall asleep, but ended up watching reruns of "Modern Family" and "The Big Bang Theory." Mail call brought me a letter from my father. The good news is he sent me money; the bad news is I wrote to him requesting advice, and he said:

You asked for my advice, but I really have nothing meaningful to offer. Whether you deserve the treatment you are receiving, or not, the prison authorities clearly hold all the cards. I would think that your interests would be best served trying not to piss them off. When you find a bucket of shit, the last thing in the world you should do is get a stick and stir it; that just makes the smell worse.

I know my litigation has brought hard times, but if a cause is just, is it not worth fighting? Clearly my dad does not think so. Then again I doubt he realizes that the only voice an inmate has is through civil litigation. Concerning my pen-pal writing, what I most need is a sense of belonging, and only people who can understand me liking boys can really know me. They need not be themselves attracted to boys. I have had pen-pals who like young girls, or who are homosexuals or lesbians and such. Very few people are blessed to have sexual attractions that are what society says is correct – same age/opposite sex. Those who are blessed with "normal" attractions seem to be closed-minded to any other option.

I think of my father's example of the bucket of shit. If it is left alone, it dries on top, but rots underneath, but if properly mixed, it will compost into a fertilizer capable of producing the most beautiful gardens. I just don't get it. My father was born in 1938. He was a teenager in the 50s, in his 20s during the 60s, and raised a family in the 70s. Then again, he also did well during Reaganomics of the 80s and is now retired. Not to mention he was a vice-president of accounting for a major insurance firm. Still, I wish I could have known my dad

who had a bong in the 60's. (I found it when I was in high school while cleaning the basement.)

[*Later.*] Well, it is now after 11 PM. I'm up for the night, wide awake. I'll take a whore bath in my sink, eat lunch at midnight, hope there is a good late night movie, and if not, read until I go to sleep.

[*Later.*] Hello again, the TV let me down last night, and I went to sleep just after my midnight feeding of bologna sandwiches. All the same, like clockwork I woke up at 3 AM. I spent some time cleaning my toilet, and then used the bowl as a wash basin to do laundry. I know it must sound gross, but the rinse cycle is easy. I just need to be careful to hold on tight during flush. It is easy to lose clothing. Now I'm waiting for breakfast.

Prison diet prevents malnutrition, but it is far from being adequate to enjoy a feeling of being full. I will say we get more food on the tray than we did at Lovelock. At Lovelock, other inmates served meals, and they figured any food they do not serve could be stolen. Here at Ely, the guards prepare the trays, and any extra is questioned if returned, so they put it on the trays. At Lovelock I was a good cell cook with canteen items. I would cook for anyone willing to buy ingredients, as long as my cellie and I ate. (He did the clean-up.) Well, being in solitary confinement makes that hustle a thing of the past. Once my Christmas money clears, I'll be able to supplement a bad meal, but for now, the 11 cents on my inmate trust fund leaves me eating state food.

Well after laundry and writing, I think I may not be able to get a nice nap in before breakfast wakes me up.

[*Later.*] I've been laying in bed since I stopped writing. Breakfast finally came at 7:30. Scrambled egg, bologna, potato mix, cream of wheat, canned pears, milk substitute (fortified kool-aid) and coffee cake. In the sack is a 2 oz tube of peanut butter, 2 restaurant jelly squares, 4 slices bread, carrot & celery stick and a brownie. I learned a good trick for carrot & celery, the cold water on my sink drips. If I hang a baggie over the spout it catches it, so I can put veggies in it and they stay in a continual flow of cold, fresh water. I really like Saturday morning TV. The religious channels have their kid programming, and there are some super cute boys singing and dancing. :)

[*Later.*] Hello again, I fell asleep about 10am and just now woke-up for dinner. I slept soundly all day. Dinner was carrot & grease soup, a chicken patty w/bun, 2 lettuce leafs, 2 pickle slices, and cake.

Not much of a meal. It looked like a grade school hot lunch. It is going to be a long wait until I eat my lunch at midnight, but if I don't save it, I'll suffer waiting for breakfast. Saturday night TV sucks, so I turn it off. The one radio station we get out here usually plays country, but on Saturday nights, it is classic rock, so I'm jamming to tunes while I write.

Well, I assume that you can piece together my daily routine from what I've written. Lots of inmates spend hours and hours a day doing a work-out. I hate to exercise, but to each his own. I see no reason to prolong life through healthy practices. A heart attack is like being granted parole. I could never put my family through the heartbreak of my committing suicide, but a nice quick cardiac event would be nice. Sadly, my family tends to live long lives. My grandma was 98 when she passed, both of my parents are well into their 70's and healthy, as are numerous aunts and uncles. So I expect to spend a long, long time in prison. Who knows, I may live long enough for society to one day accept me and set me free. How cool would that be?

[*Later.*] Hello once again, several days have passed since I wrote about my pondering the possibility of society one day accepting me and being free. I just do not see it happening within my lifetime. I had to put this letter away, as I had to wait to mail it due to postage limitations, but I guess it is time to finish it up.

For the second time in three years I ate Thanksgiving dinner alone in my cell. The food was good, but the holiday is not meant to be spent in solitude. Who would have guessed I would miss eating with other inmates, but after 10 years, some of those inmate friends become family. I really miss my cellie Oscar. Even though we had so many differences, he was my best friend. I think it is really sad that prison regulations forbid me to write to him, but those are the rules. :(Thinking about it is too depressing, so I'll end this train of thought, as well as this letter.

An uneventful day

I went to court on Monday the 26th of May for a sentence hearing. It was a totally uneventful day. The judge gave me life, with parole possible after a minimum of 20 years, but he ran it concurrent to the time I am already doing, except he did not give me credit for the time I already served. In effect he added 104 months, or eight years, eight months to my minimum time. If Nevada ever decides to

show compassion, I could get out of prison before my 62nd birthday. By that time I will have spent about 47% of my life in prison, and will have no savings, retirement, or marketable skills. I hate to use the word "institutionalized" but I really do not want to leave here. I'm fed, housed, and provided clothing. On the streets I will not have such basic things.

The one hard part of going to court was reading the victim's account of the crime in the prosecutor's report. It was not at all what I expected. Before I tell you what he said, I'd like to give my version of the events.

I first met Oliver at church. He was a classmate of my son in the fourth grade, but not really a friend. Still, being a fellow congregation member, I wanted the two of them to get to know each other. My son was having a large sleepover party to watch a USC fight on pay-per-view, and he invited Oliver. There were about 30 boys coming over, friends from school, church, and his wrestling team. Oliver was thrilled; my son was sort of indifferent.

I quickly learned that Oliver was an unusual boy. I don't want to say a 10-year-old boy was "gay" but between his being a gifted piano and violin player, owning a Shih Tzu, wearing sweater vest to church, and showing a love of musicals and theater, I began to wonder. Having three older sisters and a single mother did not help. I saw a very isolated boy, and my heart melted. That weekend while most of the boys would play capture the flag, go rollerblading, or play Super Smash Brothers on the Nintendo, Oliver hung out with me. I encouraged my son to include Oliver in future sleepovers, even though my son protested. I forced his hand in the name of his being a fellow Christian. I really grew to enjoy being near Oliver.

The most sensual memory I have of Oliver was a day at a water park. We had purchased season passes for the family, which had grainy black-and-white photographs. It was easy to pass him off as my own son. My son was visiting his grandma in Florida with his mom. By this time I had known Oliver and his family for over a year. I was his Sunday school teacher, and his mom thought nothing was out of place for me to invite her 11-year-old son for a day of fun at the water park. While sharing a two-man inner-tube in "The Lazy River," I asked Oliver about how his summer reading was going. He had read *Where the Red Fern Grows* and began to tell me about it. Two hours later he was still talking, and I was intoxicated with the beauty of him.

It did not matter that we had physical contact as his legs draped over mine, nor that he was wearing just a swimsuit. The day was in no way sexually charged. I fell in love with him emotionally.

At sleepovers we cuddled. I would hug him openly, give back rubs and massages, and rent whatever film he asked for. He loved "The Music Man" and would sing along. As I rubbed him, it became ever more obvious that he was getting erections, and quite naturally, my hand would gravitate to them. We often fell asleep in each other's arms during the movies. One night I awoke to find him dry hump my leg, his erect penis poking my thigh. I rolled him unto his back, lowered his pajamas, and sucked his dick. I also guided his hand to my own penis and showed him an appropriate milking motion.

In the morning I felt it best to clear up any and misunderstandings about the importance of not telling anyone. I told him I was sorry for doing that to him if he did not like it, but I felt he wanted it. I told him that if he told anyone, I would get into all kinds of trouble. I would not be allowed in church and we would not see each other again. He seemed to agree. Later that morning he came into my room, and flopped down on my bed, his crotch at my hand level. I began to feel him grow erect in my palm. I lowered his pants and played with it. Then looking him in the eye I asked, "Do you want me to stop or to keep going and you never tell anyone?"

His response was to smile and say, "Duh, it's not like I would tell anyone," which I took as an invitation to continue. I once again gave him head, and as I lay behind him holding his penis I ejaculated between his thighs. I never tried anal sex, as I was pretty sure it would harm him. Over the next couple of years Oliver was a frequent house guest, and he always slept right beside me with his head in the crook of my arm. When he said that my beard made his face itch, I shaved, and we had many more sexual encounters. They ended when I was arrested based on another boy's accusations.

Now here are parts of Oliver's account as presented by the prosecution.

The victim stated that between the ages of 11 and 12, in 2000 to 2003, Tony Henderson sexually abused him. The victim informed officers he was now coming forward because he had been seeing a therapist in Utah for a year, and was home from college on the spring break. He decided to report it because he felt if he did not do it now, he never would.

He told officers that he would spend the night at his friend's house and during the sleepover he would watch movies in the defendant's bedroom. The victim told officers the first time the abuse happened was while he was watching a movie. The defendant was lying behind him, rubbing his stomach until he "got hard." Then the defendant put his hand on the victim's penis, rubbing it under his clothing. He then rolled the victim over onto his back and Henderson started giving oral sex to the victim. The next morning, he brought the victim into the kitchen and told him that he was sorry, giving him a hug. Then he told them it was his fault because when the defendant was rubbing him over his clothing, the victim became erect and pressed his penis into his hand. This made him feel the victim wanted it. Henderson told the victim not to tell anyone.

The victim stated the abuse occurred every time he would spend the night. The victim remembered that the abuse always started when he was asleep at the defendant's residence. He would awake the defendant, lying behind him rubbing his penis. Eventually he would start grabbing the victim's hand making him masturbate the defendant until he would ejaculate. The victim would stay almost every weekend with his friend. During the sleepover the victim would be confronted by the defendant and was forced to masturbate him, sometimes two or three times a night. The victim also told officers that the defendant would either masturbate him or give him oral sex. He stated that the abuse would occur in the morning after the night of the abuse also. The victim stated that on two separate occasions the defendant attempted to have anal sex, but couldn't remember if penetration was made in his rectal area. He told officers that he knows the defendant's penis went through his butt cheeks and he ejaculated between his thighs.

The victim stated that some time in 2003 the abuse suddenly stopped. He told officers that he was approached by church leaders and his parents and asked if he had been abused, but he denied the allegations. He stated he was embarrassed about what happened over the years and has still not disclosed what happened to the Church or his mother. He told officers he told a friend in high school.

The victim's friend was interviewed and relayed the same information. He stated that the victim was very closed off when speaking about the abuse, and would break down crying, shaking, and apologized for doing these things. He stated the victim told him the defen-

dant told him that if he told anyone the church would throw him out.

This is not a verbatim account of the prosecution description, but it is the most accurate reconstruction of that account that I'm able to remember.

I'm amazed at how different his memories are from mine. I guess facts get distorted in 10 years time. I am sure the truth is somewhere between his account and mine. I wondered if I could fight the charges, but I didn't. I pleaded guilty because I did not want to cause him the embarrassment of a trial. I realize I should not have done it, no matter what my intentions were. He was too young to consent. I just wish the legal system could see the difference between what I did and rape. Had it been rape – violent, scary or traumatizing – why would he come over almost every weekend for two years? The state does not see it that way. I'm trying to get the actual transcript of his interview. I'm curious regarding how close it is to the state's summary.

I do know this much. I still love him. I know better than to try to contact him, but I really miss him. I own a copy of *Where the Red Fern Grows* and each time I read it, I smile. I hope Oliver finds therapy helpful, and that he knows I hold no anger toward him. I did wish that he had come to court. I would have liked to apologize for any harm I caused, but he was not there. I did not apologize to the state. I believe it to be between Oliver and me. I guess all I can do is enjoy fond memories of our time together, and hope he has a good life. He is 21 now – attending college and in therapy. I do wonder if he turned out gay or not

.

The groin pull

My senior year I was one of two students who worked in the trainer's room. Pretty basic stuff, like ankle and wrist taping or ice packs. The other student was a girl named Viola Bonnet. She liked to think of herself as being French. She spoke French, had armpit hair, and stank to high heaven. Well, after practice one day, the freshman team quarterback had a sore shoulder. Naturally I volunteered to give it a Ben Gay rubdown. As I was doing so, the varsity practice ended, and one of the running backs, an outspoken young man named Patrick came in the training room to get the tape cut off his ankles. As Viola was cutting off the tape, Patrick said, "Oh good God! Something stinks in here!"

Viola said to him, "That's not a very nice thing to say to me."

Patrick flipped and started yelling, "I wasn't talking about you, I was smelling the Ben Gay. I am way too polite to mention that you smell like a dead goat. But if you know, why don't you get in the shower? Why would someone knowingly stink as bad as you do?"

Patrick went on and on. Viola cried but he did not let up one bit. To Viola's credit she did not quit the training room.

Another day before practice a freshman soccer player came in with a groin pull. I was busy taping up an ankle and Viola asked me to trade. Being a groin pull, the school insisted on same gender treatment providers, so I had him follow me to the back room, where the steel tub whirlpool was set up. We looked at each other and I said, "Groin pull?"

He nodded.

"Which leg?"

He pointed to his right leg.

I said, "I can wrap that with an ace bandage which should help during practice. Okay?"

Again he nodded.

I said, "Lower your shorts for me," and he dropped them a few inches.

"No, I need room to work. Take them off and set them on the bench."

When he did his T-shirt hung down below his knees.

I said, "Now lift your T-shirt."

He shook his head from side to side.

"Okay, go to practice without the ace bandage. It doesn't matter to me."

He thought for a few moments, then lifted his T-shirt.

It all became crystal clear. He was wearing Scooby Doo briefs.

This was not a grade-school kid. He was a freshman in high school. No wonder he wanted to keep them hidden. Well I maintained professional composure, and did not say anything. I acted as if it were nothing unusual, and began to wrap his injured leg. The ace bandage would wrap around his waist, then once around his thigh, weaving in and out. Not really meaning to, but also not trying to avoid it, the back of my hand brushed the front at each pass. Like any boy of 14 in his underwear and with someone's hands down there, nature took its course. Scooby Doo's nose began to stick out at me in 3D. I was so deep in denial that I never even considered moving forward in

pleasure. I looked in his eyes and said, "You make that go down right now!"

With tears in his eyes he said, "I can't," and he tried hard not to cry.

I called him a "fag" and finished up. Oddly enough a groin pull is normally painful for several days, but I cured his injury that day. He did not come in for getting it re-wrapped.

What was I thinking? Prison life is full of time to contemplate regrets. I'm sure I could have handled the situation better. Calling him a "fag" was so wrong, seeing as how I was as gay as a May Pole. How many same-sex attractions would it take to get me to see who I was?

From letter – March 20, 2016

I really do not know what to write about anymore. I feel as if I have said all I have to say about every topic, and nothing new ever comes up. I feel badly even mailing you these letters, as all I do is gripe. I'm unsure what exactly the prison expects us to do. There is literally nothing offered. No classes or programs, no groups, no sports – just wasted, empty time.

Chapter 18 – Pedophiles are Supposed to be Hated

by F.B.

I voluntarily enrolled in the Sex Offender Treatment Program (SOMP) back in the year 2013, and after two years of meetings, completed it successfully. Even though I was helped by it in some ways, there was, and is, much of the SOMP program I disagree with. But, more on that later.

First, I want to give you a little bit of background on me.

I grew up in a very rural area of Pennsylvania near the Mason-Dixon line. I am 42 years old.

My parents, both mother and father, were very conservative and religious. My father much more so than my mother. Sex was seldom talked about, and if it was, it was always considered bad. My brother (who is three years younger than me) and I were never allowed to have any girlfriends, not even through high school. Normally, kids would find ways around this, but my brother and I were having every aspect of our lives controlled and restricted. This control was enforced by the totalitarian rule of my father who physically and emotionally abused my brother and me. I could go into the detail about this abuse, but would rather not for many reasons. I'll just say that, in general terms, emotional abuse meant things like calling us names, telling us we were not going to amount to anything, and lots of screaming and yelling. Physically abusive meant bloody noses, black eyes, and scratches in various places.

How young was I when this was being done to me? I am told it began at age 5. I say I am told because I can't remember anything

before the age of 12 except flashbacks of little things here and there. I used to think not remembering anything before 12 was normal. That was until I talked with others about this and found it was anything but normal. In talking with others I found out that usually the earliest memories go back to about three or four years old. What this tells me is that, for some reason, most of my earliest childhood memories were blocked out.

While I was in the SOMP program here, none of these issues were addressed. I am reluctant to get any help (real help) for this – or for anything else for that matter – because a lot of us are warned that the Federal Bureau of Prisoners (FBOP) is more interested in punishing us, shaming us, and/or scolding us, than in actually helping us. Also, we feel that anything we say might be used against us in some way. Since the Adam Walsh law (2006), the government has the power to civilly commit someone for sexual offenses whether he was convicted of them or not.

Don't get me wrong. There are people that are sexually dangerous to the public. But, most if not all, are being punished but not helped. For example, in the last 5+ years I've been in prison, I have seen many individuals who should not be in here at all, but should be in a mental institution instead. Also, even when the government civilly commits somebody (successfully), they end up being civilly committed in a prison! How is this help? It is my opinion that these civilly committed individuals are being criminally detained in a punitive FBOP facility, in violation of their habeas corpus and civil rights! The point is, they are using the prisons to warehouse mentally ill people, since the US government underfunded the mental hospital industry back in the 80s. And now, I am seeing the result of these failed policies in real time. Unbelievable!

Anyway, back to my childhood. I had no self-esteem and lived in an antisocial, anti-sex, and generally oppressive environment. Was it any surprise that this would cause me problems later on?

When my past childhood abuse was brought up in our psychology group, Dr. Holt (the SOMP psychologist) told me that "I was cheating myself." This was his way of putting all the blame on me, and trying to make me not claim any "excuses" as to why I did what I did. I was the only one to blame. Any other factors involved, including the past childhood abuse which happened to me, absolutely did not vindicate me in any way.

I told him that it must have been really convenient to have lived life in his shoes, instead of mine. I told Dr. Holt that I wondered what kind of person he, or anyone else for that matter, would have been had they gone through traumatic and dysfunctional childhood experiences.

As it turns out, empathy was an entire module of the SOMP program, which I went through much later after this incident with Dr. Holt. I was told that it was I that did not have any empathy, and that was one of the reasons why I sexually offended. In the empathy module of the program, I was given instruction on how to detect when you do not have empathy, and the proper way to exhibit empathy.

Later on I challenged Dr. Holt on the belief that sexual attraction to children by adults is voluntary. After trying to goad me into hanging myself (figuratively speaking) by putting myself on record on the issue of pedophilia (which I did not fall for), he explained to my SOMP process group members that pedophilia was not a sexual orientation.

It was after the interactions in the SOMP program that I began to realize that it was the program's philosophy to promote "healthy adult sexual fantasies." Yet any material featuring adults that is deemed sexually suggestive or explicit is contraband, no matter how modest or mainstream it may be. Mrs. Kellogg (SOMP psychologist) burst into my cell one day to shake it down (a thorough search of my property) for any suspected contraband. In the process of tearing everything in my area into scattered piles of debris, she came across a *Rolling Stones* magazine. On the front cover of the *Rolling Stones* magazine was a almost nude picture of Neil Patrick Harris, with him covering his genital area with a hat. She became furious and threw the magazines down on the table as she screamed, "This is inappropriate!" All the other guys that were around the area when she said this, wondered what was so wrong for me (or anyone) having a picture of a semi nude 40-year-old man in the first place? Mrs. Kellogg confiscated the *Rolling Stones* magazine, and she never mentioned anything about the incident afterwards.

If she had taken the magazine to the lieutenant's office and showed them what I had, they probably would have thought she was nuts. But this is the mentality of the psychology here, and just one tiny example of the absurdity of sex offender treatment philosophy.

Anything that promotes "healthy adult sexual fantasies" is taken away from us. And, there are no suitable sexual outlets allowed.

Even masturbation can earn you an incident report and disciplinary action. The psychology department's position on masturbation is, it's not needed. They tell us that we don't have to masturbate. In other words, abstinence is their official policy. One of the biggest abstinence supporters, Sarah Palin, doesn't seem to understand that this philosophy fails miserably even with her own immediate family.

Bristol Palin gives birth to her second child – *Alaska, December 27, 2015 – Bristol Palin, a daughter of 2008 Republican vice presidential candidate, Sarah Palin, has given birth to a second child out of wedlock. Palin, 25, who has been an advocate of sexual abstinence before marriage, tweeted on Thursday that she had given birth to a girl, Sailor Grace. "My heart just doubled," she wrote.*

The father was not named. Palin announced she was pregnant in June, a few weeks after her engagement to Medal of Honor winner Dakota Meyer was called off. Her first pregnancy as a teenager gained widespread attention in 2008 when it was disclosed during her mother's campaign as the running mate of Republican presidential nominee Sen. John McCain.

We can put the abstinence theory to rest. It doesn't work. Abstinence didn't work for the Palin's daughter. It didn't work for the hundreds, if not thousands of Catholic priests involved with the perpetration of child sexual abuse.

So why do all these people preach a proven failed ideology to the rest of us? I know for a fact that a lot of psychiatrists here at this federal institution have religious backgrounds. Shouldn't "professionals" in the field of psychology be impartial, and be doing research on the basis of factual evidence, not faith? Taking pictures is treated like it is a lot more harmful to the child than aggravated assault with a deadly weapon and injury to a child. This is what happens when you let the "thought police" or "sex police" make the laws.

The wide discrepancy in the sentencing raises an important question. Is this really about protecting the children, or is it something else? Consider this article, from ElPasoTimes.com January 9, 2016:

Thrift store worker get 60 years for child pornography
– Corpus Christi – A Texas thrift store worker must serve 60 years in prison for producing child pornography by recording customers

changing clothes in the dressing room.

Daniel H. Allman II was sentenced Thursday by a federal judge in Corpus Christi.

Allman, who worked at a Goodwill Industries store in nearby Portland, was convicted last year of two counts of producing child pornography.

Twenty years ago, this thrift store worker could have received a misdemeanor voyeurism charge. It would have carried a fine, and little to no jail time. Instead, the religious right crusaders and the fem-Nazis have been successfully advancing their agenda for decades. And this is the result: sex laws that are increasingly encompassing every aspect of a person's private life.

As a paralegal (soon to be), I have had to research large amounts of case law. It is an ongoing process. I have learned through all of this that the definition of child pornography has changed over the last three decades. It is now possible for any judge to interpret child pornography to be any photograph of someone under the age of 18 which shows either "sexual suggestiveness," or lascivious exhibition (whatever that means) of the genitals. Even the intent of the photograph is open to interpretation. Intent means that if the child in the picture is just nude, but is intended to induce a sexual response, it is, by the government's definition, "child pornography."

The psychologists here tell us that if we look at the pictures and fantasize about the children sexually, then it is the same as if we were actually doing it. I'm not kidding. I challenged them on this. I found it bizarre that "psychologists" were actually trying to say "thoughts" were the same as "actions."

In the recent *Criminal Law Reporter* publication we see documentation that the FBI is now going to pursue bestiality. They say in the documents that "they have found a connection between those who sexually abuse animals and those who sexually abuse children." Get ready. The next sex crusade is already on the way.

It is my belief that what we are witnessing is a type of Stalinism. It was Stalin of the former Soviet Union who created laws to imprison whomever he chose, based on whether they were his political enemies. In the gulags there were many political prisoners who, if it weren't for the creation of such laws, could not be incarcerated legally and with the public's approval.

Let's face it. With the social attitudes of the brainwashed public, just accusing someone of a sex crime can destroy a person's life. With this most effective tool, the government can silence an individual permanently, take away their assets, and justify more laws and surveillance, with the public's approval!

I recall an incident while I was in our third phase of the SOMP program, which is the last phase before the SOMP program can be successfully completed. Dr. Baronowski is the coordinator here. I remember her clearly telling us that men don't need sex. Normally, in the past, if someone had told me that with a straight face, I would have burst out laughing. At this latter stage of the program however I was highly conditioned and quite good at focusing all my energy staring at a square tile on the floor and without any visible outward emotion. She told us that "if a man did not have sex it was not like they were going to die by not having it." She continued by quoting from a study in which chimpanzees or apes had wanted sex more than food. I thought to myself, "Hmmm. Someone, or in this case an animal, wanting sex more than food. Sounds like a need to me!" But alas, because I was on my latter stages of programming I did not want to challenge anyone at this juncture, and especially not the SOMP coordinator. I continued in silence like a good sheep and focused on the tile.

If we challenge the psychiatrists on any issue for too long of a duration of time we are told that we are becoming a "parking lot." This means that we are spending too much time with intellectual debate. According to the SOMP program documentation, we are not supposed to use any intellectual arguments at all. And it is easy to see why. Feminist and religiously motivated individuals are given a platform on which to dictate and enforce their ideology under the guise of "treatment." The anti-male feminists and a group of religious men called "The Promise Keepers" found a loophole through the separation of church and state principle. By using the sex laws and psychology they were able to weasel their way into people's private lives. And the government has gladly obliged them. Historically, it seems that sometimes during the 70s and early 80s the "Promise Keepers" had allied together with the leading feminist groups to wage war on pornography.

When I first got here in 2011, the SOMP was not here. It didn't get here until early 2012. There were many individuals I knew who

went through their first SOMP. Two of these individuals told me that in the SOMP classes in 2012, the psychologists were telling group participants (inmates) that homosexuality was "sexually deviant." In 2014 they dropped the issue altogether and have never mentioned homosexuality since. I'm thinking that when the issue of same-sex marriage became national news in 2014, and the US Supreme Court ruled in favor of same-sex marriage, the psychologists here must have felt they lost the fight and became tight-lipped.

"Men don't need sex." "Homosexuality is deviant." "If you think about it, it's the same as doing." Is this *Alice in Wonderland*?

Haters (inmates who are in prison on a non-sex offense conviction) refuse to allow any sex offenders to sit in their area because sex offenders are the worst of all inmates. But they are more than happy to let a rapist (of adult females) to sit in their area. No problem. Yes, that actually is happening here! A rapist of adults is looked at as okay. But, if you are someone who viewed child pornography, or committed an act of sexual contact with the child, even if it was consensual, then you are the worst of the worst. Welcome to 21st century American rational thinking.

Check this out. I was told at my sentencing hearing that during the investigation of my child pornography collection they had notified over 120 victims. These are not just victims, but they were *my* victims. Even though I did not know or do anything physically with any of these children in the photographs, they are all my victims. What makes this possible? A change in the law on July 27th, 2006. This is when the "Adam Walsh Child Protection and Safety Act of 2006" was made law. There we read:

"Every instance of viewing images of child pornography represents a renewed violation of the privacy of the victims and a repetition of their abuse." Adam Walsh Child Protection and Safety Act of 2016, published L. No.109 – 248 SS501 (2) (D)102 stat 587, 624 (2006) codified at 18 USC SS 2251 note.

Based on this mentality, anyone who has viewed violent acts on YouTube, news broadcasts, movies, videos or adult pornography has repeated the act. George Orwell's thought police are here, in reality, now. It's only a matter of time before they create a device that can read your thoughts. Then this statute will be applied to thoughts, just

as in viewing pictures.

New laws that treat thoughts as though they are actions have became the justification for quadrupling of the sentencing guidelines for child pornography offenses:

Before 2006 (years)	After 2006
Possession	
0	0-10 (usually 5)
Distribution	
5-20	5-20
Production	
5-20	15-40

Not only did sentencing guidelines go up by a factor of four, but the definition of child pornography came to include parents taking pictures or videos of children nude or naked in bathtubs. Children and teenagers taking nude pictures or videos of themselves with webcams, cell phones, or other devices now fit the definition of producing child pornography as well.

At one group SOMP session I had here, I asked the psychiatrist at what point do I stop being punished? I felt like the system wanted to punish me even after I served my sentence. The response was that "your victims will have to live with it the rest of their lives."

I thought:

- First, I've never touched this person in my life.
- Second, do they feel like they are my victims?
- Third, it's the government that is actually sending out the notices.

Victim notification letters are sent to the "victims" by the National Center for Missing and Exploited Children when a person is found to have pictures of them on a computer or cell phone. A lot of them ask the government to stop sending them the notices. Some have sued the government to get them to stop. But the notices keep coming. So who's really doing the victimizing?

Because a thought becomes an action, someone on the receiving

end of the thought abuse can sue civilly for punitive and compensatory damages. This has amounted to hundreds of thousands of dollars. Sometimes millions depending on how deep the pockets of the one sued are, and how motivated the one suing is. The assets now available for forfeiture becomes widely expanded, even unlimited . It's a cash cow of unprecedented proportions.

I've tried to challenge the rational basis for any of the dogmas I have mentioned thus far before the psychologists in the SOMB program. I've had them sweating, pulling at their ties, rolling around in their chairs, and sometimes speechless. In the end, though, I had to conform to their ideology. Or at least pretend like I did.

Being in the SOMB program in here or on the outside requires a poker face at times. Challenging them too much can get bad things written in your file. The more you question, the more they claim you'll re-offend. They can use whatever nonconforming attitudes you have as evidence against you in civil commitment proceedings. At least while I am in the BOP's custody, or am on supervision with the treatment program, I won't have the First Amendment right to say what I feel, even after I've served my sentence.

Protecting children from sex? Yes. Protecting children from being blown to bits by a hellfire missile? No. But you can be assured that the "pedophile crusade" is to protect the children, at all cost.

Let me return to what I was sharing earlier about my childhood, and what transpired as a result. I never had any girlfriends through middle school and high school. I knew I wasn't allowed to interact socially or sexually with girls so I didn't bother. I never went to my high school prom.

I joined the US Air Force shortly after my 18th birthday to escape the oppressive atmosphere I lived in. Being in the military further isolated me, and I continued to repress any "sexual issues" I was having. Admitting to any problems I had while serving in the military seemed to be futile to me at the time, as it would have been considered weakness in the ranks. So I kept the issue to myself.

I was stationed at a remote Air Force Base in Idaho for almost 3 1/2 years. I began to explore my sexuality by having sexual relationships with other young men. It was something I thought was natural (to me anyway) but I had to hide and repress again. I was always in fear that I might be found out and kicked out of the military. This was 1992 through 1995 and "don't ask don't tell" was in effect. Up until

this point in my life I had to hide everything sexual from other people around me. Whether it was family, coworkers, or the general public.

One of the reasons why I decided to not re-enlist and to get out of the military was that I felt I could never live a free life – a life that I did not have to live in the shadows. For this and other reasons, I felt I was not appreciated for my service. I received a Good Conduct Medal, good recommendations by senior noncommissioned officers, and was offered a generous reenlistment bonus. I respectfully turned down the offer and separated with an honorable discharge in July 1995.

At age 22, I started my non-military life back in Pennsylvania. It was also at this time (July 1995) I had my first interaction with a computer and the Internet. Using AOL I chatted with various guys on line. At some point, somebody sent me a picture of what looked like a 15-year-old boy, nude with an erection. From that point on I was hooked.

One year later, after receiving a new computer and getting an apartment with my boyfriend (we had an openly gay relationship) I managed to meet up with an old acquaintance of my childhood. His name was Eric. He was three years younger than me, and I showed him pictures of some of the young teenagers and children people were sending each other in AOL chat rooms. He was shocked, and excited too.

Eric was an electronics genius by the time he was 11 years old. I was also an electronics guru, but Eric was light years ahead of me. At age 17, he went to the vo-tech (vocational school in high school) national competition and won the gold medal for the electronics area.

Now, at age 21 and seeing what I had showed him, he became enthusiastically interested in getting back into the computer world, and on the World Wide Web. Something that only existed as "BBS" (dial-up computer hosts) sites when he was a kid had now morphed into something much bigger. In 1996 I moved out of my boyfriend's apartment, and moved in with my friend Eric who began to build computers out of our spare parts. He was also the one who taught me the beginnings of what I would become much later on in life. Eric and I went to computer shows and electronics flea markets together. He quickly self taught himself "Linux Red Hat" and I saw him become a super hacker in a very short time. At some point "child pornography" got brought up. We actually didn't use the words "child pornography"

to describe what we were downloading and looking at. We thought that we were simply looking at naked children and that it was a normal thing to do. You might ask why would we think that? When I first started using AOL in 1995, the Internet was rampant with child/adult pornography. It was openly being traded in private messaging and through the SMTP mail servers. It was so frequently traded that at no time did I think that what I and others were doing was breaking the law or wrong.

By the end of year 1996 I was introduced to "newsgroups." Most of these groups were very lightly posted on, and a lot of them remained completely dormant. But the alt.binaries.sex and alt.binaries.erotica groups were very active with hundreds of thousands of posts. Out of all of the sex-related groups, the ones that were most massively posted on were the child sex-related groups.

What did all of this tell me? That not only was it normal for people to be interested sexually in children, but it was highly sought after. IRC was a UNIX-based chat server that posted various chat rooms in which you could connect up to chat, trade files, or whatever. This chat server environment was very active for child pornography rooms where people could use "DCC," "FTP," or "FSERVE" to trade files.

It was around this time that my friend Eric admitted to me that he was a pedophile. I was shocked and at first got angry at him. But shortly afterwards, I realized that I was doing the same thing as he was! For some reason, I had never done a full introspection of myself, but now I fully realized what I had been looking at and fantasizing about, and what that all meant. I admitted to him that I was probably the same. From that point on we had detailed conversations about what we were looking at, and what we liked sexually. I was 24 and Eric was 21 years of age. One night in our conversations, Eric said "I feel like during all my childhood, adults all hid their sexual attractions to children away from me, and it was a fake world. Now, I find out the truth, and it seems enlightening."

These times were the late 90s. The Internet was a blooming flower of freedom, free exchange of ideas, and sexual liberation. One time a young guy who worked as a cop (ironically) came over to visit me and find out how he could locate the same stuff that I had on my computer. I showed him my computer and network set up, the newsgroups, IRC, and some of the pictures I had as examples of what was

out there. He was very happy with me helping him on this. I never saw him after that day, but in my 20s it was normal for people to come and go. As crazy as all this might sound, that's how open, tolerant, and free the atmosphere was on the issue of child pornography in the late 90s on the Internet. People really didn't care about it.

Then came the busts. First, the FBI busted a bunch of individuals on AOL in 1997. In 1998 various newsgroups and newsgroup servers were raided. Then, in 1999 the FBI infiltrated the IRC networks. Through all of this, I remained unscathed. Being very technologically savvy, I always remained one step ahead of them. I feel the government authorities felt a little blindsided by the fact that all of this was going on under their noses for so long without any limitations whatsoever. It was partly their technological ineptness that allowed people to think and speak freely. This made them very angry.

People working for the government at the time were old school and technologically ignorant (for the most part). The Internet was new and being commandeered by a bunch of young school dropouts – people like Eric and me. The authorities were ill-equipped to do anything about it, and they knew that. They needed new tools and new people to be on top of the "problem." Also, they had to get around the US Constitution. Having to get warrants from judges before they could violate a person's privacy was a very tall order indeed.

In the following years of 1999 to 2000 the child pornography market got skittish after the recent past that all people like me (and there were lots of us) operated with anonymity without any problems.

Then came September 11, 2001.

It it is my opinion that September 11th was an "inside job," as many have claimed. I believe it was allowed to happen for many reasons. One of the main reasons it happened, was to eliminate a lot of "Bill of Rights" provisions through the passage of the "Patriot Act" and the creation of a mammoth police state that would make Joseph Stalin blush, and the former Soviet Union and Nazi Germany in the 1940s seem like amateurs by comparison.

When I talked about this stuff back in the early 2000's I was considered a kook. After the revelations of Edward Snowden, I am seen as a prophet. And they still want him dead. Why? Because it was one of their own who revealed to the world that the US government was doing a lot more than just going after "terrorists." The recent NSA surveillance program and warrantless wiretapping program was in

fact ensnaring thousands of people on domestic crimes.

But, before I get too much off track, I want to continue with what I was doing in the years 1995 to 2001.

I refined my computer and network skills on my own spare time. After getting out of the Air Force in 1995, I worked as an industrial mechanic/technician. I had good trouble-shooting skills, and a vast amount of electrical, electronic, pneumatic and mechanical skills to boot. All of this worked well for me in my career until the manufacturing sector really took a beating under trade agreements, and a lot of manufacturing sector jobs were eliminated. I was angry about this, as I had been affected early on just as I was starting out in life to establish myself. The deterioration of the job market was a significant factor in why I stopped caring. I decided to break the law, or at least to continue to break the law. When the "system" shuts you out from opportunity, oppresses you financially, and exploits your labor, you ask yourself why you should conform to a system of laws when it is the system that is making you miserable. One of the ways I alleviated my stress was through my pornography world. As my work-related difficulties increased, so did my Internet pornography world. Eventually, I had devoted so much time and skill to creating and maintaining a pornography server that it became one of the largest in the world at the time.

Around the year 2000, I was attracting more hacker attacks from a growing number of people on-line. This was because I had begun posting much of my child pornography collection through peer to peer programs (P2P), and I became more visible to the general public. One hacker attack resulted in a loss of my four-disc array. All the data was lost. The backup I had failed as well. I learned a lot from this experience. However, I was very angry, and vowed to wage war on the ones who successfully sabotaged me. I vowed that I would create a child pornography collection larger than anyone had ever seen and that my network security measures would be impenetrable to any hacker.

Year 2000. My friend Eric (the hacker) had created his own "black box" using Linux, and he showed me his set up. For the last four years, Eric hadn't worked or had a job of any type. He focused all his energy into coding and hacking. He was brilliant beyond imagination. I told him that he could make more money than anyone I knew personally if only he conformed to society's rules and got a job.

His response was that he felt that America and its capitalistic system were corrupt, and that he did not want to have any part of it. I then asked him what he thought would work better. He said socialism – or a more socialistic system. At the time I was still under a sort of brainwashing which made me criticize him and attack his political views – just as I had done years earlier when he revealed to me his pedophilic sexual persuasions. Once again, my programmed and conditioned mind would not let me see the light.

Shortly after this time, I found out that Eric had been attending the local Carroll County Community College. I found out that he had gone into theater/drama, and this seemed odd to me. Eric had always been highly technical. Why theater? I asked him this, and he told me why. Apparently, some of the acting crews involved younger people in a lot of the shows they did, including children. He showed me some videos of their performances. Some of the top kids involved in the shows were seven to twelve year old girls and boys. Then I found out he was getting close to some of them, and was bringing some of them back to his place. I told him that he was taking some real chances. Even though this was well before the "pedophile crusade" had officially begun, there were still risks of getting busted, depending on how far you took it. But that was Eric. He was a risk taker and a daredevil from as far back as I can remember, even when we were young kids ourselves. I was the exact opposite. I was conditioned to conform and play by the rules. I then found out that Eric was attending NAMBLA meetings in the library at the college. At the time it was still considered a right of free speech to discuss different views about sexual attraction toward minors. As the latter half of the year 2000 approached, no one knew how this would all change very soon.

Leading up to the presidential election of the year 2000, Eric started to go through a state of depression. At the time, I did not know what was the cause of this. I was too busy serving my corporate masters. I had very little free time for myself, and whatever free time I did have, I was building, modifying, and/or repairing computer-related hardware. That, porn, and computer game activities occupied my time. I had the misguided impression that if I conformed to society's rules, good things would happen to me. The crumbs they threw me off the table allowed me to barely afford a tiny townhouse that was built in 1984, and to buy simple pleasures. I thought I was living the American dream.

My response to his depression was the same that I expected others would have if I had asked for help for my issues. I considered it weakness. Eric had started to take medication for his condition. This included opium, plus some sort of tranquilizers. Whatever this medication was, it didn't help. I say this because most of the time he was a zombie. But there were sporadic episodes of anger and rage. I couldn't tell when he would go into a mad yelling spree or go crazy. So, I distanced myself from him, and stopped visiting him altogether. Sometime after mid-2000, I cut off communications with him. He was my best friend but I feared for my own safety at this point. I had learned a lot from Eric. I wished for him to go on a better route. But instead of helping him and supporting him, I took the road my corporate masters wanted me to take: continue to make profits for my bosses and their shareholders, and not waste my time on someone else's mental illness.

With the scraps they threw me, I was on my way to buying my first house. Not the house I wanted, but the only one I could afford. Ms. Miller who was my real estate agent told me that I was "lucky" because apparently most people my age couldn't do what I was doing. I was 22 years old.

In November 2000 I was beginning to move out of my apartment and into my new house. I remember waking up one morning to move my stuff. I played a message on my answering machine that sounded like Eric's sister, Kim, asking me in a frantic voice if I knew anything about Eric. I dismissed it as nothing important. I had more important things I had to do. I only had two days to move my stuff before I had to go to work again. Eric and I weren't talking anymore anyway. I began the arduous process of filling my stuff into a U-Haul with the help of my brother.

By 2001 my porn server was going full steam. I had built four computers just for myself. But, most of my computer activities were for games, not pornography. I was too busy working for my corporate masters to really do much of anything else anyway. But that was about to change.

In February 2002, on a day that started out just like any other day, I got a call from my brother. It was in the morning before I went to work, and that was odd. My brother almost never called me at that time. He told me that a former acquaintance of my friend Eric had told him that Eric was dead . He had killed himself. I was shocked. At

first I couldn't believe it, so I called Eric's mother to verify. She did, and I broke down in tears.

I went into shock and had to call my boss at work to take a day off to deal with this loss. But instead of getting sympathy and support from my employer, I was told that by not coming to work I was the one not being supportive! Apparently, all the years of support I gave to the company, and to my boss, in the end didn't matter. For him to ignore the pain I was going through, after I had just had a bombshell dropped on me, caused something in me to snap. I hung the phone up on him after telling him he wouldn't see me that day. I then immediately drove to Eric's mother's house, where I embraced her and cried.

She told me what had happened. Eric's sister had tried to contact me, but apparently I had been too busy with work and the move to my house. Then my phone number had changed, so I was never told. My friend had died over a year earlier. Eric sometimes went into seclusion for long periods of time, which is what I thought he had done, so I never bothered to check on him. I felt horrible and somewhat responsible. If anyone could have prevented the suicide, I could have. It was at this time I had a watershed moment. All the things that Eric had told me, being very critical of capitalism, started flashing through my head.

I returned to work the following day and nobody at work said a word to me about what had happened. What they didn't realize was that something inside me changed. A year and a half later, I was fired from this job because I started to stand up for myself and because I stopped caring about the company that didn't care about me. A negative reference from the supervisor at this job screwed me over for future jobs and caused a downward spiral in my career. All of this reinforced the criticisms of Eric's view on the American system as a whole.

Eric was right about everything. I was just too ignorant to see it. And now he was dead.

After analyzing the situation I suppose I got depressed too. I stopped caring about the corporate world. I got more entrenched in my computer world and the Internet. I fortified my network and built bigger and faster computers. I began to use a person-to-person program called Napster. One day this program updated itself and scanned my hard drive for all media files. In the process, a lot of

my child pornography files were automatically shared, without my knowing it. Then I noticed my network bandwidth traffic skyrocketed. When I expanded my Napster menu and looked at the download upload queue, people were downloading child pornography files like crazy. I freaked out and shut down the program and the computer. I then hid the computer for a month, and laid low. Eventually, I got back on line.

I thought about the situation. Why were so many people downloading something illegal, and in such huge amounts? So I conducted an experiment. I went on WinMX (another P2P program) and searched for child pornography terms. I discovered the WINMX network was rampant with child pornography. I started a WINMX server and ran it for almost 10 years. I wasn't caught until I ran a Giga-Tribe account, and that drew too much attention to me, and exposed my identity.

When the FBI finally came in on me, they calculated that I had over two million child pornography files. It was more files than any of them had ever seen in the past. I faced up to 30 years but managed to hire attorneys from California, and they did a wonderful job for me. I received a nine year sentence and I have served 5 1/2 of it so far. I do get some good-time credit and should be out of here in or around mid-2018. I'm only hoping that the economy and country is in better shape then when I left it.

How kids started coming over to my house is a story in itself. I'm a big kid myself. The neighbors knew me well and trusted me. I never did anything inappropriate with any kids that were over at my house. I was a model citizen of the community. The kids in the neighborhood all loved me. A lot of them loved to spend time at my place because I had so many things they liked: my yellow car, 55-gallon fishbowl tanks, king-size water-bed, and mostly my computers and computer games. Even though I am sure the FBI tried their best to get the kids to say bad things about me – things that weren't true – instead they said really good things. This must've made the feds really angry. After all, pedophiles are supposed to be hated not loved.

Chapter 19 – **Prejudicial Treatment**

By C.J.

A drug offender who continues to sell drugs and medication, even in prison, is still able to self-carry their medication. Someone who commits mail fraud still has access to mail. A physical abuser, a murderer, an arsonist – all are able to go out and have the opportunity to reintegrate into society and be accepted, though they have committed vile crimes. The murderer, the drunk driver, the drug abusers, assaulters, are all able to exit prison and live among potential victims without having their few freedoms in prison restricted prior to release. They can live among others who they MAY rob, kill, steal from, assault or otherwise abuse. They are all accepted with the HOPE that they've learned their lessons.

The sex offender is NEVER really free, and never given the opportunity to fully reintegrate into society and be accepted as "normal." With disproportionately long years of Supervised Release and on a public registry, the sex offender is continually oppressed and held back by societal fear – even though studies have shown, along with statistical data, that sex offenders are one of the least likely to re-offend after incarceration. Most of us do not seek to harm or injure, nor to perpetuate any cycles of aggression. We just want the opportunity that most others are provided, both out of prison and within: the opportunity to not be oppressed needlessly, the opportunity to do the time we were given and to move on in life with a new vision.

Chapter 20 – **An Impossible Love**

by H.A.

In this selection H.A. meditates on the meaning of the great love of his life.

ଓଃ

I have a single photograph of the person I loved the most in this sad life. His name is Caspian and he is eleven and one-half years old. He has been eleven and one-half for more that twenty-six years now, and I keep his picture in my Seifer T'hilim (Psalter), but I don't permit myself to look at it except on the New Moon[1] and a few other occasions. I cry each time.

Until yesterday, my photograph of Caspian weighed heavily on my soul, an albatross around my spiritual neck. I know that I am bound eternally to this boy who has not existed for decades – and perhaps who never existed at all as I remember him – and I have imagined that impossible love pulling me earthward again and again in a ceaseless repetition of gilgulim, incarnations, from which I could never escape because I never would relinquish my love.

Yesterday I laughed out loud when I realized that my incomprehension was a terrific joke on God's part. The very fact that this child of my enthrallment has had no counterpart in manifest reality – in

---

[1] The new moon symbolizes that which is apparently lost or consumed, but then re-appears. It also is the day when the Book of Psalms customarily is begun anew each month.

the Explicit Order[2], the Olam Ha-'Asiva[3] – for so long means that the "letting go" I had deemed forever beyond my reach had already been accomplished for me long ago by God. The Caspian who brought forth and defined for me the quintessence of love is the Caspian of the Implicate Order2, the Olam Ha-y'tzira[4], where time has no meaning, and "simultaneity" is literally in the eye of the beholder. There, like his photograph, my Caspian remains unchanged and unchangeable, "contemporary" with every instant at which the set of divine aspects, Midot, which defines him is activated. Now God projects through that template directly into my consciousness without physical intermediary, and the awareness of that presence is experienced as love and longing. Is not all love naught but the sensation of awareness of God? Of course the Caspian resident in my soul is more unblemished than the one whose flesh I treasured in my youth! Of course my love for him is more pure and perfect! Is not the film itself more veridical that its projection on a dusty screen? Is not light on God's immanence more beautiful and coherent when appreciated directly than when filtered through the senses?

My physical form, together with the whole universe, dies each instant and is re-created through God's will, never exactly the same. As I loosen my identification with this world of transience and transfer it to the world of permanence[5], I move not away from the Caspian I love, but toward him. My "letting of" is not of him, but of that which separates me from him; it is not a relinquishing at all, but a re-uniting. For I am to become my Eternal Self, as he has become for me

---

[2] As used by David Bohm, cf. Talbot, Michael, *The Holographic Universe*. The basic metaphysical thesis, not necessarily theistic, is that there is a superordinate level of reality, the Implicate Order, of which our perceived universe, the Explicate Order, is a "projection," roughly analogous to a hologram.

[3] The world of doing/making, i.e. the spatial-temporal universe. This is the level at which the true nature of reality, which ultimately is only God himself, is most obfuscated.

[4] The world of "Forms," used in a sense similar to Plato's. This is one level "up" from the Olam Ha-'Asiva, and includes both "Forms" or "Ideas," which are then projected into the physical universe, and entities whose final level of existence is on the "astral" or "subtle" level itself.

[5] Contrast Rabbi Shimon bar Yochai's observation after emerging from his long retreat in a cave with his men, as reported in the Talmud. When he saw that ordinary persons had set aside matters of eternity, i.e. Torah, in favor of transitory concerns, his reproving glance burnt them to a crisp.

the Puer Aeternus, the Child-ness of the divine, which I believe is the means of my tiqun, the completion/rectification of my n'sbama, my soul. The great love I first experienced then as two persons entwined, is the same love I experience now in heart-rendering contemplation of a frayed icon of my spirit's complement, and it is the very same love that will fill me and surround me and redress me if I but open to it – because it is the sensation of the presence of God.[6]

---

[6] Cf. a central aphorism of Swami Muktananda: Love is the sensation of awareness of God.

Afterword

by Prof. Thomas K. Hubbard

Several observations come to light from listening to these men. Many of them reveal a genuine delight in associating with boys even when sex is not the motive. K.J. had a long career as a camp counselor (and ultimately director) and admits an erotic fascination with boys, but never had sex with them. He is in prison because he was falsely accused by a nephew who later formally recanted his testimony; the boy at the age of eight was coerced by investigators into making a statement because the man's wife incorrectly suspected him after finding boy-love literature in his car. S.R. was a teacher and active in his church. G.D. tells of a popular assistant scoutmaster. H.D. as a 20 year old continued to enjoy all of the things younger boys did: skateboarding, video games, racing dirt bikes, playing at the beach. Sex seems not to have been the dominant motive in his associations with the many boys he discusses, but in some cases came about almost incidentally. There were others like Glenn, with whom he maintained a 3.5 year friendship without ever having sex. Did these men become scoutmasters, camp counselors, teachers, or even just friends to gain ready access to boys they could groom, as the popular narrative alleges, or is it because they were so often around horny boys that temptation and opportunity arose?

I. The boys
One is also struck by the unambiguous willingness of many pre-pubescent boys to become physically intimate with these men, such that they came back on multiple occasions, not due to any bribery or coercion, but because they genuinely enjoyed the physical in-

teraction and wanted to repeat it. In none of these narratives is the boy in such a position of emotional or financial dependence on the adult that he had to come back. Even K.T., who has found Jesus and regrets his past life, and now even thanks the FBI for having stopped him, concedes, "To be honest, I never hurt a boy – never made a boy do something he didn't want to do. They were always happy, always having fun." This challenges the traditional assumption that premature sex is necessarily "traumatic" for children; as the Harvard psychologist Susan Clancy (2009) found in a study that also included many female survivors, psychological distress seldom occurs at the time of the act itself, but later on, when the minor becomes more self-conscious about sexuality and aware of society's dominant narrative that such relations must be manipulative and harmful. Clancy finds that the discrepancy between this hegemonic social construction and the earlier experience, which they may have enjoyed to some degree, is what is most discomfiting and confusing to adults and adolescents coming to terms with childhood abuse.

Indeed, it is in many cases the younger partner who initiates the sexual aspect of the relationship. H.D., whom most observers would classify as a serial pedophile, says that his first sexual experience of any sort was at age 16, when a six year old introduced him to sex play. Similarly T.J., also a serial pedophile who is now confined by civil commitment, says he first experienced sex with a younger child at 13, when a nine year old came onto him. In today's ubiquitously sexualized culture, even very young children are far from innocent of curiosity: C.F. tells us about his nephew, who at the age of five asked him to show the child how to download porn from the Internet. IW's narrative is a detailed account of his first sexual exploration, when as an 11 year old he admits aggressively and repeatedly soliciting sexual contact with an adult neighbor whom he helped in remodelling an old farmhouse. His neighbor kept putting the boy off, telling him "that's serious stuff," but finally relented and gave him what he wanted. Is it really correct to view the older partner in such incidents as a manipulative predator? The Kinsey Institute studied court transcripts from a number of mid-century child molestation cases and found that 52.3% of cases involving younger boys and 70.3% of cases involving male teens showed evidence of the minor encouraging the sexual contact (Gebhard et al. 1965, 795-97, 821), even from a period long before the ubiquity of children's exposure to sexual content in music, media,

and the Internet.

Not all of the writers discuss how they came to be discovered and arrested, but of those who do, only P.A. says it was in virtue of a child complaining or intentionally turning him in. Even that case concerned a 15 year old who came into his video store wanting to look at porn and who quite willingly engaged in sex contact after watching it, but later grew jealous of P.A.'s involvement with some younger boys. Two of the boys with whom H.D. was involved talked about their sexual experiences with a school counselor or psychologist, who as a mandatory reporter had to go to the police with the information that these boys had been molested. Similarly, S.R.'s downfall came about as a result of one child admitting his own "sins" to a church counselor and another, many years later as a college student, discussing his sexual past with a therapist. H.D.'s and K.J.'s accounts both emphasize just how threatening and abusive police and prosecutors can be in interrogating children who have no desire to inculpate their partner, but finally do so to take the pressure off themselves for having committed "naughty" acts. Two of the 11-year-old boys with whom P.A. was involved refused to testify even despite the pressure placed upon them; some of H.D.'s "victims" were also adamant in defending him. After reading about these juveniles compelled to testify against their will, one is justified in wondering whether it is not the criminal justice system that is more guilty of manipulating and coercing children than their supposed "abusers," and whether therapists who betray a young patient's trust by informing police authorities of the most intimate details do more psychological harm than any derived from the sexual act itself.

II. The offenders as boys

Another conclusion we can draw from listening to these men is the importance of their own childhood experiences in framing their adult desires and identity. O.D. and F.C. recognized an attraction to younger boys as soon as they reached puberty at age 13. Several admit to having positive experiences with older male partners (G.D. at 12, I.W. at 11, K.T. at 12, T.J. at 8 to 10, B.C. at an unspecified age). The conventional explanation for this continuity of childhood experience with adult behavior is the "abused-to-abuser" hypothesis, whereby adults compensate for the powerlessness and victimization they experienced as children by asserting dominance over others when they

become older (Bolton et al. 1989; Garland & Dougher 1990; Glasser, Kolvin, et al. 2001). However, this accords very poorly with what these men tell us about their memory of the juvenile experiences, which they did not in any way see as abusive, but positive and pleasurable. A much more straightforward explanation is that because of their own positive experience with intergenerational sex, it became normalized and acceptable in their minds, leading them to assume that it would also be positive for the youngsters with whom they later became involved. It is perhaps significant that men tend to become involved with boys right at the same age as their own first extended sexual experience, as in the case of K.T., who had a romance with a "Big Brother" at the age of 12 and then later in life became involved with two 12-year-old boys when he got out of the army.

What we find in almost everyone's account of their childhood is a sense of being different or excluded by other kids their own age: G.D. was diagnosed with ADHD and dyslexia, S.R. was a lonely child and overweight, F.C. admits to being an awkward child who didn't fit in, and later had his hair styled into a mohawk and joined the punk scene. H.G. says that his self-esteem as a child was so low that he would allow older boys to have sex with him, even though the same boys called him names and treated him with contempt in public. Sometimes family environment was a factor creating estrangement: T.J. was separated from his vagabond family at the age of 10, F.C. did not have a father-figure in his life, and K.T.'s father was a troubled military veteran who committed suicide in front of the whole family, after which he grew up amid poverty, crime, and frequent changes of address. H.D. and I.W. were youngest children in large families with no siblings even close to their own age. M.D. and F.B. grew up in very strict, abusive, religious families that afforded them little freedom: the situation with M.D.'s homophobic parents was so bad that he ran away at age 16, and F.B. says his father was so violent that he has blacked out virtually all memories from before the age of 12.

Could it be that these men felt a special attraction to troubled boys out of empathy, remembering the loneliness and unhappiness of their own childhood? R.R., who was a practicing psychotherapist prior to his arrest, theorizes that boy lovers like himself are characterized by an "internal timidity" that delayed their transference to normative adult heterosexuality, often as a result of various forms of abuse in their childhood; he postulates that the boy lover has a spe-

cial empathy for boys right around the age of his own childhood crisis. Not all would agree with the first part of this Freudian approach, pointing to the many cases of men who feel attracted to boys as well as to adult women (e.g. B.C., K.J., O.D., S.R.).

The nature of MAPs' childhood experiences with sex and other environmental factors is in need of more quantitative as well as qualitative analysis, and is a focus of the Percy Foundation's ongoing collection of data from its prisoner questionnaire. [1]

III. Consequences

After reading these narratives, one is also struck by the recognition that none of these men appeared to worry about being caught, even after becoming intimate with multiple boys. This engenders doubt about the deterrent value or effectiveness of the harsh punitive sanctions American law places on statutory rape. H.D. continued to associate with boys even after being convicted and serving out his first prison sentence; he found that his post-release status as a registered sex offender was no impediment to gaining access to boys, who in many cases knew about it.

M.D. does say that he would break off his friendship with boys before becoming sexual with them, but his motive seems to have been ethical and religious rather than a fear of legal consequences. As his chapter tells us, he was raised in a deeply religious family and later went to a Bible college, but at the same time joined NAMBLA and bought boy-love literature. Similarly, H.G. admits struggling with intense self-loathing over his pedophilic attractions, and immediately admitted his guilt when the police finally confronted him. As we have noted, K.T. now thanks the FBI for stopping him; B.C. says that prison was good for him in that it prompted deep soul-searching. Could it be that more compassionate approaches like those of B4U Act or Stop It Now! might be more effective in raising doubts that will hinder MAPs from behavior that could damage themselves or others? However, mandatory reporter-laws in the US make it difficult for MAPs to

---

[1] The largest sample with which I am familiar is that of Glasser, Kolvin, et al. (2001), based on patients referred to a London psychiatric clinic: 35% of the male perpetrators of child sexual abuse had been "victims" in childhood, but 65% were not. For other family background factors, see Bentovim & Boston (1988).

seek therapy or admit their desires to anyone, much less discuss their actual experiences.

We have discussed in the previous section just how wide of the mark conventional clinical wisdom about the aetiology of sex offending is (with specific reference to the "abused-to-abuser" hypothesis). Two of the writers specifically discuss the sex-offender therapy that is available in prison, which they regard as worse than ineffective. F.B. complains that it is intensely sex-negative, grounded in either feminist or religious dogma that is patently ridiculous in the eyes of even modestly educated inmates. Prisoners are told that fantasies or thoughts are just as bad as acts, that sex is a luxury rather than a biological necessity, and that any abuse they may have suffered in their own childhood is irrelevant. They are told that they must learn to change their sexual orientation to whatever the therapist defines as "healthy adult desires," yet are to do so without access to any sexually explicit materials (which are banned in prison) or even voluntary sexual interaction with other adult prisoners (which is also against the rules). Any attempt to question or engage in intellectual debate is marked as a sign of "resistance to therapy" and thus inhibits the goal of gaining earlier release. This encourages prisoners to stare at the floor and dissemble their true thoughts by passively engaging in ritual repetition of the therapist's mantra. Rather than promote any real change of internal attitude or thinking, it trains prisoners in the art of deception, which in turn renders most prison-administered studies of sex offenders worthless. Aware of its hectoring negativity, E.J., himself a trained therapist, found the prospect of mandated sex-offender therapy so degrading that he seriously contemplated suicide rather than subject himself to it.

Even if released, the sex offender's path to social reintegration is extremely difficult. B.C. wrote his essay as he was about to be released, and expressed the hope that he could be an activist who would write on MAP issues. However, since his original crime involved internet communications, the terms of his parole block him from accessing the internet or even using a computer. This of course makes it virtually impossible to obtain employment in his profession or find an adult romantic partner, not to mention all the other disadvantages of being a registered sex offender. Rather than deal with these challenges, some sex offenders are content to remain incarcerated for the rest of their lives; however low their stature within prison, they

can at least expect free food, shelter, clothing, and basic health care at taxpayer expense. Others simply disappear into the ranks of the homeless and nameless, where no one can monitor or counsel them.

All of the issues these contributions raise are in need of further investigation: the deterrent effect of severe punishments, the impact and success of various therapeutic interventions, the best strategies for social reintegration that lessen the odds of recidivism, as well as the nature of the harm derived from child sexual abuse compared to other forms of childhood abuse and neglect. Patiently listening to what these men have to tell us and collecting more stories like theirs, including those of men who were involved with underage girls, can provide a useful screen against which academic theories concerning the causes and effects of sex offending must be tested.

Works cited

Bentovim, Arnon, and P. Boston. "Sexual Abuse – Basic Issues." In *Child Sexual Abuse Within the Family: Assessment and Treatment,* edited by Arnon Bentovim et al. London: Wright, 1988. 1-15.

Bolton, Frank G., Jr., Larry A. Morris, and Ann E. MacEachron. *Males at Risk: The Other Side of Sexual Abuse.* Newbury Park: Sage, 1989.

Chaffin, Mark, Stephanie Chenoweth, and Elizabeth J. Letourneau. "Same-Sex and Race-Based Disparities in Statutory Rape Arrests." *Journal of Interpersonal Violence* 31, no. 1 (2016): 1-23.

Clancy, Susan A. *The Trauma Myth: The Truth about the Sexual Abuse of Children – and its Aftermath.* New York: Basic Books, 2009.

Garland, R., and M. Dougher, "The Abused/Abuser Hypothesis of Child Sexual Abuse: A Critical Review of Theory and Research." In *Pedophilia: Biosocial Dimensions,* edited by Jay R. Feierman. New York: Springer, 1990. 488-519.

Gebhard, Paul H., John H. Gagnon, Wardell B. Pomeroy, and Cornelia V. Christenson. *Sex Offenders: An Analysis of Types.* New York: Harper & Row, 1965.

Glasser, M., I. Kolvin, D. Campbell, A. Glasser, I. Leitch, and S. Farrelly, "Cycle of Child Sexual Abuse: Links Between Being a Victim and Becoming a Perpetrator." *British Journal of Psychiatry* 127, no. 6 (2001): 482-94.

Rind, Bruce, Philip Tromovitch, and Robert Bauserman. "A Meta-Analytic Examination of Assumed Properties of Child Sexual Abuse Using College Samples." *Psychological Bulletin* 124, no. 1 (1998): 22-53.

Rind, Bruce. "Gay and Bisexual Boys' Sexual Experiences with Men: An Empirical Examination of Psychological Correlates in a Nonclinical Sample." *Archives of Sexual Behavior* 30, no.4 (2001): 345-68.

Rind, Bruce. "Pederasty: An Integration of Empirical, Historical, Sociological, Cross-Cultural, Cross-Species, and Evolutionary Perspectives." In *Censoring Sex Research: The Debate over Male Intergenerational Relations,* edited by Thomas K. Hubbard and Beert Verstraete. Walnut Creek: Left Coast Press, 2013. 1-90.

William A. Percy Foundation. "Highlights on Prisoner Study (2016)." Last modified September 29, 2016. http://wapercyfoundation.org/?page_id=75.